Music Query

Contents listings for previous volumes of *Computing in Musicology* may be found online at

www.ccarh.org/publications/cm/

Music Query
Methods, Models, and User Studies

Computing in Musicology, Volume 13

edited by Walter B. Hewlett and Eleanor Selfridge-Field

Copublished and distributed by
The MIT Press
Cambridge, Massachusetts
London, England

MIT Press books may be purchased at special quantity discounts for business or sales promotional use. For information, please email special_sales@mitpress.mit.edu or write to Special Sales Department, The MIT Press, 5 Cambridge Center, Cambridge, MA 02142.

ISBN: 0-262-58256-2
Library of Congress Control Number: 2004115776

10 9 8 7 6 5 4 3 2 1

Music Query: Methods, Models, and User Studies
(Computing in Musicology 13)

Foreword

The topic of music query received only minor attention, at least under that name, before the distribution of music on the internet became widespread. The purpose of music analysis, however, has always been to answer questions about music. One chief difference between analog and digital methods of analysis is that the first uses notated scores as its basis and the second uses encoded data. Another follows from the first: computer-based searches can process more data in less time and can process it systematically.

A lot of thinking remains to be done about the value of standardizing music query. Query methods are inevitably dependent on the quality of the data they query. The "quality" can vary not only according to its method of representation and the rigor with which it has been error-checked but also according to the characteristics of the repertory to be searched. For some, rhythmic features may be essential to basic identity (to differentiate, let us say, a tango from a fox trot). In other cases rhythmic features may play a slight role or be poorly recorded in the data. The defining features of other repertories could be harmonic, tonal, scalar, accentual, and so forth. The high degree of diversity among different repertories can limit the transfer value of a procedure tuned to one repertory and its prized features. At the current stage of development of music query, that is an acceptable condition. Procedures that work well on one repertory are still scarce.

As with so many other technologies focused on music, there is no common agreement on what "working well" actually means. In music query, an approach that works well in the practical sense must first of all work consistently well with large quantities of whatever kind of music it is designed to search. The scarcity of large quantities of data has been one of the impediments to some of the intended research in this field. Studies of scalability for music-search algorithms remain very few. That is, procedures that show promise on 100 examples may not work in a meaningful way for 10,000 examples. For example, a hit rate of 2 per hundred seems respectable, but 200 hits, even if representing a search of 10,000, is the intellectual equivalent of "spam." It is impractically large. In some cases, a more precise query may be available to the user. Providers need to be sure that the user has such tools.

One of the least well explored aspects of query research, the user interface, is, we feel, given due attention in this issue. Micheline Lesaffre and her colleagues at the University of Ghent show experimental results which challenge the widely held notion of technologists that users looking for music find humming the most natural form of query. In an unstructured situation, they may change search methods in the middle of a query. Humming is not the most prevalent method either, as the table on the front cover indicates.

Also contributing to our understanding of the querying user are Daniel Muellensiefen and Klaus Frieler (University of Hamburg), who compare a large number of algorithms for searching musical data with experimental results for human judgments of melodic similarity. A statistical procedure for sorting and ranking similar melodies based on a paradigm from earth science is presented by Frans Wiering and his associates at the University of Utrecht. Eleanor Selfridge-Field offers a provisional measure of "cognitive" distance between comparable melodies derived from a meta-study of one expert user.

The first four articles consider a wider range of topics: the automatic synchronization of recorded music, MIDI files, and symbolic data in the case of Vlora Arifi and her colleagues (University of Bonn). The use of fuzzy logic in modeling rhythmic motifs in considered in Tillman Weyde's contribution. Wei Chai (MIT Media Lab) brings thoughtful consideration to several recent approaches to feature identification (oriented towards web applications). Olivier Lartillot and Emmanuel Saint-James examine the use of perceptual rules in facilitating motivic analysis, particularly in the *OpenMusic* environment used at IRCAM (Paris).

[Volume 13 of *Computing in Musicology* was unavoidably delayed by a series of technical problems. This volume was scheduled for publication in 2003 and will be followed at a short interval by Volume 14.]

These contributions barely scratch the surface of a field bursting with new ideas and interdisciplinary research. We believe that they represent an instructive cross-section which will introduce readers to several of the most promising and important dimensions of the field. We emphasize again, however, that this area of enquiry is in its infancy. If this publication encourages further initiatives, it will have served one of its primary purposes.

Stanford, CA
September 10, 2004

1 Automatic Synchronization of Musical Data: A Mathematical Approach

Vlora Arifi, Michael Clausen, Frank Kurth, and Meinard Mueller

Institut für Informatik, Abt. III
Universität Bonn
Römerstrasse 164
D-53117 Bonn, Germany
{arifi, clausen, kurth, meinard}@cs.uni-bonn.de

Abstract

Digital music libraries typically contain the same piece of music in different data formats (a printed score, MIDI files, and performances on CD recordings). The heterogeneity and complexity of such music data make content-based browsing and retrieval in digital music libraries a difficult task with many as yet unsolved problems. One important step towards a solution could be the use of synchronization algorithms which could automatically link data streams from different formats representing a similar kind of information.

We introduce algorithms which can automatically link any two data streams given in score, MIDI, or CD format (*.wav) representing the same polyphonic piano piece. This series of algorithms involves steps for extracting note parameters such as onset times and pitches from CD data. These discrete parameters make the physical audio data comparable with symbolic score data. We also give a summary and specification of further problems related to the synchronization problems discussed.

Music Query: Methods, Models, and User Studies (Computing in Musicology 13). Published by CCARH and The MIT Press, 2004.

1.1 Introduction

Modern digital music libraries contain textual, visual, and audio data. Among these multi-media-based types of information, musical data poses many problems, for musical information is represented in diverse data formats, which, depending upon the application, differ fundamentally in their respective structures and content. For example, the score—encoded in a formal language and depicted in a graphical-textual form—gives a specification of what we commonly refer to as the "piece of music." In a score the notes are fixed by parameters such as pitch and duration. The global and local tempo variations are specified by textual notations, such as *allegro* or *moderato* for global tempo and *accelerando* or *ritardando* for local tempo modifications. Similarly, loudness and dynamics are described by terms such as *piano, forte, crescendo,* or *diminuendo.* Hence the score is a description of the piece of music which leaves a lot of room for various interpretations implemented in performance. These may concern not only the tempo or dynamics of individual passages but also the multi-note execution implied by such single signifiers as a trill, arpeggio, or grace note. Figure 1.1, which is the basis of later discussion, shows a score representation containing some of these features. It comes from the beginning of the "Aria con variazioni" (BWV 988) by J. S. Bach.

Figure 1.1. Beginning of the "Aria con variazioni" (BWV 988) by J. S. Bach.

From a physical point of view, the musician, by means of his voice or instrument, generates an *audio signal.* This audio signal has the form of a sound wave emerging at its source and spreading through the air. Graphically, such an audio signal may be represented by its *waveform,* which depicts the amplitude of the air pressure over the time (see Figure 1.2 for an example). The Pulse Code Modulation (PCM) format, as used for CD recordings, is an encoded version of such a waveform. In the following commentary, we do not distinguish between the waveform and its PCM representation.

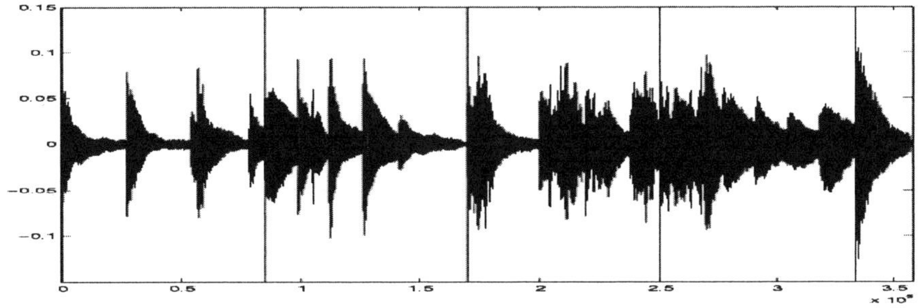

Figure 1.2. Waveform representation of an interpretation [i.e., recording] of the Bach aria shown in Figure 1.1.

The waveform representation, as opposed to the score representation, encodes all information needed to reproduce the acoustic realization of a specific musical interpretation. This includes the temporal, dynamic, and tonal micro-deviations that make the music seem to be alive. However, in waveform note parameters such as onset times, neither pitches nor durations are given explicitly. Even worse (when considering that even a single note of the score becomes a complex sound when played on an instrument), waveforms may contain several harmonics as well as noise components and vibrations. This renders the task of determining note parameters from the waveform of a polyphonic orchestral piece formidable.

The *MIDI format* (see, e.g., Selfridge-Field 1997) may be thought of as a hybrid of the score and the waveform-based PCM format: it can encode all relevant content-based information in the notes of the score as well as agogic and dynamic niceties of a specific interpretation. However, MIDI is quite limited, especially in modeling the timbre of a sound. MIDI data streams are very often visualized by the piano-roll representation as shown in Figure 1.3.

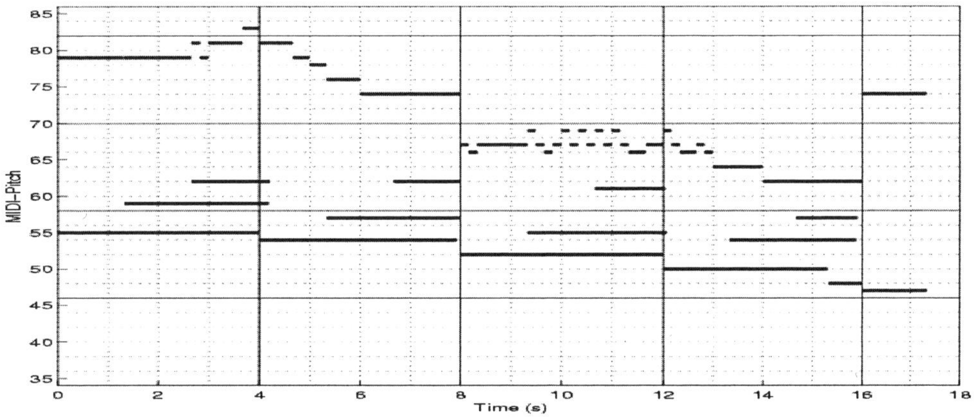

Figure 1.3. Piano-roll representation of a performance of the Bach aria.

A musical work is, in the digital context, far from simple or singular, since it can exist both in multiple formats and in multiple realizations in each of them. This heterogeneity makes content-based browsing and retrieval in digital music libraries a challenging task. Thus the value of synchronization algorithms which automatically link diverse data streams lies in their promise of coordinating the multiple information sets related to a single piece of music. In the audio framework *synchronization* is taken to mean a procedure which, for a given position in one representation of a piece of music, determines the corresponding position within another representation (e.g., the coordination of score symbols with PCM data). In theory, such algorithms could extend score-based music retrieval to facilitate access to a suitable audio CD. Automatic annotation of music documents which are available in different data formats could further assist content-based retrieval. Synchronizations could facilitate the investigation of tempo studies. Temporal linking of score and audio data could be useful for automatic tracking of the score position in a performance.

Here we concentrate on the three representative data formats—symbolic score data, physically-based data in the PCM format, and semi-symbolic MIDI data. The following five types of synchronization problems are considered:

1. Score-to-MIDI (here called SM),
2. Score-to-PCM (SP),
3. MIDI-to-PCM (MP),
4. MIDI-to-MIDI (MM), and
5. PCM-PCM (PP).

Figure 1.4 presents a schematic view of all the possible relations between score, MIDI, and PCM data.

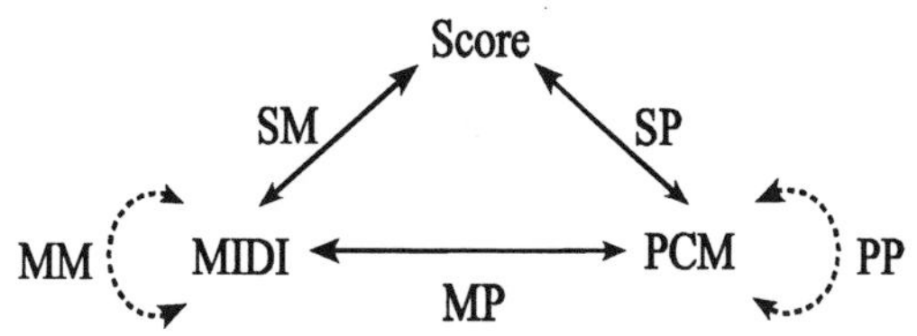

Figure 1.4. Schematic view of the elements of temporal synchronization.

Since the PCM format does not contain any explicit information about discrete events, one first has to extract event-related data such as note onsets and pitches in order to make PCM data comparable with symbolic representations and thus usable for synchronization. The problem of extraction of note information from the waveform of polyphonic music is solved for only a few special cases.

We have concentrated on polyphonic piano music. In contrast to many other research projects, we do not restrict ourselves to PCM data generated by MIDI pianos. We allow PCM data generated by any acoustic piano including audio data from a CD of piano music. This leads to many extraction results which are not suitable in a transcription of the original work. However, the extracted data is of sufficient quality to serve in synchronization algorithms.

1.2 Synchronization

To define and classify the synchronization problem it is helpful to delimit this problem to related problems in computational musicology such as segmentation, extraction, and musical transcription.

1.2.1 Segmentation

Cognitive segmentation could refer to the partitioning of a sonata into its movements, or of the first movement into its exposition, development, and recapitulation sections, or of the exposition into its A and B themes. The rendering of a piece of music into measures might be considered a type of logical segmentation. In audio-signal processing segmentation refers to the temporal partitioning into logically coherent sections. In audio-signal processing segmentation requires the decomposition of a sound stream into more elementary units. While in a speech signal the segments might be phonemes, in monophonic music they might correspond to notes. The segmentation boundaries consist of the initial and endpoints [onsets and offsets] of the corresponding notes (Raphael 1999). In audio signals of polyphonic music (e.g., in the PCM format) it is not clear how to define the segmentation boundaries in a meaningful way. Audio signals are complex sound mixtures. In combination with resonance effects, the intermingling and superposition of sounds results in such phenomena as a sudden increase of the intensity of certain harmonics even though no new notes are played (Blackham 1998). Apparently, a more general notion of segmentation is needed. *Segmentation boundaries* are here defined to be points of time where sudden changes in the spectrum as well as in the energy of the signal occur. Within a segment, the signal may be assumed to be quasi-periodic and the segmentation boundaries are candidates for the onset times of notes. The distance between onsets is the inter-onset interval (IOI).

1.2.2 Extraction

Segmentation can be considered as one element of the more general problem of *extraction*. When in audio-signal processing one tries to extract a suitable set of parameters from a waveform representation which describes the musical content of the underlying piece of music, the parameters include not only onset candidates but also spectral parameters for the description of pitch and parameters for the description of note duration, loudness, and so on. In this context, *beat* and *tempo tracking* can be considered as special cases of the extraction problem where temporal and dynamical parameters are suitably interpreted (Cemgil et al. 2000, Goto 2001). Alternatively, repeating spectral patterns are used (Foote et al. 2001). For the task of *automatic accompaniment*, spectral parameters are used to determine the pitch (Dannenberg et al. 1988, Raphael 1999), sometimes in combination with energy parameters (Cano et al. 1999). The extraction of the pitch from the corresponding spectral parameters constitutes a more or less unsolved problem in the domain of polyphonic piano music because the harmonics cannot be uniquely assigned to the single notes. Possible approaches to pitch extraction are based on the usage of note templates (Bobrek et al. 1998, Ortiz-Berenguer et al. 2002) or additional score information (Scheirer 1995). We use a technique similar to that described by Bobrek et al. (1998).

1.2.3 Transcription

Transcription (the conversion of an audio recording into score notation) and extraction, while similar in many ways, differ in one essential point: the score data are "standardized" parameters which allow room for local interpretations in performance, whereas the extracted note parameters of a music signal include both the score information and the features specific to a particular recorded interpretation.

For transcription the following steps seem to be feasible:

(1) Extraction of parameters for onset times, pitch, and note duration;

(2) Reassessment of the extracted data by suitable quantization and normalization methods.

(Other approaches to music transcription are discussed in Cemgil et al. 2000).

Synchronization is generally defined as the temporal coordination of two independent processes when coming into interaction. In the context of this article synchronization refers to the temporal coordination of two different realizations or variations of the same piece of music which are given as two independent data streams in possibly different data formats. This coordination obviously requires a suitable linking structure.

The problem of *synchronization* can be considered to be complementary to the problem of *transcription*. While in music transcription there is only *one* data stream from which the score parameters have to be determined, in synchronization one starts with *two* data streams. The goal of transcription, when seeking to obtain "pure" score data, is to reconcile the deviations in the extracted data resulting from the specific underlying interpretation. The goal of synchronization (particularly of SP synchronization) is to pick up just those local time deviations in the underlying interpretation of the PCM-data stream required to accomplish the linking with the uninterpreted score-data stream.

A number of recent approaches are based in part on techniques similar to those presented here. In general, however, there are important differences in the details. For example, in the problem of automatic accompaniment, one typically has a solo part played by a musician which is to be accompanied in real time by a computer system. Dannenberg et al. (1984, 1988, 1994) describes one of the first algorithms for automatic music accompaniment. He reduces the task of synchronization to a longest common subsequence (LCS) model which is implemented using dynamic time programming. Vercoe (1984) has developed a system for the automatic accompaniment of a transverse flute. Raphael (1999, 2001) has developed a system for automatic accompaniment of an oboe based on Hidden Markov Models. Desain et al. (1997) describe some general sequential and tree-based score/performance matching algorithms. A similar problem is addressed by Large (1993) using dynamic programming to study music-production errors. In all of these approaches, the data streams involved in synchronization either contain explicit note parameters or consist only of monophonic music (in which case the note parameters are comparatively clean and error-free). In our case, we allow PCM data of complex polyphonic piano music where there are no such explicit and clean parameters. We also take a few cues from the comprehensive study of Mazzola (2002), which gives a detailed account of local tempo variations resulting from expressiveness in performances.

Two recently proposed algorithms compute the alignment of a MIDI-data stream with a score-data stream which is somewhat similar to our approach: Turetsky et al. (2003) first convert the score-data stream into an audio-data stream using a suitable synthesizer and perform the alignment in the audio domain. Soulez et al. (2003) use the score to design a sequence of suitable filter models which then can be compared with the audio-data stream. In contrast to these two approaches, we perform the synchronization purely in the score-like domain, which has advantages in view of efficiency and accuracy: due to the expressiveness of score-like parameters, only a relatively small number of such features is sufficient to solve the synchronization task.

1.3 Extraction of Note Parameters from PCM Data

Our synchronization algorithms use only the onset times and pitches of the note objects. While one could also think of exploiting note durations or dynamics parameters, the restriction to onset times and pitches is sufficient for obtaining good synchronization results. Our experience that a staccato performance of a piece contains most of the information needed for work identification accords with that of many other researchers. Our extraction algorithms use established techniques from audio signal processing. Our main contributions are a refined template-matching algorithm for polyphonic pitch extraction and a two-step algorithm for note-onset detection.

In the extraction of note parameters the onset times are estimated using suitable attack-detection algorithms. Ideally, this yields a sequence of time intervals, each containing a note event. This may be a single note, a superposition of several simultaneously sounding notes (with possibly different onset times), or a chord. In a second step, we examine each of these events and try to determine the pitches of all notes contained in the event.

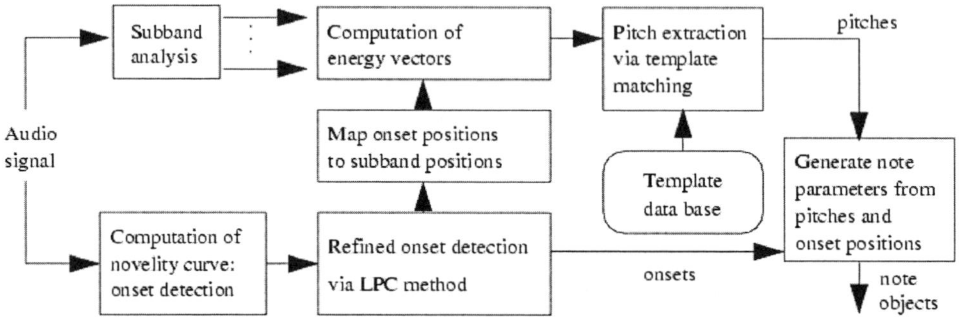

Figure 1.5. Diagram of the feature-extraction algorithm.

Figure 1.5 gives an overview of the components of our feature-extraction algorithm. Methods proposed for detecting onsets of musical notes, which may be classified into frequency- and time-domain approaches, were investigated. In frequency-domain approaches such as linear prediction, we found that several notes with relatively low energy (mainly repetitions of notes and chords) could not be detected. In pure time-domain approaches, such as creating coarse signal approximations using sliding windows, we found inferior detection results in passages containing strong variations in dynamics.

After eliminating these single-domain approaches, we developed a compromise between them to detect attacks. For this we used novelty curves (similar to those in Foote 2000), which describe an approximation to the change of a signal's frequency contents in time by summing over the absolute changes of the last two steps' magnitude spectra. Figure 1.6 shows the novelty curve extracted from an interpretation of the aria shown in Figure 1.1.

As the time resolution resulting from this procedure is relatively coarse, a post-processing is performed based on the concept of linear prediction. Using a method proposed by Foster et al. (1982), we refined the estimated coarse onset positions to a reasonable time resolution of up to 10 ms. In Figure 1.6, the peaks corresponding to the refined onset times are marked by circles. Figure 1.7 shows the detected onset times in the context of the physical waveform corresponding to the particular interpretation of the Bach aria.

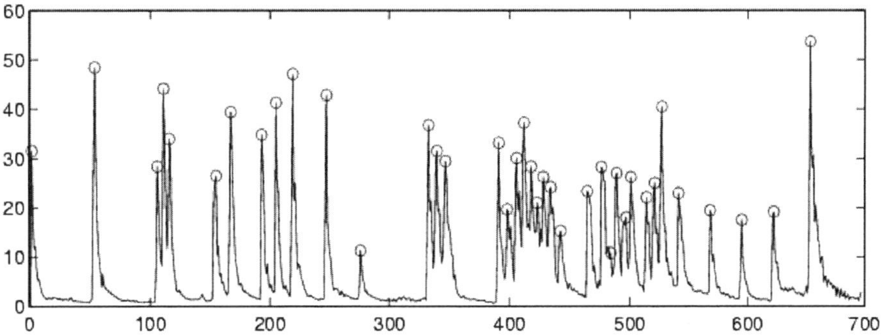

Figure 1.6. Novelty curve extracted from an interpretation of the aria shown in Figure 1.1.

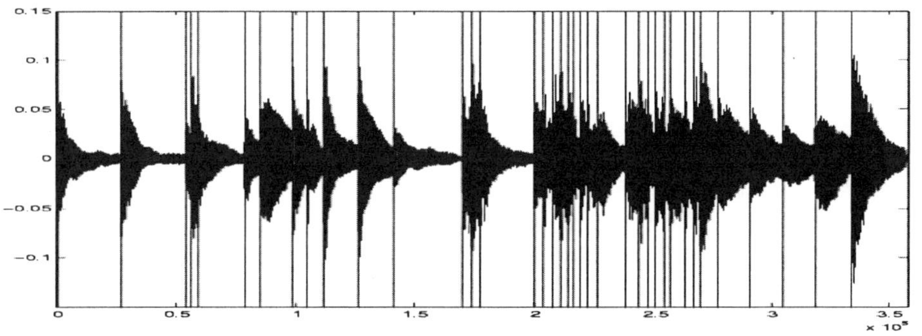

Figure 1.7. Detected onset times in the context of the physical waveform corresponding to the particular interpretation of the Bach aria (Figure 1.1).

The polyphonic pitch detection which is performed at a second stage uses a template-matching algorithm. This algorithm is subsequently applied to each time segment between two successive detected attack positions. The purpose of template matching is to successively compare the target interval (in a suitable representation) with a collection of pre-trained templates stored in a database. The template database (TDB) consists of one template for each possible note (it corresponds intuitively to the keyboard of the piano). The time interval is assigned to those notes whose templates yield a "good" match with respect to a suitable criterion.

The templates are created using fingerprints of the frequency-energy distributions of the single notes. Technically, we use a tree-structured filter bank (Bobrek et al. 1998) to transform the signal into a sub-band representation. The tree structure of the filter bank and hence the frequency ranges of the sub-bands are chosen such that the fundamental frequency of one piano note (in equal temperament) falls into one sub-band. This guarantees that in the template-matching algorithm templates can be uniquely assigned to energy vectors (Arifi 2002, Bobrek et al. 1998).

Our templates were recorded using a Yamaha GranTouch E-Piano. We also evaluated templates generated by two acoustic pianos (Steinway and Schimmel). However, the E-Piano's templates turned out to be the most robust for our purposes.

Our template-matching algorithm starts with an initial energy vector of the signal on the time segment in question. Then the algorithm tries to select an approximate template from the TDB which optimally fits the energy vector with respect to a particular criterion. If successful, a corresponding energy fraction is subtracted from the energy vector to yield a modified vector, which is used to recursively process the data until the remaining residual energy falls under a lower boundary.

We used the following criterion for selecting a template which optimally fits an energy vector $E \in \mathbb{R}^M$: find the lowest sub-band index k such that

$$E(k) \geq (c / M) \sum_{i=1}^{M} |E(i)|$$

(for a suitable prior constant c). If such a k exists, search the TDB for a template S_k with fundamental frequency in this sub-band. If E contains S_k to a significant extent, select S_k as a matching template. Bobrek et al. (1998), instead of using the lowest significant sub-band, choose the sub-band containing the highest energy component for selecting the template. In our experiments this criterion turned out to yield several octave-interval errors in pitch detection, especially when applied to recordings from acoustic pianos.

Figure 1.8 shows the piano-roll representation of the note parameters extracted from the interpretation of the Bach aria using the algorithms proposed. The explicit parameters of the first two measures can also be found in Figure 1.9. Note durations are not derived in our extraction process. We note that our algorithms require a careful choice of parameters (e.g., thresholds for template extraction, peak picking, or the minimum IOI [Arifi 2002]).

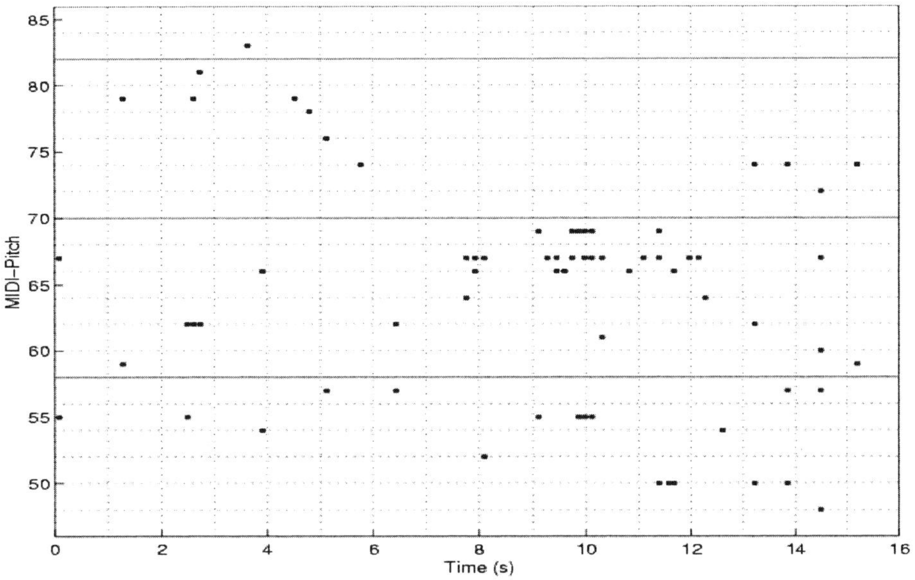

Figure 1.8. Piano-roll representation of the note parameters extracted from an interpretation of the Bach aria.

1.4 The Synchronization Algorithm

Our notions of tempo, time flow, and synchronization follow in part Mazzola (2002). We specify the *steady tempo* T by the formula $T = \#\text{beats}/\text{minute}$. Independent of such a tempo annotation one can allocate each metric position within any measure of a score to a *musical onset time* (MOT). Suppose there are b beats per measure and the position in question is the kth beat in the mth measure, then this position has the MOT

$$E = b \cdot (m-1) + k.$$

As an example, Figure 1.9 shows the onset times of the first few notes in the right hand of the aria, where $b = 3$ beats per measure.

If E_0 and E are MOTs with $E \geq E_0$ then, presupposing a uniform tempo T, the *physical onset time* $e(E)$ corresponding to E relative to the physical onset time corresponding to E_0 is given by

$$e(E) = e(E_0) + \frac{E - E_0}{T} \tag{1}$$

In reality one seldom has a uniform tempo. Slight local tempo deviations as well as tempo changes prescribed by the score have to be considered. Closer to reality is the uniform tempo of the piece.

ith note	1	2	3	4	5	6	7	–	8	9	10	11	12
E_i	0	1	2	$2\frac{3}{4}$	3	$3\frac{1}{2}$	4	5	6	7	$8\frac{1}{2}$	$8\frac{3}{4}$	9

Figure 1.9. Onset times of the first twelve note objects in the right hand of the Bach aria.

Suppose $E_0 < E_1 < \ldots < E_n = E$ are the MOTs, so that the tempo between E_{i-1} and E_i is uniformly given by T_i.

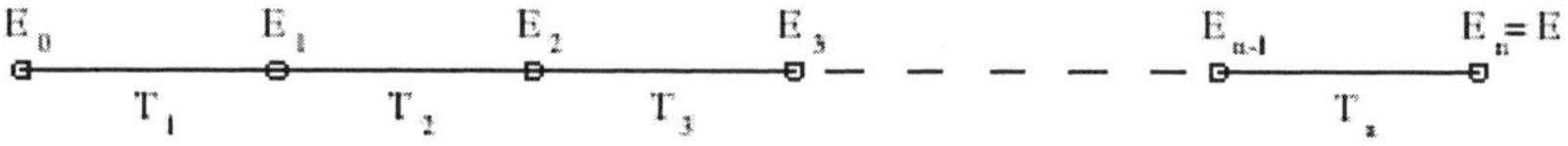

Then the physical onset times of E are given by the formula

$$e(E) = e(E_0) + \sum_{i=1}^{n} \frac{E_i - E_{i-1}}{T_i}.$$

Considering a finer and finer subdivision, the sum

$$\textstyle\sum_{i=1}^{n}(E_i - E_{i-1})/T_i$$

may be regarded as a Riemann sum and T_i may be interpreted as instantaneous tempo. Under suitable assumptions the *time flow* at musical onset time $E \geq E_0$ which is based on the tempo function T is given by

$$e(E) = e(E_0) + \int_{E_0}^{E} \frac{dx}{T(x)}.$$

Hence, given time flow e, the *tempo* in E is the reciprocal value

$$T(E) = \left(\frac{de}{dE}(E)\right)^{-1}.$$

We illustrate these principles with two typical examples. If $T(x) = T$ is constant, then the tempo is uniform and $e(E)$ reduces to the formula $e(E) = e(E_0) + (E-E_0)/T$. If $T(x) = \alpha \bullet (x-E_0) + T_0$ (for any $\alpha \neq 0$, a constant T_0, and all $x \in [E_0, E]$), then one gets

$$e(E) = e(E_0) + \frac{1}{\alpha} \ln \frac{\alpha(E - E_0) + T_0}{T_0}.$$

In other words, for $\alpha > 0$ one has, from the musical onset time E_0, a uniform *accelerando*, whereas for $\alpha < 0$ one has a uniform *ritardando*.

Now, suppose two given tempo functions T_1 and T_2 from two different interpretations of the same piece are known to lead to the time flows

$$e_1(E) = e_1(E_0) + \int_{E_0}^{E} \frac{dx}{T_1(x)} \quad \text{and} \quad e_2(E) = e_2(E_0) + \int_{E_0}^{E} \frac{dx}{T_2(x)}.$$

Then the (ideal) *synchronization* of the two interpretations consists in linking the point of time e_1 (E) with the corresponding point e_2 (E) of the second interpretation for each musical onset time E of the score. This is illustrated in Figure 1.10.

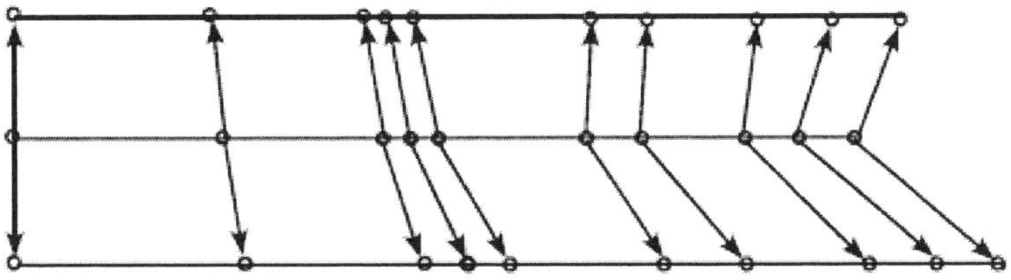

Figure 1.10. Ideal synchronization of two interpretations with time flows e_1 (E) and e_2 (E) via the score.

In score-based synchronization, the reality is remote from this model because of the vagueness of tempo indications and the modifications suggested by directions such as *ritardando* or *accelerando*. The exact course of the tempo in performance may vary greatly from what the score implies. Since there is no canonical tempo function present in the score, each tempo function has to be derived from a concrete interpretation.

1.4.1 Synchronization Problems

We are now able to specify the problems particular to each synchronization path. These are listed by increasing degree of difficulty.

Score–MIDI Data (SM)

In the easiest scenario a score and a MIDI data stream are given. Here the synchronization problem boils down to computing the tempo function of the MIDI recording. This task is comparatively easy since MIDI files contain key numbers which can usually be translated to accurate sounding pitches. Articulations (trills, arpeggios, grace notes) indicated symbolically in a score may be rendered by additional events to fulfill the expectation of listeners. We call such event-groups *fuzzy notes.*

Score–PCM Data (SP)

Here the synchronization problem consists of computing the tempo function of the PCM data stream. This requires the extraction of the note parameters from the PCM file, a process which can produce erroneous results. We address this problem using cost-optimal partial matches based on a suitably designed cost function which takes such possibilities into account.

The score, a MIDI- and PCM-data stream are given. The MIDI and PCM interpretations are to be synchronized. In this case, the MP synchronization can be done by combining the solutions of the two previous tasks.

MIDI–PCM DATA (MP)

In the absence of score information, the MIDI data is used as a reference. The procedure is similar to the Score-PCM case, with the difference that MOTs are lacking.

Further, MM synchronization and PP synchronization (the synchronization of two MIDI versions to two PCM versions of the same piece) may be realized by combing solutions of above problems via

$$\begin{array}{lcl} \mathrm{SM}_1 \ \& \ \mathrm{SM}_2 & \longrightarrow & \mathrm{M}_1\mathrm{M}_2 \\ \mathrm{SP}_1 \ \& \ \mathrm{SP}_2 & \longrightarrow & \mathrm{P}_1\mathrm{P}_2. \end{array}$$

Owing to space limitations, we give a detailed account of only the second case (SP synchronization). The other cases can be done in a similar fashion (Arifi 2002). Figure 1.11 shows the steps performed in our algorithm.

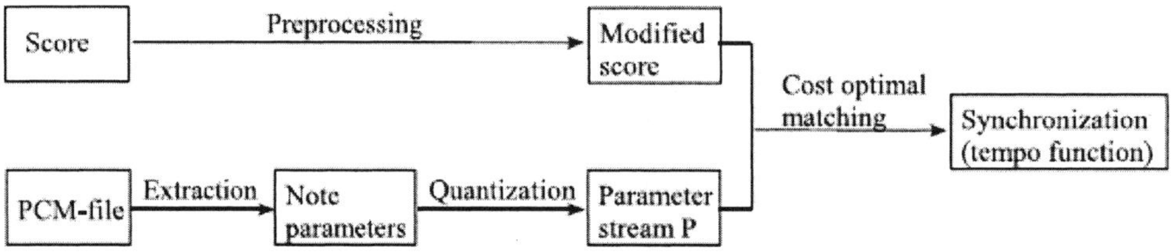

Figure 1.11. Algorithm for score-PCM synchronization.

1.4.2 The Preprocessing of Score Data

We assume the score data to exist in an electronic form (e.g., as *Capella*, *Finale*, or *Sibelius* files; *Capella* was used in the analysis). We seek to establish only two parameters, the MOT and pitch. The MOT of the kth beat in the mth measure is given by $E = b + (m-1) + k$, where b denotes the number of beats per measure. Hence $E \in \mathbf{Q}$, where $\mathbf{Q}$ denotes the set of rational numbers. Furthermore, we identify a pitch p with the corresponding MIDI key number (MKN) in the integer range 0 to 127. Defining $[0{:}127] := \{0,1,\ldots,127\}$ one writes $p \in [0{:}127]$. For example, the standard pitch A [440 Hz] is represented by the number $p = 69$.

We distinguish between two kinds of notes: *explicit* ones, in which all the parameters are given directly, and the *implicit* ones, which we call *fuzzy notes*. [In the Bach aria the ornamented and graced notes are fuzzy objects.] All explicit objects at a given onset time E will be represented by a pair (E, H_0) which consists of the onset time E and a set of pitches $H_0 \subseteq [0{:}127]$ containing all the pitches of the corresponding notes. For example, the explicit notes at onset times $E = 0$ and $E = 1$ of the Bach aria in Figure 1.1 are represented by $(0, \{55, 79\})$ and $(1, \{59, 79\})$ respectively.

Implicit objects allow multiple realizations, for performance depends on the epoch and the specific individual interpretation. We define a *fuzzy note* as a pair (E, H_1) consisting of a musical onset time $E \in \mathbf{Q}$ and a set of *alternative* pitches $H_1 \subseteq [0{:}127]$. Then an implicit note object, such as a trill, is represented by the MOT of the associated main note and the set of all pitches appearing in a possible realization of this object. Figure 1.12 illustrates the definition. Here, the two fuzzy-note pitches are given by $(0, \{67, 69\})$ and $(1, \{71, 72, 74\})$.

Figure 1.12. Appoggiatura and trill, (a) notation, (b) possible realization, (c) fuzzy notes containing all the pitches involved in the articulation of the symbols in (a).

To simplify the discussion we assume that there is at most one implicit note object at a given musical onset time E. It is a straightforward generalization to admit several implicit note objects at a time. Then after preprocessing we may assume that a score is given by a subset $S \subset \mathbf{Q} \times 2^{[0:127]} \times 2^{[0:127]}$, where $2^{[0:127]}$ denotes the set of all subsets of [0:127]. Here, in a triple $(E, H_0, H_1) \in S$ the subset $H_0 \subseteq 2^{[0:127]}$ consists of all pitches of explicit note objects having music onset time E and similarly the subset $H_1 \subseteq 2^{[0:127]}$ consists of all pitches of implicit note objects having musical onset time E. We want to emphasize that H_0 is a set of pitches which certainly appear in an interpretation of the score at onset time E, whereas H_1 represents just a set of *alternatives* of possible or likely pitches. Table 1.1 shows the encoding of the first few notes of the Bach aria.

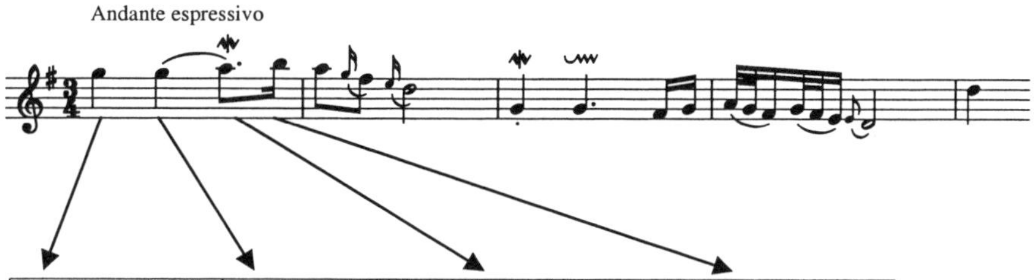

$(0, \{55, 79\}, \emptyset)$,	$(1, \{59, 79\}, \emptyset)$,	$(2, \{62\}, \{79, 81\})$,	$(2\frac{3}{4}, \{83\}, \emptyset)$,
$(3, \{54, 81\}, \emptyset)$,	$(3\frac{1}{2}, \emptyset, \{78, 79\})$,	$(4, \{57\}, \{74, 76\})$,	$(5, \{62\}, \emptyset)$.

Table 1.1. Representation of fuzzy notes (pitch sets) in the Bach aria. [Lower voice shown in MIDI key numbers (MKN); see Figure 1.1 for music.]

1.5 Matching and Cost Function

The SP synchronization algorithm is based on dynamic programming. The decisive ingredient for our approach is a carefully designed cost function. After preprocessing the score, we extract a set of possible note objects consisting of physical onset times (POTs) and pitches from the PCM data. The POTs are then quantized. We pool all note objects by suitably adjusting those POTs which differ by only a small value (i.e., smaller than a suitably chosen $\Delta > 0$), since these note objects are likely to have the same MOT in the corresponding score format. After quantization, we may assume that the extracted PCM data is given by the subset $P_\Delta \subset \mathbf{Q} \times 2^{[0:127]}$. Note that the PCM data contains only explicit note objects.

Altogether, we may assume that the score and the Δ-quantized PCM data are given by the sets

$$S = [(s_1, S_{01}, S_{11}),\ldots,(s_s, S_{0s}, S_{1s})]$$

and

$$P_\Delta = [(p_1, P_{01}),\ldots,(p_p, P_{0p})].$$

Here, the s_i, $1 \le i \le s$, denotes the MOTs and the p_j, $1 \le j \le p$, denotes quantized POTs. Furthermore, S_{0i}, S_{1i}, $P_{0j} \subseteq [0:127]$ are the respective sets of pitches (MKNs) for the explicit and implicit objects.

On the basis of S and P_Δ we can now perform the SP synchronization. Since the score and the PCM data represent the same piece of music, it is reasonable to assume $s_1 = p_1 = 0$ by shifting the onset times. The goal is now to partially link the onset times $s_1,\ldots,s_s$ to $p_1,\ldots,p_p$ by maximizing the matches of the corresponding pitch sets. In the following, we formalize this approach.

Definition 1.1. A *Score-PCM match* (SP match) of S and P_Δ is defined to be a partial map $\mu : [1:s] \to [1:p]$, which is strictly increasing in its domain satisfying $(S_{0i} \cup S_{1i}) \cap P_{0\mu(i)} \neq \emptyset$ for all $i \in$ Domain (μ).

The fact that objects in S or P_Δ may not have a counterpart in the other data stream is modeled by the requirement that μ is only a partial function and not a total one. The monotony of μ reflects the requirement of faithful timing: if a note in S precedes a second one this should also hold for the μ-images of these notes. Finally, the requirement $(S_{0i} \cup S_{1i}) \cap P_{0\mu(i)} \neq \emptyset$ prevents onset times from being linked if the objects are completely unrelated with respect to their pitches.

Obviously, there are many possible SP matches between S and P_Δ. By means of a suitable cost function we can compare different matches. The goal is then to compute an SP match minimizing the cost function. To simplify the notation we identify the partial function μ with its graph Graph $(\mu) := \{(i_1, j_1),\ldots,(i_\ell, j_\ell)\}$, where $\{i_1 < \cdots < i_\ell\} \subseteq [1:s]$ and $\{j_1 = \mu(i_1) < \cdots <$

$j_\ell = \mu(i_\ell)\} \subseteq [1:p]$. In the following definition we assign costs to each SP match μ. In doing so, we make use of a parameter vector $\pi := (\alpha, \beta, \gamma, \delta, \zeta, \Delta) \in \mathbb{R}^6_{\geq 0}$ consisting of six real parameters which will be specified later.

Definition 1.2. Let $\pi := (\alpha, \beta, \gamma, \delta, \zeta, \Delta) \in \mathbb{R}^6_{\geq 0}$ be a parameter vector. Then the *SP cost* of an SP match μ w.r.t. π between a score S and a Δ-quantized set P_Δ of the corresponding PCM document is defined as

$$
\begin{aligned}
C_\pi^{\mathrm{SP}}(\mu|S, P_\Delta) \;:=\; & \alpha \cdot \sum_{(i,j)\in\mu} \Big(|S_{0i} \setminus P_{0j}| + \lambda(i,j) \Big) \\
& + \beta \cdot \sum_{(i,j)\in\mu} \Big(|P_{0j} \setminus (S_{0i} \cup S_{1i})| + \rho(i,j) \Big) \\
& + \gamma \cdot \sum_{k \notin \mathrm{Domain}(\mu)} \Big(|S_{0k}| + \sigma(k) \Big) \\
& + \delta \cdot \sum_{t \notin \mathrm{Image}(\mu)} |P_{0t}| \\
& + \zeta \cdot \sum_{(i,j)\in\mu} \Big| s_i - p_j \cdot \ell(S)/\ell(P) \Big| .
\end{aligned}
$$

This definition requires some explanations. The sum corresponding to the factor α represents the cost of the non-matched explicit and implicit note objects of the score S. More precisely, the cardinality $|S_{0i} \setminus P_{0j}|$ measures the cost arising from the difference of the set S_{0i} of explicit note objects at the ith onset time of S and the set P_{0j} of explicit quantized note objects at the jth onset time of P_Δ. In addition, $\lambda(i, j)$ is defined to be 1 if and only if the score S has an implicit note object at the ith onset time and $P_\Delta \cdot P_\Delta$ has no counterpart at the jth onset time, i.e., $S_{1i} \neq \emptyset$ and $S_{1i} \cap P_{0j} = \emptyset$. In all other cases $\lambda(i, j)$ is defined to be 0. Next, we consider the sum corresponding to the factor β. The first summand in the brackets measures the cost of (possibly erroneously) extracted notes at the jth physical onset time whose pitches do not lie in $S_{0i} \cup S_{1i}$. Further, $p(i, j)$ is defined to be $|P_{0j} \cap S_{1i}| - 1$ if $P_{0j} \cap S_{1i} \neq \emptyset$. Otherwise, $p(i, j)$ is defined to be 0. In other words, for the implicit note objects only *one* match is free of cost; each additional match is penalized. (This is motivated by the idea that all notes belonging to a possible realization of a fuzzy note are expected to have pair-wise distinct POTs.) The sum corresponding to γ accounts for all onset times of the score which do not belong to the match μ. The first term within the brackets counts the number of explicit note objects at the kth onset time, $k \in \mathrm{Domain}(\mu)$. Furthermore, $\sigma(k)$ is defined to be 1 if there is a non-matched implicit note object and 0 if there is no implicit note object at the kth onset time. (The idea is that a non-matched fuzzy note should only be penalized by 1 since it only represents one set of alternatives.) The sum corresponding to δ accounts for the cost of those notes in P_Δ which do not have a counterpart in S. Finally, the last sum corresponding to ζ measures an adjusted ℓ^1-distance (known as Manhattan distance) of the vector pairs $(s_i, p_j)_{(i,j)\in\mu}$, where $\ell(S)$ and $\ell(P)$ denote the differences of the last and the first musical respectively physical onset times (a kind of musical and physical duration). By this sum one penalizes matches with large relative time deviations, thus preventing large global deviations in the synchronization.

In the following we fix a parameter vector π, a preprocessed score S, and quantized extracted PCM data P_Δ. Note that if μ is an SP match, then $\mu' := \mu \setminus \{(i, j)\}$ for some $(i, j) \in \mu$. An easy computation shows

$$\begin{aligned} C_\pi^{\mathrm{SP}}(\mu|S, P_\Delta) - C_\pi^{\mathrm{SP}}(\mu'|S, P_\Delta) \;=\;& \alpha \cdot \Big(|S_{0i} \setminus P_{0j}| + \lambda(i,j) \Big) \\ & + \beta \cdot \Big(|P_{0j} \setminus (S_{0i} \cup S_{1i})| + \rho(i,j) \Big) \\ & - \gamma \cdot \Big(|S_{0i}| + \sigma(i) \Big) \\ & - \delta \cdot |P_{0j}| \\ & + \zeta \cdot \Big| s_i - p_j \cdot \ell(S)/\ell(P) \Big| . \end{aligned} \qquad (2)$$

Now one can determine a cost-minimizing SP match by means of dynamic programming. We recursively define a matrix $C = (c_{ij})$ with $i \in [0{:}s]$ and $j \in [0{:}p]$.

First, initialize $c_{0j} := c_{i0} := C_\pi^{SP}(\emptyset \mid S, P_\Delta)$ for all $i \in [0{:}s]$, $j \in [0{:}p]$. Note that this accounts for the costs that there is no match at all between S and P_Δ. At position $(i, j) \in [1{:}s] \times [1{:}p]$ the value c_{ij} expresses the cost for a cost-minimizing SP match within the subset $[1{:}i] \times [1{:}j] \subset [1{:}s] \times [1{:}p]$. Hence, c^{sp} expresses the minimal cost of a global SP match. For $(i, j) \in [1{:}s] \times [1{:}p]$, the value c_{ij} is defined as

$$c_{ij} := \min\{c_{i,j-1}, c_{i-1,j}, c_{i-1,j-1} + d_{ij}^{SP}\},$$

where

$$d_{ij}^{\mathrm{SP}} := \begin{cases} \text{right hand side of Eq. (2),} & \text{if } (S_{0i} \cup S_{1i}) \cap P_{0j} \neq \emptyset, \\ 0, & \text{otherwise.} \end{cases}$$

Using the resulting matrix C, the procedure of Figure 1.13 computes a cost-minimizing SP match.

```
SCORE-PCM-SYNCHRONIZATION(C,s,p)
   i := s,  j := p,  SP-Match := ∅
   while (i > 0) and (j > 0)
      do if c[i,j] = c[i,j-1]
            then j := j-1
         else if c[i,j] = c[i-1,j]
            then i := i-1
         else SP-Match := SP-Match ∪ {(i,j)},
              i := i-1,  j := j-1
   return SP-Match
```

Figure 1.13. Procedure for computing the cost-minimizing SP match.

SM and MP synchronization can be done similarly to the SP case. Other synchronization problems, such as synchronization of two PCM data streams P_1 and P_2 (P_1P_2 synchronization), may be achieved by using a score S as a reference and carrying out both an SP_1 and an SP_2 synchronization.

In the parameter vector $\pi := (\alpha, \beta, \gamma, \delta, \zeta, \Delta)$ of most of our experiments, we set the quantization constant to $\Delta = 50$ ms. This threshold was chosen as a good compromise between psychoacoustically distinguishable asynchronisms of chords and the shortest possible musical note durations. With the parameters α and β one can weight the cost for the symmetric difference of pitch sets corresponding to matched onset times, whereas with the parameters γ and δ one can weight the cost of those note objects which do not have a counterpart in the other data stream. One meaningful standard choice of the parameters is $\alpha = \beta = \gamma = \delta = 1$. However, if one wants to penalize non-matched onset times, for example, one may increase γ and δ. If $\zeta = 0$, the last sum of the cost function remains unconsidered. Increasing ζ will hamper matches (i, j) whose onset times s_i and p_j differ too much with respect to their relative positions in their respective data streams. In other words, excessive global time divergence in the synchronization of the two data streams can be controlled.

1.6 An Example

We illustrate the SP synchronization by means of the Bach aria shown in Figure 1.1. After the preprocessing step the score is given by the data stream $S = [(s_1, S_{01}, S_{11}),\ldots,(s_s, S_{0s}, S_{1s})]$ with $s = 23$. For example, the set $S_{01} = \{55, 79\}$ contains the two pitches at musical onset time $s_1 = 0$ corresponding to the first note g (MKN 55) in the left hand and the first note g'' (MKN 79) in the right. As another example, the mordent in the right hand of the first measure is modeled by a fuzzy note (implicit note object) at musical onset time $s_3 = 2$ given by $S_{13} = \{79, 81\}$, or a'' and g'', the notes involved in the ornament. Table 1.2 shows all the note objects of S corresponding to the first two measures of the Bach aria.

S				P_Δ		
i	s_i	S_{0i}	S_{1i}	j	p_j	P_{0j}
1	0	{55, 79}	∅	1	0	{55, 67}
2	1	{59, 79}	∅	2	1.23	{59, 79}
3	2	{62}	{79, 81}	3	2.44	{55, 62}
				4	2.56	{62, 79}
				5	2.68	{62, 81}
4	2.75	{83}	∅	6	3.58	{83}
5	3	{54, 81}	∅	7	3.86	{54, 66}
6	3.5	∅	{78, 79}	8	4.47	{79}
				9	4.75	{78}
7	4	{57}	{74, 76}	10	5.06	{57, 76}
				11	5.71	{74}
8	5	{62}	∅	12	6.39	{57, 62}

Table 1.2. Matching of the preprocessed score data stream S and the data stream P_Δ consisting of the quantized note parameters extracted from the PCM data stream for the first two measures of the Bach aria.

The PCM-version P represents a recording of the Bach aria performed on a Steinway grand piano. The physical length is $\ell(P) = 13$ seconds. After extraction of the note parameters (shown in Figure 1.8) and Δ-quantization ($\Delta = 50$ ms) one obtains $P_\Delta = [(p_1, P_{01}),\ldots,(p_p, P_{0p})]$ with $p = 38$ note objects. Note that the number $p = 38$ in P_Δ is much greater than the number $s = 23$ in S. The reason is that P_Δ not only contains several note objects for each trill and appoggiatura (which correspond in S to a single implicit note object) but also erroneous extraction results. Table 1.2 shows all the note objects of P_Δ corresponding to the first two measures of the Bach aria. Here p_j denotes the POT for the positions $j = 1,2,\ldots,38$ measured in seconds.

Table 1.2 also illustrates some of the difficulties which occur in the extraction step. For example, at position $j = 1$ the set $P_{01} = \{55, 67\}$ contains MKN 67 instead of the expected 79 (an octave higher). This is because at onset time p_1 the notes g (MKN 55) and g'' (MKN 79) are played simultaneously. The sound corresponding to the note g contains the harmonics g' and g''. It is nearly impossible to decide whether g' or g'' are fundamental frequencies of independent notes or just harmonics of g. At position $j = 1$ the extraction algorithm has, instead of g'', mistakenly interpreted g' (MKN 67) as an independent note. Such octave errors are typical for the extraction step. To tackle this problem one may restrict oneself to considering only pitches which are reduced modulo 12 when using the note parameters as input for the synchronization algorithm. The extraction of the note g (MKN 55) at position $j = 3$ may be attributed to the fact that this note has been played at onset time p_1 and continues to sound at time p_3. The extraction algorithm mistakenly rediscovers this note as a "new" object at time p_3. The mordent over a'' in the first measure, corresponding to the fuzzy note $S_{13} = \{79, 81\}$ in the score, has several counterparts on the PCM side, namely P_{03}, P_{04}, and P_{05}. In passages with many short notes having similar spectral components, the extraction algorithm is prone to produce additional pitches.

In spite of its tendency to produce superfluous note parameters, the SP synchronization algorithm performs well overall. Using the cost function $C^{SP}_{\pi}(\mu|S,P_\Delta)$ from Definition 1.2 with the prototypical parameter vector π = (1, 1, 1, 1, 0, 50) leads to the cost matrix $C = (C_{ij})$, which is shown in Table 1.3 for the note objects of the first two measures.

We recall that the number c_{ij} expresses the costs for a cost-minimizing SP match of the note objects of S up to position i with the note objects of P_Δ up to position j. (For c_{ij} all note objects above the positions i and j respectively are not considered and remain unmatched.) For example, the number $c_{00} = 102$ is the cost for the empty match, i.e., the cost where there is no match at all. Hence c_{00} is maximal among all numbers c_{ij}. When the first note object S_{01} at position i = 1of S is matched with the first note object P_{01} at position j = 1 of P and all other note objects are left unconsidered, one gets the cost $c_{11} = 98$ which is lower than c_{00}, and so on. Now, using dynamic programming, one gets the cost-minimizing global match μ. In Table 1.3 the matrix entries c_{ij} corresponding to a matched pair $(i,.j)$ [i.e., μ (i) = (j)] are written in boldface, i.e., the matches of the first two measures are **{(1,1),(2,2),(3,3),(4,6)}**, **{(5,7),(6,8),(7,10),(8,12)}**. In this example, the fuzzy note S_{13} is matched with the "first note" P_{03} of the three note objects belonging to the mordent realization of the interpreted PCM version. Furthermore, the SP algorithm has matched the appoggiatura of the score S modeled by the fuzzy note S_{16} at position i = **6** with the corresponding first note object P_{08} of the appoggiatura of P_Δ at position j = **8**, and similarly S_{17} with $P_{0,10}$.

	0	1	2	3	4	5	6	7	8	9	10	11	12
0	102	102	102	102	102	102	102	102	102	102	102	102	102
1	102	**98**	98	98	98	98	98	98	98	98	98	98	98
2	102	98	**94**	94	94	94	94	94	94	94	94	94	94
3	102	98	94	**90**	90	90	90	90	90	90	90	90	90
4	102	98	94	90	90	90	**88**	88	88	88	88	88	88
5	102	98	94	90	90	88	88	**85**	85	85	85	85	85
6	102	98	94	90	88	88	88	85	**83**	83	83	83	83
7	102	98	94	90	88	88	88	85	83	83	**79**	79	79
8	102	98	94	90	88	86	86	85	83	83	79	79	**77**

Table 1.3. Cost matrix $C = (c_{ij})$ for the note objects of S (row index $i = 0,\ldots,8$) and P_Δ (column index $j = 0,\ldots,12$), corresponding to the first two measures of the Bach aria.

In Figure 1.14 the computation of an optimal SP match is illustrated by means of a 3D plot which visualizes the cost matrix C. The right coordinate represents the indices j for the onset times s_j, $1 \le j \le s$, $s = 38$. The middle coordinate represents the indices i for the onset times p_i, $1 \le i \le p$, $p = 23$. Finally, the vertical coordinate shows the values c_{ij} of the matrix C. The path indicates the cost-minimizing match representing the solution of the synchronization problem.

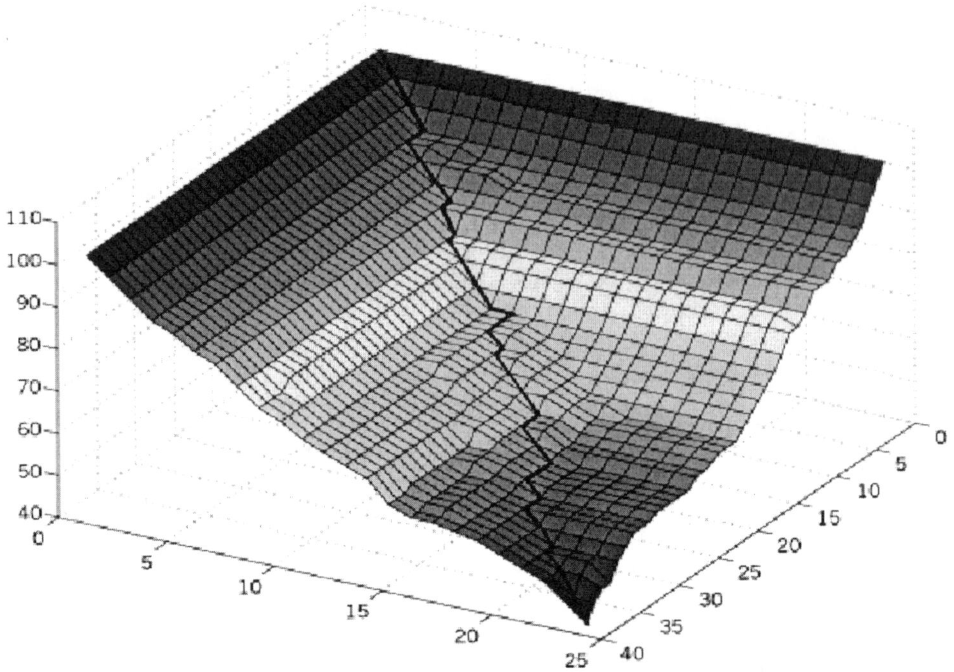

Figure 1.14. The cost matrix C and a cost-minimizing SP match for the Bach aria.

1.7 Implementations

We have implemented a prototype of the extraction algorithms from section 1.3 and the synchronization algorithms in the MATLAB programming language and tested our algorithms for SM, SP, and MP synchronization on a variety of classical polyphonic piano pieces of differing complexity and length (ranging from 10 to 60 seconds) played on various instruments. We have also systematically generated a library of more than one hundred test pieces both in MIDI and PCM format played on a MIDI piano, a Steinway grand piano, and a Schimmel piano. In some of these pieces our player has deliberately included excessive *accelerandi*, *ritardandi*, rhythmic distortions, and wrong notes. Even in these extreme situations, where one unsurprisingly has many "erroneously" extracted note objects which differ considerably from the score data, our SP synchronization algorithm resulted in good overall global matches, which are sufficient for the applications mentioned in the introduction. Also, in the case of relatively accurate extracted note parameters, our synchronization algorithms could resolve subtle local time variations in an interpreted version of the piano piece. For further details and results of our experiments, see Arifi (2002).

We describe here one of our experiments where we started with an uninterpreted score-like MIDI version and an interpreted PCM version of a piano piece. Using the results of our MP synchronization, we automatically modified the onset times of the MIDI stream to correspond to the PCM stream in view of the global and local tempo variations. This resulted in an "expressive" MIDI version which represented a sonification of our synchronization results. The modified MIDI version sounded rhythmically like a real interpretation of the underlying piano piece.

1.8 Conclusions

Our implementation yields good synchronization results even for complex PCM-based polyphonic piano CD recordings. One of the decisive features is a carefully designed cost function which penalizes not only non- or partially matched note objects but also large relative global time deviations (in case $\zeta > 0$). The parameter vector π allows us to weight different aspects in the matching process and leaves room for experiments.

Our cost function may be improved and extended in various ways. One improvement may result if one allows that a fuzzy note of the score data stream S may be assigned to several note objects of P_Δ. For example, in Table 1.2 a simultaneous match of the mordent S_{13} at position $i = 3$ with all three note objects P_{03}, P_{04}, P_{05} (leading to the matches [3,3], [3,4], and [3,5]) would better reflect the correspondence of the score parameters and the extracted note parameters of the PCM data. In this case the match μ would be a relation rather than a partial function.

Another improvement may be achieved by emphasizing note objects with a high probability of correct detection. Such objects might be low notes whose fundamental pitch cannot be mixed up with harmonics of other notes, or notes with unusual spectral components. Here, prior knowledge of the score may be used to determine such objects which should then be matched preferentially. This can be achieved by modifying the cost function in such a way that non-matching of notes likely to be unambiguous leads to disproportionately higher costs. In the Bach aria, for example, the first notes of each measure in the left hand are good candidates for these anchor positions.

Finally, we note that our current system works off-line, where the bottleneck lies in the preprocessing step needed to extract parameters from the PCM files (where we up to now have not used any score information). An ongoing research project is to exploit the score information in the extraction step (see also Scheirer [1995] for a similar approach.) This prior knowledge allows us to use prediction methods, in particular Kalman filtering, which, in connection with time-varying comb filters, may result in extraction algorithms running in real time. Such fast algorithms may be at the expense of the quality of the extraction parameters. However, even low-quality and coarse parameters may be sufficient for a successful synchronization when using a suitably designed cost function which is robust for erroneous parameters.

References

Arifi, Vlora (2002). "Algorithmen zur Synchronisation von Musikdaten im Paritur-, MIDI- und PCM-Format." Ph.D. thesis, University of Bonn (Institut für Informatik).

Blackham, E. D. (1998). "Klaviere" in *Die Physik der Musikinstrumente*, 2nd edn., Spectrum, Akademischer Verlag.

Bobrek, Miljko, and Daniel Koch (1998), "Music Signal Segmentation Using Tree-Structured Filter Banks," *Journal of the Audio Engineering Society*, 46/5, 412–427.

Cano, P., A. Loscos, and J. Bonda (1999), "Score-Performance Matching Using HMMs," *Proceedings of the International Computer Music Conference 1999*, pp. 441–444.

Cemgil, A. T., P. Desain, and B. Kappen (2000), "Rhythm Quantization for Transcription," *Computer Music Journal*, 24/2, 60–76.

Cemgil, A. T., B. Kappen, P. Desain**Error! Bookmark not defined.**, and H. Honing (2000), "On Tempo Tracking: Tempogram Representation and Kalman Filtering," *Proceedings of the International Computer Music Conference 2000*, pp. 352–355.

Dannenberg, R. B. (1984), "An On-Line Algorithm for Real-Time Accompani-ment," *Proceedings of the International Computer Music Conference 1984*, pp. 193–198.

Dannenberg, et al. (1994). "Automated Musical Accompaniment with Multiple Input Sensors," US Patent #5521324.

Dannenberg, R. B., and H. Mukaino (1988), "New Techniques for Enhanced Quality of Computer Accompaniment," *Proceedings of the International Computer Music Conference 1988*, pp. 243–249.

Desain, P., H. Honing, and H. Heijink (1997), "Robust Score-Performance Matching: Taking Advantage of Structural Information," *Proceedings of the International Computer Music Conference 1997*, pp. 377–380.

Foote, J. (2000), "ARTHUR: Retrieving Orchestral Music by Long-Term Structure," Proceedings of the First International Symposium on Music Information Retrieval (ISMIR), *www.fxpal.com/people/foote/papers/allpapers.html*.

Foote, J., and S. Uchihashi (2001), "The Beat Spectrum: A New Approach to Rhythm Analysis," *Proceedings of the International Conference on Multimedia and Expo (ICME)*, pp. 1088–1091.

Foster, S., W. A. Schloss, and A. J. Rockmore (1982), "Towards an Intelligent Editor of Digital Audio: Signal Processing Methods," *Computer Music Journal*, 6/1, 42–51.

Goto, Masatako (2001), "An Audio-Based Real-Time Beat Tracking System for Music with or without Drum-Sounds," *Journal of New Music Research*, 30/2, 159–171.

Large, Edward W. (1993). "Dynamic Programming for the Analysis of Serial Behaviours" in *Behaviour Research Methods, Instruments, & Computers* (1993), pp. 238–241.

Mazzola, Guerino, ed. (2002). *The Topos of Music*. Basel: Birkhäuser Verlag AG.

Ortiz-Berenguer, L. I., and F. J. Casajús-Quirós (2002), "Pattern Recognition of Piano Chords Based on Physical Model," *Proceedings of the 112th AES Convention*, pp. 10–13.

Pickens, Jeremy, Juan Pablo Bello, Giuliano Monti, Tim Crawford, Matthew Dovey, Mark Sandler, and Don Byrd (2002), "Polyphonic Score Retrieval Using Polyphonic Audio Queries: A Harmonic Modeling Approach" in *ISMIR 2002 Proceedings*, (Paris: IRCAM, 2002), pp. 140–149.

Raphael, C. (1999), "Automatic Segmentation of Acoustic Musical Signals Using Hidden Markov Models," *IEEE Transactions on Pattern Analysis and Machine Intelligence*, 21/4, 360–370.

Raphael**Error! Bookmark not defined.**, C. (2001), "A Probabilistic Expert System for

Automatic Musical Accompaniment," *Journal of Comp. and Graph. Statistics*, 10/3, 487–512.

Scheirer, E. D. (1995). "Extracting Expressive Performance Information from Recorded Music." M.S. thesis, MIT Media Laboratory.

Scheirer, E. D. (1998), "Tempo and Beat Analysis of Acoustic Musical Signals," *Journal of the Acoustical Society of America*, 103/1, 588–601.

Selfridge-Field, Eleanor (ed.) (1997). *Beyond MIDI: The Handbook of Musical Codes.* Cambridge, MA: MIT Press.

Soulez, F., X. Rodet, and D. Schwartz (2003), "Improving Polyphonic and Poly-instrumental Music-to-Score Alignment" in *ISMIR 2003 Proceedings*, *http://ismir2003.ismir.net/papers/Soulez.pdf.*

Turetsky, R. J., and D. P. Ellis (2003), "Ground-Truth Transcriptions of Real Music from Force-Aligned MIDI Synthesis" in *ISMIR 2003 Proceedings*, *http://ismir2003.ismir.net/papers/Turetsky.pdf.*

Vercoe, B. (1984), "The Synthetic Performer in the Context of Live Performance," *Proceedings of the International Computer Music Conference 1984*, pp. 199–200.

2 Modeling Rhythmic Motif Structure with Fuzzy Logic and Machine Learning

Tillman Weyde

Research Unit for Music and Media Technology
University of Osnabrück
Osnabrück
D-49069 Germany
tweyde@uos.de

Abstract

Analyzing the motif structure of rhythmic sequences is a central issue to music psychology, music theory, and computer applications in music. There are many approaches to the topic by music theorists, psychologists, and computer scientists, yet a model capable of integrating the different findings is still missing. The Integrated Segmentation and Similarity Model (ISSM) presented here is a newly developed model designed for this integration. It is based on a structural representation with detailed information on individual parts, a fuzzy system for rating structural alternatives, and algorithms for computationally efficient structure-recognition and system-optimization by machine learning. The design of the ISSM is described with a focus on musical motivation, and some results of the implementation and evaluation are discussed.

Music Query: Methods, Models, and User Studies (Computing in Musicology 13).
Published by CCARH and the MIT Press, 2004.

2.1 Introduction

The analysis and comparison of rhythmic sequences is a fundamental task for research and application in musical computing, like music tuition, music information retrieval, and score-following. Several aspects of rhythmic motifs have been studied empirically, mostly investigating the effect of particular factors on perceived segmentation or similarity. A number of algorithms have also been developed that analyze sequences, most taking little account of rhythm. What is missing so far is a computational model of rhythmic structure that allows the integration of the different aspects in a way that is psychologically adequate, computable, efficient, extensible, and testable.

The Integrated Segmentation and Similarity Model (ISSM) aims to provide such a general model, consisting of three main parts.

- a structural representation of motif relations, which is designed to be as general as possible and largely independent of specific musical or algorithmic approaches
- a fuzzy rule system, which models preferences for alternative structures using expert knowledge
- selection and learning algorithms applied to representation and rule system

The description of the ISSM focuses on the structural model and fuzzy rules and their musical motivation, and some results of the implementation and evaluation are discussed.

2.2 Rhythmic Motif Structure

The ISSM models the structure of an Input sequence by describing motifs and their relations to other motifs, which may be from the Input (Analysis mode) or from another sequence, the Model (Comparison mode). See Figure 2.1.

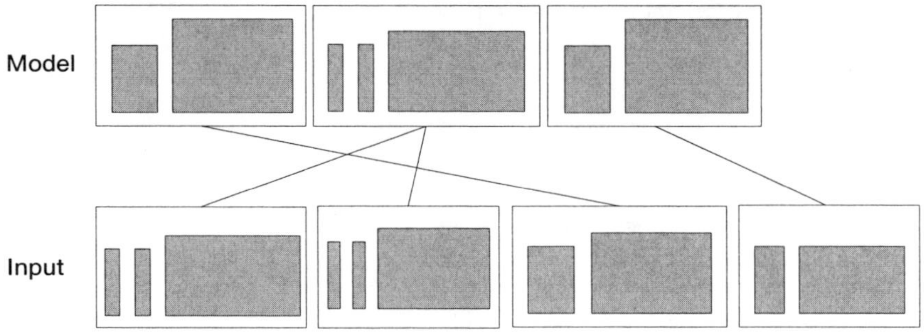

Figure 2.1. Two sequences of notes (depicted as gray boxes with time from left to right and height representing loudness), segmented into motifs (shown as rectangles), and assignments of Input motifs to Model motifs (lines connecting rectangles).

The Analysis case can be subsumed under Comparison by identifying the Input with the Model. Thus the motif structure representation is of the form shown in Figure 2.1. The relation of assigned motifs is described by assigning notes within Input motifs to notes in the assigned Model motifs, as shown in Figure 2.2.

Modeling rhythmic-motif structure independently of metrical structure enables the analysis of performed music, while the open architecture of the ISSM still allows the integration of metrical information. Here sequences of notes with physical time values are used as Input, enabling the system to handle rhythms played by a user on a MIDI keyboard.

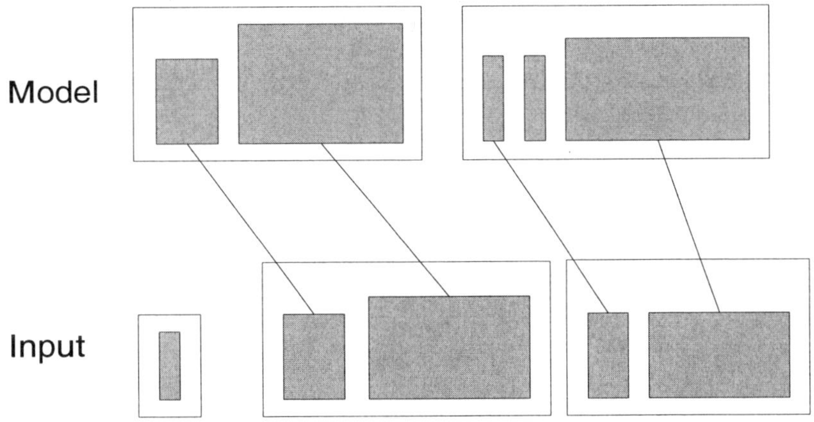

Figure 2.2. Assignment of notes within assigned motifs.

For recognition of rhythmic structure, the ISSM generates structural interpretations (SI), that is, structural descriptions associated to the given sequences. The best SI is found by searching through all alternatives and rating their appropriateness to the sequences. This approach corresponds to the preference rules introduced by Lerdahl and Jackendoff (1983) and used by Temperley (2001).

So far only two representational levels are used in the ISSM, the *motif level* on which notes are assigned, and the *phrase level*, i.e. the whole SI comprising the motif assignments. Although the use of more structural levels is possible, it would exceed computing time-limits for interactive applications. Two levels are sufficient for many applications and it is methodologically sound to start with simple models, as their properties can be tested more easily.

For the same reasons some restrictions are imposed on the segmentation and assignments:

- overlapping motifs are not allowed
- an input motif cannot be assigned to more than one model motif
- a note-object cannot be assigned to more than one sounding pitch

Additionally, in *analysis* mode the segmentations of *model* and *input* are required to be equal and an assignment of a motif to itself is not allowed. The intention was not to build constraints into the structure representation, but to realize them as filter functions based on a general representation, which can be varied and experimented with. Therefore the ISSM does not rely in general on these constraints.

Feature values are assigned to the structural elements, indicating for instance tempo deviations, deviations of note positions, etc. These low-level features are used as input to a fuzzy-logical system describing the properties of the structural interpretation. The fuzzy-logical rules offer a way to model expert knowledge in a form similar to natural language, e.g. an expert statement 'a good segmentation of a motif has long inter-onset intervals (IOIs) and long rests at its boundaries and starts with a loud note' can be written as:

$$GSegment \leftarrow GLongIOI \wedge GLongRest \wedge GStartLoud. \qquad (1)$$

The rules use one operator, either $\vee$ or $\wedge$, to connect the premises on the right side. The rule has a truth-value itself that is used in the implication operator when calculating the conclusion on the left side (see Weyde and Dalinghaus [2003] for details on the fuzzy-logical system). By convention, names of rules on the phrase level begin with a C while the rules on the motif level have an initial *G*.

To use the non-negative feature values as fuzzy truth values, they need to be fuzzified, i.e. transformed to the range [0,1], for which the normalization function

$$norm(x) = \frac{x}{x+1} \qquad (2)$$

is used. To simplify the rule system, the negation

$$not(x) = x - 1 \qquad (3)$$

is used in the feature pre-processing, if necessary, to describe the quality of the SI positively. The use of *norm* and *not* will be omitted in the following descriptions for clarity.

2.3 Features of Rhythmic Structure

The preference for a certain rhythmic structure is based on features of the structure in relation to the sequences. The features used here are designed according to music psychology and music theory, but like the segmentation and assignment constraints, they are not fixed parts of the system, but can be altered and extended.

2.3.1 Segmentation

The segmentation of an event sequence into motifs is a fundamental characteristic of rhythmic perception, because it defines the basis of note assignments and motif assignments. There are three main characteristics to be taken into account: note distances, individual motif duration and length, and the global distribution of motif length and duration.

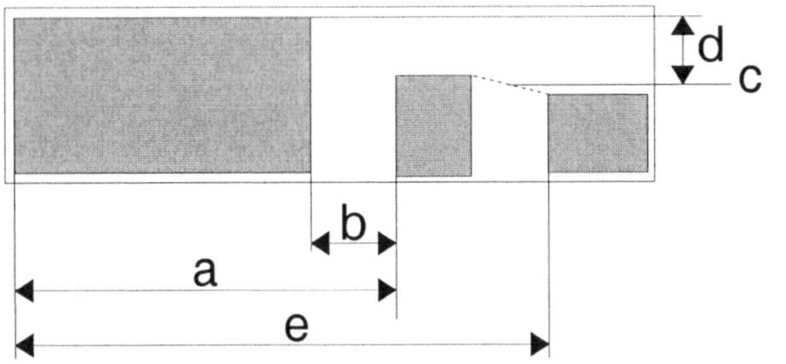

Figure 2.3. Measures for segmentation.

The classical *Gestalt* approach to segmentation follows the principle of proximity, which puts boundaries between distant events (Wertheimer 1923). In the case of monophonic rhythms, this leads to motif boundaries at local-distance maxima. Yet unlike for spatial objects, there is no natural definition for the distance between notes. A common approach to measuring note distances is treating the notes with duration, loudness, and pitch as points in a three-dimensional space and using a metric, e.g. the Euclidian or "city-block" metric (e.g. Tenney and Polansky 1980).

One problem with metrics is the scaling of the components. It is not clear which units should be used to measure loudness or time, but this greatly affects the influence of each parameter. Relating to time there are two possible measures of distance: rests and IOIs. IOIs and rests (see 'a' and 'b' in Figure 2.3) need to be treated differently but it is not clear exactly how. Thus the weighting of the individual parameters in the ISSM is part of the fuzzy rule system, where it can be fine-tuned by expertise or machine learning. For IOIs the accordance of the motif with grouping by proximity is measured by dividing the average of the IOIs at the motif boundaries by the maximum of IOIs within the motif. For a motif M consisting of notes $n_k,\ldots,n_l$ the feature value is calculated as

$$GLongIOI\,(M) = \frac{avrg\,(ioi(n_{k-1}),\ldots,ioi(n_l))}{\max_{i=k}^{l-1}(ioi(n_i))}, \qquad (4)$$

where $ioi(n_k)$ is the IOI between n_k and n_{k+1}. If M consists of a single note the value is set to 1. The feature *GLongRest* is defined analogously.

In addition to the problem of scaling, a metric is required to be symmetric by definition (i.e. $\mu(a,b) = \mu(b,a)$), but the effect of note differences on segmentation is asymmetric. Woodrow (1909) found already that a loud note tends to start a new group, so the distance measure is not appropriate here. The feature value for the loudness is

$$GBeginLoud(M) = loud(n_k) - \frac{\sum_{i=k+1}^{l} loud(n_i)}{l-k-1} \quad (5)$$

(see 'c' and 'd' in Figure 2.3) and is 1 for motifs containing only one note.

2.3.2 Motif Length and Duration

Factors not reflected in considerations on note distance are the length and duration of motifs (length referring to the number of notes while duration describes the temporal extent). Length and duration are limited by memory, and there are perceptual and cognitive preferences.

Miller (1956) found that subjects tend to confuse the order in groups of more than four elements, and elementary musical motifs of more than four notes are rare according to Swain (1986) and Handel (1989); a maximal length of 5 is used in the ISSM. It models the preference for individual length values by using a feature for each length from 1 to 5, which is defined to be 1 when the motif has the respective length and 0 if not. For the duration there are four features that correspond to duration values 0.4, 0.7, 1.2, and 2.0 sec, which are approximately evenly spaced on a logarithmic scale. The motif duration is compared to the corresponding value using a fuzzy *equal* function

$$GDur04(M) = equal(dur(M), 400) \quad (6)$$

where *dur*(*M*) is the duration of the motif (see 'd' in Figure 2.3), and

$$equal(x, y) = gauss(x, y, q \cdot \frac{x+y}{2}). \quad (7)$$

and

$$gauss(x, m, s) = e^{-\frac{(x-m)^2}{2s^2}} \quad (8)$$

The several features are combined with one feature per motif for length and one for duration using $\vee$ since one motif can only have one length and duration. Conversely the overall segmentation value is combined using $\wedge$ because a segmentation is best if it is good in all features. The combined segmentation quality of a motif is then modeled by the following rule set:

$$GSegment \leftarrow GrpLength \wedge GrpDuration \wedge GLongIOI \wedge GLongRest \wedge GBeginLoud \quad (9)$$

$$GrpLength \leftarrow GrpLen1 \wedge GrpLen2 \wedge GrpLen3 \wedge GrpLen4 \wedge GrpLen5 \quad (10)$$

$$GrpDuration \leftarrow GrpDur04 \wedge GrpDur07 \wedge GrpDur12 \wedge GrpDur20 \quad (11)$$

2.3.3 Global Segmentation Features

In addition to the local-motif properties, there are global properties of segmentation that are of importance. Listeners prefer segmentations with evenly distributed length (Handel and Todd 1981) and durations (e.g. see Handel 1990, ch. 11). The evenness of the length distribution in a segmentation is measured by dividing the standard deviation of the length by the average length:

$$CConstantLength(S) = \frac{\sqrt{\sum_{i=1}^{s}(len(M_i) - avrg(M_1,\ldots,M_s))^2}}{avrg(len(M_1),\ldots,len(M_s))} \quad (12)$$

where S is a segmentation consisting of Motifs $M_1,\ldots,M_s$ and $len(M)$ is the length of M. The feature *CConstantDuration* for motif duration as indicated in Figure 2.3 is defined analogously. The whole segmentation of a sequence is rated by this rule set:

$$CSegmentation \leftarrow CConstantLength \wedge CConstantDuration \wedge CSegment \quad (13)$$

$$CSegment \leftarrow GSegment_1 \wedge \ldots \wedge GSegment_n \quad (14)$$

Rule 13 is an example of the transition from the motif level to the phrase level. The varying number of motifs in a phrase has some implications for the fuzzy processing as will be discussed in Section 2.4. The segmentation feature value is calculated for Input and Model in the same manner.

2.4 Motif Similarity

Based on note assignments, the similarity-related features of the motifs are calculated. The degrees of similarity are described by measuring deviations that can be divided into three feature groups:

- structural deviations
- gradual deviations
- tempo and position

The approach used in the ISSM is to integrate these different aspects by describing transformations required to convert one motif into another and assigning a rating to each transformation.

2.4.1 Structural Deviations

In the ISSM, notes in Input-motifs are assigned to notes in the assigned Model-motif, where notes may be skipped, but a note may only be assigned to one other note. Although the replacement of several notes by one or vice versa is a common technique of variation, its effect can always be expressed by erasure or introducing notes. No intersections or bifurcations of assignments are allowed to avoid the ambiguity of notes changed by property or position.

Structural deviations are those related to notes that are not assigned. A classic measure for this is the Levenshtein distance defined as the minimal number of editing operations (deletions and insertions) needed to transform one sequence into another. In order to apply it to musical rhythms, it is necessary to take timing and dynamics into account. Approaches to this problem have been to assign different values to operations depending on differences in the note's parameters and to introduce special operations that depend on the timing of the notes (e.g. Orpen and Huron 1992 and Smith et al. 1998).

Concerning the temporal structure, there are two concepts of editing operations. E.g. when removing a note, the following notes can be changed in position, leaving IOIs and rests constant, or they can remain unchanged, affecting the IOI and the rest following the previous note. The former is called *Deletion*, the latter *Subtraction*, and the analogs for added notes are called *Insertion* and *Addition*. Each choice leads to a different temporal structure and all variants have to be rated. The feature values corresponding to these operations are calculated as

$$GAddition(M) = \sum_{n \in M \cap Add} \frac{loud(n)}{avrgLoud(M)} \tag{15}$$

$$GInsertion(M) = \sum_{n \in M \cap Ins} \frac{ioi(n) \cdot loud(n)}{avrg_{m \in M}(ioi(m) \cdot loud(m))} \tag{16}$$

where *Add* and *Ins* are the sets of all notes in the Input which are added and deleted. *GDeletion* and *GSubtraction* are defined analogously.

2.4.2 Gradual Deviations

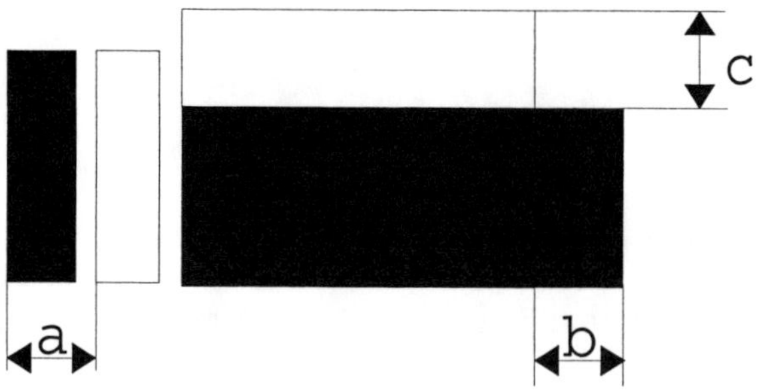

Figure 2.4. Note deviations of two motifs (one with black, one with white notes): (a) onset, (b) duration, and (c) loudness.

Since the relation of the individual parameters to each other is unclear, the feature values are calculated individually for the parameters. Perception is not symmetrical. In order not to penalize small deviations which are normal in performance and do not affect recognition, the values are collected individually for positive and negative deviations. The feature values are computed as the sum of squared values for each note. E.g. for the timing of notes played early, the feature *GEarly* is calculated as:

$$GEarly(M) = \sum_{n \in M \cap Early} \left(\frac{onset(m(n)) - onset(n)}{ioi(m(v))} \right)^2 \qquad (17)$$

where *Early* is the set of all notes in the Input being earlier than the assigned Model note, *m*(*n*) is the Model note assigned to Input note *n*, and *onset*(*n*) is the onset time of the note *n*. The features *GLate*, *GLong*, *GShort*, *GLoud*, and *GSoft* are defined analogously based on duration and loudness.

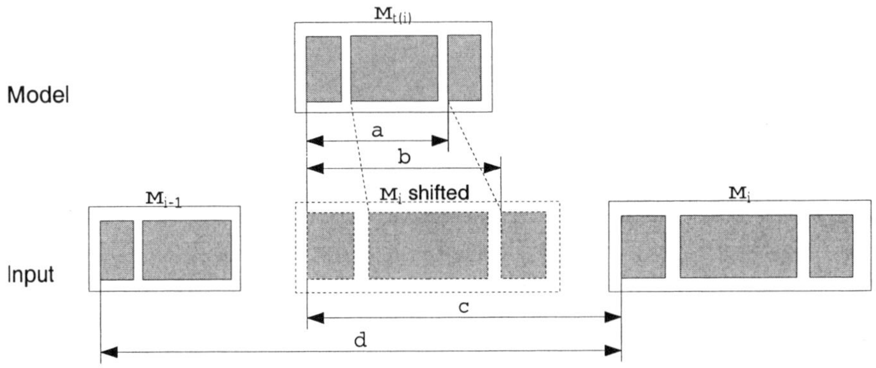

Figure 2.5. Tempo and position measurements: (a) model duration, (b) input duration, (c) position shift, and (d) motif distance.

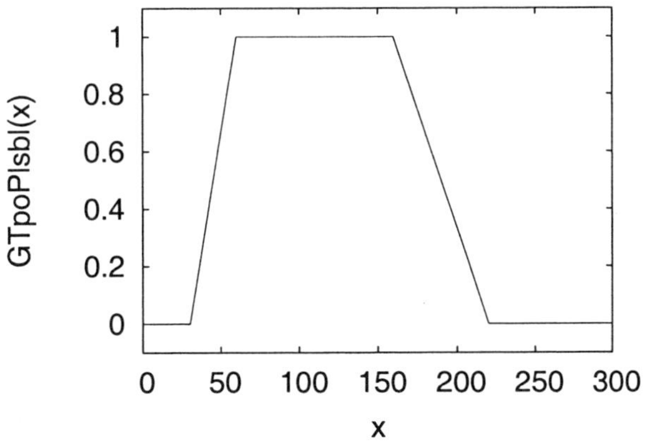

Figure 2.6. Trapezoid function for tempo plausibility.

2.4.3 Tempo and Position

Apart from deviations of the individual notes, there can be changes in tempo and position of the whole motif. The relative tempo is measured by dividing the Input motif duration by the Model motif duration (i.e. b/a referring to Figure 2.5).

If the Model has tempo information assigned, it is used to compute a feature value for the absolute tempo describing its plausibility as a musical tempo. The feature *GTpoPlsbl* is computed by a trapezoid function yielding 1 in a musically sound tempo range and decreasing to 0 at the borders (Figure 2.6).

In the tempo feature for motif assignment, the relations are compared to the preceding motif's tempo (*pre_tpo*) indicating ritardando or accelerando

$$GEqualTempo = equal(input\_tpo, pre\_tpo)\,. \tag{18}$$

The same is done with double and triple tempo values, as they are qualitatively different from the other values (see Epstein 1985), and they are combined into a tempo stability value:

$$GTpoStbl \leftarrow GEqualTempo \vee GDoubleTempo \vee GTripleTempo \vee$$
$$GHalfTempo \vee GThirdTempo \tag{19}$$

The overall tempo rating for a motif combines the stability and the plausibility values:

$$GTpoQual \leftarrow GTpoStbl \wedge GTpoPlsbl. \tag{20}$$

The position deviation of the Input motif from the Model motif (c in Figure 2.5) is put in relation to the distance from the last motif to the expected motif position (d in Figure 2.5).

The choice of tempo and position are interdependent. The problem of finding the appropriate values has been approached by Mazzola (2002) by defining the *Gestalt Distance* of motifs as the *infimum* (greatest lower bound) of distances over all tempo and position changes and over all possible uses of deletions or insertions. The Gestalt Distance is an abstract measure of similarity, since neither the tempo nor the inserted or deleted notes have an influence on the distance value. Although tempo and position are determined by this method (except from the case of several global minima), in the case of comparing motifs in context there is a need to take more factors into account.

For a given note assignment, the tempo and position values leading to minimal distance can be calculated easily if the feature values are combined using a Euclidian metric. With nonlinear operators as used in this fuzzy system, there is no general method to find a global minimum. Hence a heuristic is used, based on tempo estimates derived from combinations of two pairs of associated notes.

2.4.4 Combined Similarity Ratings

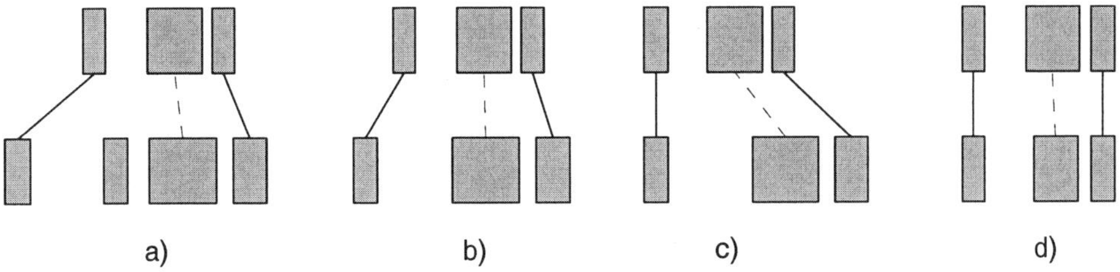

Figure 2.7. Pre-processing of notes in a motif assignment based on a pair of assigned notes (continuous lines): (a) original, (b) structure adjusted, (c) position adjusted, and (d) tempo adjusted.

To calculate the feature values for a motif assignment, all variants of the structural interpretation on the note level are generated and preprocessed in four steps as depicted in Figure 2.7. For each of these transformations the values to the corresponding features are set. With all transformations applied, the gradual deviation features are calculated.

Not all combinations of structural variants between the motifs are evaluated, instead the best-rated one is chosen individually in a left-to-right manner. This is necessary since there are many alternative structures, rendering global optimization computationally very expensive, and it is appropriate, because most of the feature values are based only on local structure, and those that include non-local information refer only to earlier events.

The overall quality of similarity of an assigned group is computed by the following rule set.

GSim is the fuzzy similarity value for the motif assignment, *GPrcsn* reflects the gradual deviations, and *GCorrect* combines the fuzzy features for structural deviations.

$$GSim \leftarrow GTpoQual \wedge GPrcsn \wedge GCorrect \wedge GRelPos \quad (21)$$

$$GPrscn \leftarrow GLoud \wedge GSoft \wedge GLate \wedge GEarly \wedge GLong \wedge GShort \quad (22)$$

$$GCorrect \leftarrow GAddition \wedge GInsertion \wedge GSubtraction \wedge GDeletion \quad (23)$$

2.5 Global Features

On the structural level, there are the already mentioned global segmentation features and a feature for order preservation. In a motif-association graph as in Figure 2.1 there can be intersections and bifurcations, which indicate structural differences. The corresponding feature value should be independent of the number of motifs assigned. Therefore the value is calculated as the number of actual intersections and bifurcations divided by the number of possible intersections and bifurcations, which for a Structural Interpretation *Int* with *asgnum(Int)* motif assignments is given by

$$crossfork\ (Int) = \frac{asgnum\ (Int) \cdot (asgnum\ (Int) - 1)}{2}. \tag{24}$$

The feature $COrder$ is then calculated as

$$COrder(Int) = \frac{|\{(M_i, M_j) \mid (M_i, M_j) \in S_I \times S_I \wedge i < j \wedge mi(i) \geq m(j)\}|}{crossfork(Int)}, \tag{25}$$

where S_I is the Input Segmentation of *Int* and *mi*(*i*) is the index of the model motif assigned to Input motif M_i.

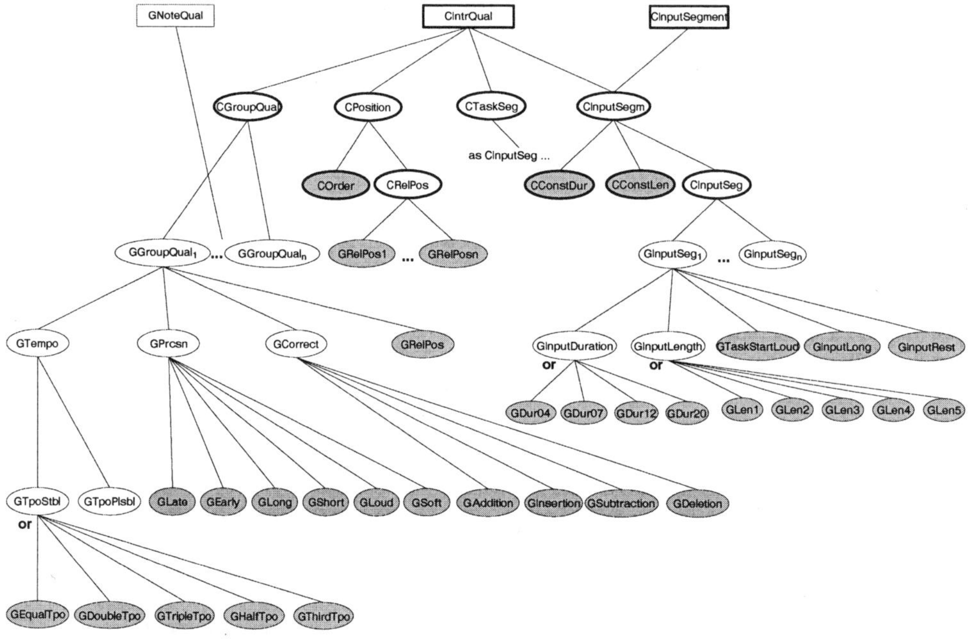

Figure 2.8. The Neuro-Fuzzy system for rating Structural Interpretations. Nodes marked with 'or' use $\vee$ *all others use* $\wedge$*. Transitional rules nodes are marked with '...'.*

2.5.1 Structure Selection, Learning, and Evaluation

The features of the structure are combined, after fuzzification and negation where necessary, by the fuzzy rule system to rate the quality of the Structural Interpretation as a whole. The fuzzy system is an extended form of Fuzzy-PROLOG, and its rules can be interpreted as a Fuzzy-Logical Neural Net (FLNN), interpreting propositions as neurons and rules as connections. The network representation of the whole rule system is shown in Figure 2.8.

In the transition from motif level to sequence level, the number of premises is variable. This is not covered by prepositional logic used here. Therefore the ISSM has been extended with a list-processing feature. Standard t-norms and s-norms as evaluation functions for the fuzzy-logical operators would have introduced a systematic preference for shorter resp. longer motifs. The operators used in the ISSM are based on the compensatory *q-Operator,* which is specifically designed to be independent of the number of arguments. The ISSM uses compensatory operators for $\wedge$ and $\vee$ to allow premise values to counterbalance for others, e.g. motifs with very different tempos may still be considered similar if the gradual and structural deviations are very small (for details see Weyde and Dalinghaus 2003).

The analysis process searches for the best of all valid Structural Interpretations, by generating and rating them using the fuzzy system. This strategy is prone to combinatorial explosion, thus filtering and algorithmic optimization techniques are employed to make the search efficient.

2.5.2 Filtering and Optimization

Filtering very much enhances efficiency, as it reduces the number of Structural Interpretations before rating them. There are filtering interfaces at several stages in the generation process. The filters active in the earliest stage, the segmentation, are most effective—they avoid the association of motifs and can be perceptually motivated:

- Motif length limiting the length of motifs to 5 notes. This is motivated by the already mentioned study by Miller (1956).
- Motif duration limiting the duration of motifs to 1800 ms. This is motivated by the fact that the sense of rhythmic coherence is lost for notes with larger IOIs (Fraisse 1982).
- Single Notes only allowing single note groups when there are long IOIs before and after (<500 ms). This is motivated by the fact that perceptual grouping cannot be avoided by listeners at will.
- Proximity1 not allowing short IOIs (<300ms) to be group boundaries if an adjacent IOI is longer (1.5 times). Deutsch (1982a) found proximity to be the dominant factor in grouping; strong temporal boundary indicators cannot be overruled by other factors.
- Proximity2 not allowing any IOIs to be group boundaries if an adjacent IOI is much longer (2.5 times).
- Proximity3 requiring long IOIs (>1200ms) to be group boundaries.

The number of unassigned notes and motifs is also restricted to avoid interpretations containing few relations. These filters have proven to work well with the sample sequences tested so far. Depending on the application, the filter parameters may need to be made more permissive.

A second technique for enhancing computational efficiency is the Branch-and-Bound method of reducing the search space based on partial solutions. Filtering together with Branch-and-Bound can reduce complexity drastically (see Weyde and Dalinghaus 2003) and it makes possible the analysis of sequences of 10-12 notes in nearly real time. This is sufficient for incipits and for many tutorial applications. For treating longer sequences it is appropriate to use a dynamic time-window, which is a goal of current development.

2.5.3 Learning and Evaluation

Transferring the fuzzy-rule system into a neural network enables the system to learn from data, by adapting the truth-values of the fuzzy rules with backpropagation. Training the net directly would mean to provide combinations of input sequences and structural interpretations with quality ratings. It is not feasible to do this with a comprehensive number of interpretations, even for one sequence. The technique employed here to use less expert input is Iterative Training (see Weyde 2002). With iterative training only the best structural interpretation for each input sequence is needed, which can be easily provided by a domain expert, e.g. a musician, musicologist, or music teacher depending on the application.

The ISSM has been implemented in an experimental application for MIDI data and tested on data collected from music students. The system has been evaluated on segmentation, comparison, and analysis tasks. It has been shown to perform well on rhythmic comparison, reaching ca. 90% correct answers on training sets, and 80% on test sets. An incorrect answer means that the system did not choose the same interpretation as the expert, but its answers were often musically acceptable, so that only about 3% of all answers were inappropriate. Further tests were conducted, comparing the Neuro-Fuzzy-System to standard Multi-Layer-Perceptrons (MLP) and a linear model, showing that the FLNN and MLP outperformed the linear model, with the FLNN (in contrast to the MLP) being interpretable and proving to be very robust (see Weyde and Dalinghaus 2003).

2.6 Conclusions

The ISSM is a model for structural analysis which provides detailed structural descriptions, integrates expert knowledge, and can be optimized by learning from data. It is designed following the findings of psychological studies and has proven to function well in evaluations. It can be extended easily, thus offering the possibility to test hypotheses from music psychology and music theory empirically. The integration of structure recognition with knowledge and machine learning offers a perspective for a wide range of applications such as music-analysis and production tools, music tuition, and music-information retrieval.

Current and future goals are directed towards extending the ISSM with more musical parameters, especially pitch, meter, and harmony. First experiments with melodies have already shown encouraging results (Weyde 2002). An interesting task is the extension of the ISSM to work with a dynamic time-window to handle arbitrarily long sequences and the addition of a memory model. Performance improvements in this context could allow the use of global search on the note level. The learning method shall be enhanced by using Bayesian methods, to enable better interpretation of results of learning from data, in order to support development and testing of theories of rhythmic and melodic structure.

References

Deutsch, Diana (1982a). "Grouping Mechanisms in Music" in Deutsch (1982b), ch. 4, 99–134.

Deutsch, Diana, ed. (1982b). *The Psychology of Music*. New York: Academic Press.

Epstein, David (1985). "Tempo Relations: A Cross-Cultural Study," *Music Theory Spectrum*, 7, 34–71.

Fraisse, Paul (1982). "Rhythm and Tempo" in Deutsch (1982b).

Handel, Stephen (1989). *Listening: An Introduction to the Perception of Auditory Events* (Cambridge, MA: The MIT Press).

Handel, Stephen, and Peyton Todd (1981). "Segmentation of Sequential Patterns," *Journal of Experimental Psychology: Human Perception and Performance*, 7, 1, 41–55.

Lerdahl, Fred, and Ray Jackendoff (1983). *A Generative Theory of Tonal Music* (Cambridge, MA: The MIT Press).

Mazzola, Guerino (2002). *Topos of Music* (Basel: Birkhäuser).

Miller, George A. (1956). "The Magical Number Seven, Plus or Minus Two: Some Limits on Our Capacity for Processing Information," *Psychological Review*, 63/2, 81–97.

Orpen, Keith S., and David Huron (1992). "The Measurement of Similarity in Music: A Quantitative Approach for Non-Parametric Representations," *Computers in Music Research*, 4 (1992), 1–44.

Smith, Lloyd A., Rodger McNab, and Ian H. Witten (1998). "Sequence-Based Melodic Comparison: A Dynamic-Programming Approach" in Walter B. Hewlett and Eleanor Selfridge-Field, eds., *Melodic Similarity* (*Computing in Musicology* 11), (Cambridge, MA: The MIT Press), 101–117.

Swain, Joseph P. (1986). "The Need for Limits in Hierarchical Theories of Music," *Music Perception*, 4/1, 121–148.

Temperley, David (2001). *The Cognition of Basic Musical Structures* (Cambridge, MA: The MIT Press).

Tenney, James, and Larry Polansky (1980). "Temporal Gestalt Perception in Music," *Journal of Music Theory*, 24/2, 205–41.

Wertheimer, Max (1923). "Untersuchungen zur Lehre von der Gestalt," *Psychologische Forschung*, 4, 301–350.

Weyde, Tillman (2002). "Integrating Segmentation and Similarity in Melodic Analysis" in K. Stevens, D. Burnham, G. McPherson, E. Schubert, and J. Renwick, eds., *Proceedings of the International Conference on Music Perception and Cognition 2002* (Sydney, Australia: University of New South Wales), pp. 240–243.

Weyde, Tillman, and Klaus Dalinghaus (2003). "Design and Optimization of Neuro-Fuzzy-Based Recognition of Musical Rhythm Patterns," *International Journal of Smart Engineering System Design*, 5/2, 67–79.

Woodrow, Herbert (1909). "A Quantitative Study of Rhythm," *Archives of Psychology*, 14, 1–66.

3 Melody as a Significant Musical Feature in Repertory Classification

Wei Chai

Media Laboratory
Massachusetts Institute of Technology
Cambridge, MA 02139
chaiwei@media.mit.edu

Abstract

This article addresses the music psychological principles and theories on melodic perception, music memory, melodic organization and melodic similarity, indicating how melody is important for recognition of songs or styles. Folk songs from different countries are classified on the basis of their melodies using Hidden Markov Models. The procedure illustrates that melody itself carries some statistical features to distinguish the styles of music. This experiment also points out some issues in melodic representation that are important for applications of this general kind.

Music Query: Methods, Models, and User Studies (Computing in Musicology 13). Published by CCARH and the MIT Press, 2004.

3.1 Approaches to Understanding Melody

3.1.1 Melodic Perception

Several aspects of melodic perception need to be considered when developing a song-recognition (or "query-by-humming") system. (1) What types of queries will users present? [See also Lesaffre et al., elsewhere in this issue.] (2) In the case of someone trying to locate a half-remembered fragment of music, it is useful to understand how people remember music, and in particular, how they remember melodies and how accurately people can produce (e.g., hum) melodies. [See also Muellensiefen and Frieler in this issue.] (3) Since most music that we hear contains both melody and accompaniment, it is necessary to determine what would be perceived as melody in an accompanied musical work. (4) Since many music queries involve finding similar but not exact matches to melodies, we need to decide what similarity means in terms of music perception.

From a technical perspective, the first concern—query type—is related to the problems of query representation and construction. The second concern—melodic memory—is related to melodic representation. The third concern—differentiation of foreground melody from background accompaniment—is related to melodic grouping and extraction. The fourth—melodic similarity—is related to melodic-matching algorithms. Here we emphasize underlying psychological principles of musical memory, melodic organization, and melodic similarity. A style-identification sample folk song classification based on melodies is then presented. It is here that the boundaries of fuzzy matching come into play. The application of these principles to the development of a query-by-humming system is addressed by Chai (2001, Ch. 5).

3.1.2 Musical Memory

There has been much research on how people build mental structures while listening to music and on how music is remembered. Dowling (1978) discovered that *melodic contour* is more easily remembered than an exact melody. He postulates that contour and scale are stored separately in memory and that melodies are mapped onto an over-learned scale structure, so that if presented a melody with an unknown scale, we map it to the scale structure with which we are familiar.

Edworthy (1985), however, discovered that the *length* of a novel melody determines whether it is easier to detect *changes in contour* or *changes in intervals*. There are also differences in terms of short-term and long-term memory for melodies: it is easier for people to reproduce a well-known melody with exact intervals than to do so for new melodies. In terms of music-database queries, a user's query melody will probably be in long-term memory, so exact intervals will be important. Memory tasks are generally performed better by experienced musicians than by those with less experience.

Dowling (1986) presented evidence supporting the notion that schematic representations of familiar tunes in *long-term memory* consist of (rhythmically organized) sets of relative pitch chromas and that such representations can be accessed by means of labels and such global melodic features as contour. *Short-term (episodic) memory* , long-term (semantic) memory, and cognitive development were investigated with respect to the roles played by pitch, interval, contour, and tonal scale.

3.1.3 Melodic Organization and Gestalt Principles

The ambiguity of melodic definition has been defined by Cross (1999) in these terms:

> "Melody seems to exist as a succession of discrete pitches in time, yet it is likely to be heard as one thing, one integrated entity, as pitch moving in time. The fact that a melody can be heard as pitch moving in time when all that a listener is confronted with is a sequence of separate pitches is something that has perplexed philosophers for centuries."

An explanation of this conundrum was suggested by Gestalt psychologists earlier in this century. They were trying to account for the perception of visual shape, but their theories seemed also to apply to melody, to auditory shape. They suggested that certain laws seemed to underlie our perception of form, laws of proximity, similarity, good continuation, and so on. These laws governed our tendencies to group elements in a visual field so as to constitute shape or form at a larger scale than the individual elements of the pattern. Several rule-systems based on Gestalt principles which can be used in melodic analysis have been developed by Lerdahl and Jackendoff (1983), Temperley (2001), and Singer (2002). Some representative rules follow lines such as these:

> PROXIMITY: Items placed in close (spatial) proximity tend to be grouped together as a unit. The importance of pitch-proximity in audition is reflected in the fact that melodies all over the world use small pitch intervals from note to note (this will be shown by the interval change histogram of any music corpora). Violations of proximity have been used in various periods and genres of both Western and non-Western music for a variety of effects. For example, fission based on pitch proximity was used to enrich the texture so that out of a single succession of notes, two melodic lines could be heard.
>
> SIMILARITY: Similar items tend to be grouped together as a unit. For example, similarity of timbre can be used to group sequences of sounds so that the melody will be perceived. Similar amplitude or loudness of notes was found to be fairly unimportant in the perception of musical parts compared to other rules, but is also used for grouping of notes.
>
> PRäGNANZ (good continuation): In perception we tend to continue contours whenever the elements of a pattern establish an implied direction. Here, good means symmetrical, simple, regular, but most

> important, familiar. The listener could attend to notes of a familiar melody even though they are not differentiated from their background on any other basis than being parts of a meaningful configuration.

Additionally, the listeners usually pay more attention to louder and higher pitch notes in a melodic line. The above rules were referred to as local pattern organization by Dowling (1986), who wrote,

> "The listener's appreciation of the global aspects of a piece of music is in terms of invariants—structural constancies underlying surface change in local pattern features. Invariants that might occur over relatively long-time periods in a piece are regularities of temporal organization such as the beat, of tonal scale organization such as the key, and of instrumentation and density of note spacing in pitch and time. One way in which the comprehension of global invariants of the structure might function as we listen to a piece is by affecting our expectancies from moment to moment."

Dowling also proposed that the local features are related to each other and to global patterns by some hierarchical structure.

3.1.4 Melodic Similarity

"The ability to recognize melodic similarity lies at the heart of many of the questions most commonly asked about music. It is melody that enables us to distinguish one work from another. It is melody that human beings are innately able to reproduce by singing, humming, and whistling. It is melody that makes music memorable: we are likely to recall a tune long after we have forgotten its text" (Selfridge-Field 1998). In this book (Hewlett 1998) conceptual and representational issues in melodic comparison are reviewed by Selfridge-Field; different melodic-matching methods—such as the geometrical algorithm, dynamic-programming algorithm, and other string-matching algorithms—are presented.

Uitdenbogerd (1998) suggested the following ordering of factors in music similarity on a continuum from good to poor evidence of similarity. The rhythmic aspect of melody was not considered in her ordered list:

1. Exact transposition (all rhythmic values preserved or ignored).
2. Exact transposition in a tonally related key.
3. Exact transposition in a tonally distant key.
4. Exact transposition except for a chromatically altered note.
5. Exact transposition except for a diatonically altered note.
6. Same contour and tonality.
7. Same contour with different (or no) tonality.
8. Same pitch-classes distributed in multiple octaves (i.e., same chroma but different contour).
9. Different contour, different note values.

3.1.5 Melodic Transitions as a Feature for Folk-Music Classification

To get at the question of *melodic discrimination* we (Chai 2001) ran one experiment in which monophonic folksongs were deduced to be from different countries through the use of Hidden Markov Models (HMMs). Folk melodies from different countries may have some significant statistical differences, which we anticipated could be captured by an appropriate statistical model. The results suggest to us that melodic similarity may have statistical explanations but also that the level of precision in melodic representation is very important for melodic discrimination in this kind of effort.

Monophonic melodies can be easily modeled by HMMs, since a Markov chain is simply a table of transition probabilities. In the context of modeling monophonic pitch sequences, a Markov chain usually expresses the probability that if the current pitch is x_t, the next pitch will be x_{t+1}. In a Hidden Markov Model, transition probabilities can be computed for unknown input states and observable output symbols, even though the intervening transitions and probabilities may be invisible to the user. Wide varieties of pitch transitions can be expressed using the relationships expected in a Hidden Markov Model.

The Hidden Markov Model (HMM) is a very powerful tool to statistically model a process that varies in time. It can be seen as a doubly embedded stochastic process with a process that is not observable (hidden process) and can only be observed through another stochastic process (observable process) that produces the time-set of observations. An HMM can be fully specified by (1) N, the number of states in the model; (2) M, the number of distinct observation symbols per state; (3) $A=\{a_{ij}\}$, the state transition probability distribution; (4) $B=\{b,(k)\}$, the observation symbol probability distribution; and (5) $\Pi=\{\pi_i\}$, the initial state distribution (Rabiner 1989).

In the classification experiment, 187 Irish folk-music pieces, 200 German folk-music pieces, and 104 Austrian folk-music pieces were used. The main reason for the choice of places was availability of data, which were obtained from two corpora:

1. The ESSEN FOLKSONG COLLECTION (first made available by Helmut Schaffrath), which contains over 7,000 European folk melodies encoded between 1982 and 1994;

2. The IRISH DANCE MUSIC COLLECTION encoded by Donncha Ó Maidín over roughly the same period of time.

The Essen collection was originally encoded in the symbolic EsAC (Essen Associative Code) and subsequently (1995) translated into another symbolic format, **kern, for processing with the *Humdrum Toolkit*. The Irish collection was originally encoded in ALMA and has also been translated to other formats.

For this experiment, we represented melodies in four different ways.

(A) With base-12 pitch class represented [12 states]. Each melody was converted into a pitch sequence by normalizing the pitches into one octave from C4 (Middle C) to B4. Pitches in different octaves but of same *chroma* were encoded with the same symbol in the sequence and thus there was a total of twelve symbols for pitch.

(B) With base-12 pitch class and duration represented. To incorporate duration, we make use of the concept behind the representation for rhythmic sequences employed by Carpinteiro (1998). Briefly, we repeated each note multiple times to express the total duration as a series of single-pitch events of a common unit.

(C) With intervallic representation. A melody was converted into a sequence of intervals. Each interval was expressed in semitones. Here 27 symbols were used in the range –13 to +13. (Intervals of more than 13 semitones were classified as being +/–13).

(D) With contour representation. For this representation, we quantized intervallic changes into five levels:

0	stasis (no change),
+/–	ascents/descents by step (1 or 2 semitones),
++/– –	ascents/descents by leap (3 or more semitones).

This representation was fairly compact and fault-tolerant in melodic identification applications (Kim 2000). Figure 3.1 shows each approach in relation to a common example.

```
A: {2, 7, 9, 11, 11, 9}.
B: {2, 7, 9, 11, 11, 11, 9}.
C: {5, 2, 2, 0, -2}.
D: {++, +, +, 0, -}.
```

Figure 3.1. The four representations of a melody used experimentally to classify folksongs.

Because the number of hidden states and the structure may impact the classification performance, we use HMMs with different numbers of hidden states and different structures to perform classifications. We then compared their performances. The different structures used and compared in our experiment are shown in Figure 3.2.

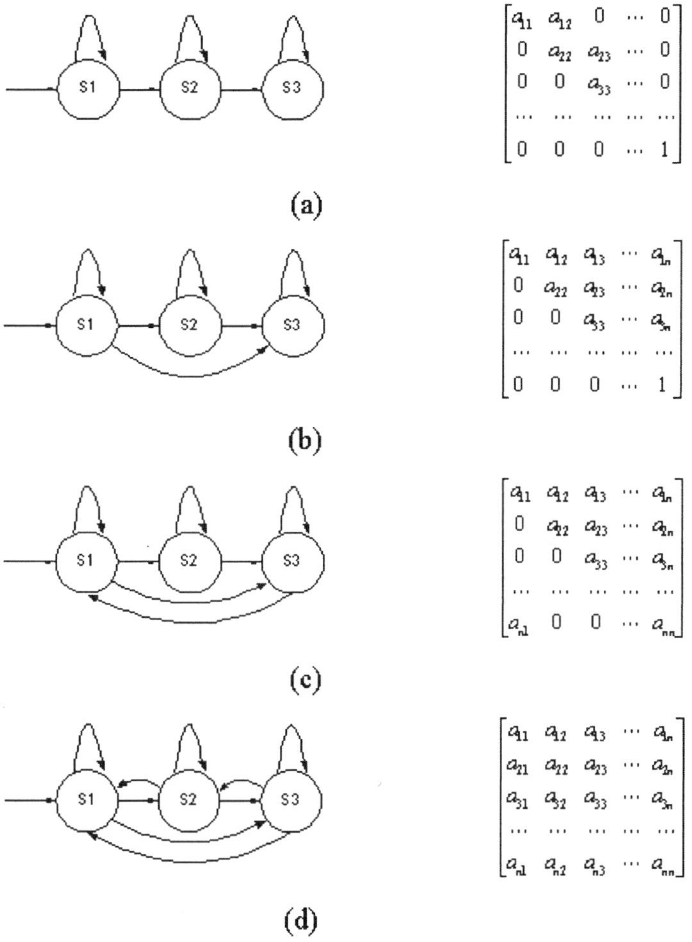

Figure 3.2. HMMs used in the experiment. (a) A strict left-right model; each state can transfer to itself and the next one state. (b) A left-right model; each state can transfer to itself and any state to the right of it. (c) A variation of the left-right model, additional to (b); the last state can transfer to the first state. (d) A fully connected model.

The Baum-Welch [Expectation-Maximization] re-estimation method was implemented to train an HMM for each country using the training set. To identify the country of an unknown melody, the Viterbi algorithm [a dynamic-programming algorithm for calculating the optimal state sequence] was used to decode the sequence and compute its log probabilities respectively using HMMs trained for different countries. We then assign the melody to the country with the highest log probability.

The results were obtained in this way: all the data were split randomly into a training set (70%) and a test set (30%). Each result was cross-validated with 17 trials using the 70%/30% splits. The classification performances are shown in Figure 3.3 (i)–(iv). The first three figures show the generalization performances of two-way classifications. The last figure shows the generalization performance of the three-way classification. The X-axis in all the figures indicates different HMMs, whose corresponding structures are shown in Table 3.1.

HMM	1	2	3	4	5	6	7	8
N	2	2	2	2	3	3	3	3
STRUC	a	b	c	d	a	b	c	d
HMM	9	10	11	12	13	14	15	16
N	4	4	4	4	6	6	6	6
STRUC	a	b	c	d	a	b	c	d

Table 3.1. 16 HMMs with different structures and numbers of hidden states used in the experiment (see Figure 3.2 for the description of the structures).

The results show that, in general, the state number (2, 3, 4, or 6) did not impact the classification performance significantly. The strict left-right HMMs (a) and the left-right HMMs (b) outperformed the other two HMMs (c and d). The representation C generally performs better than the representations A, B and D. Performances of the 6-state left-right HMM, for example, are shown in Table 3.2. It achieved classification accuracies of 75%, 77% and 66% for 2-way classifications and 63% for the 3-way classification using representation C.

The performances of two-way classifications are consistent with our intuition that it is harder to discriminate between German music and Austrian music than between German music and Irish music or between Austrian music and Irish music. Therefore, we expect that the result will improve if we use a more easily discriminated data set.

The results suggest to us a new way to think about similar musical styles. Nettl (1973) pointed out that it is difficult to quantify the difference between one kind or style of music and another. As he suggested, one way of telling that a musical style is similar to another which you already recognize, is that this style also appeals to you. This has to do with the fact that folk-music styles, like languages, exhibit greater or lesser degrees of relationship. Just as it is usually easier to learn a language that is closely related in structure and vocabulary to one's own, it is easier to understand and appreciate a folk-music style similar to one that is already familiar. Here we presented a method to measure the musical-style similarity quantitatively. The two styles that are less easily discriminated in classification are deemed more similar. The method can be based on the classification accuracy, as was done here, or on the distance of their statistical models directly—for example, the distance of two HMMs (Juang 1985).

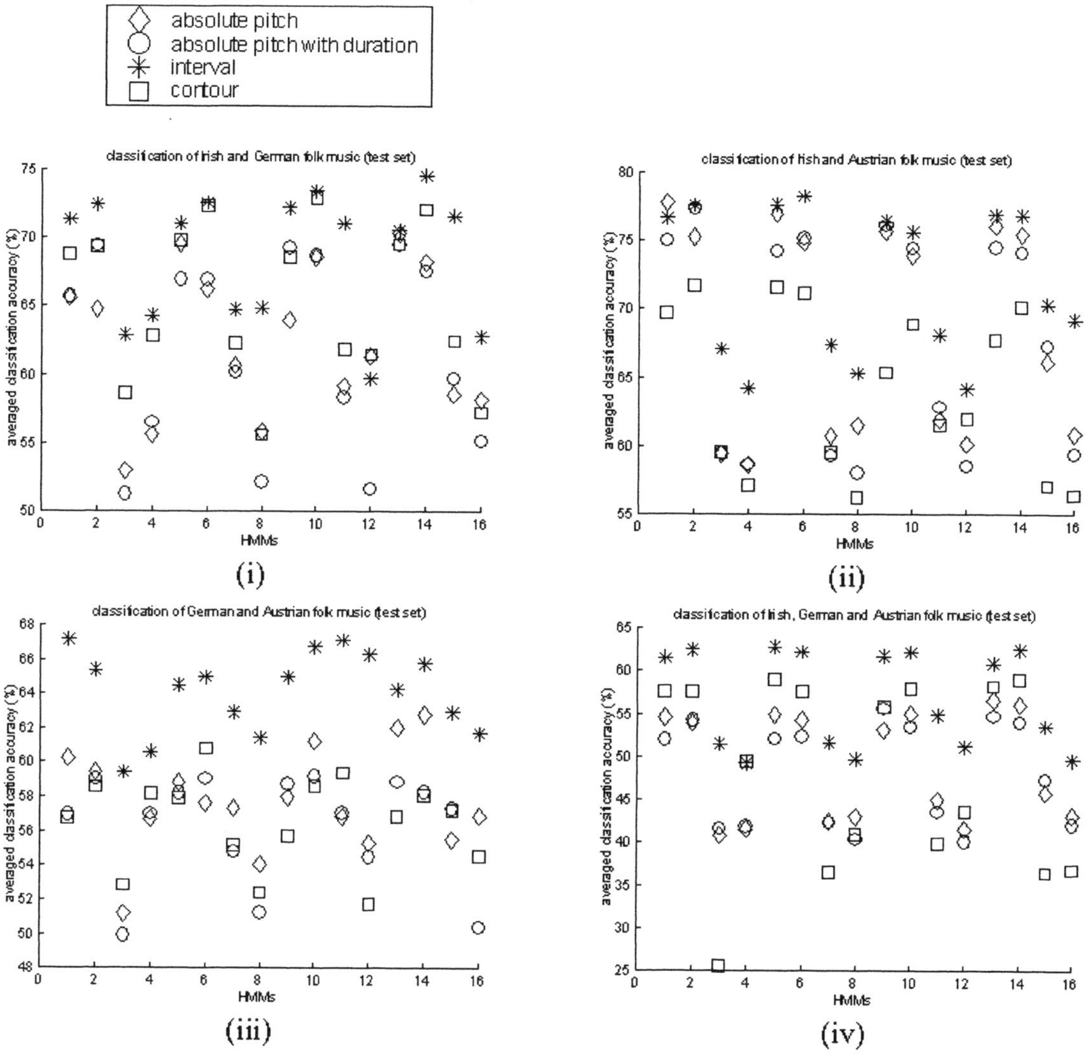

Figure 3.3. Classification performances using different representations and HMMs. (i), (ii) and (iii) correspond to 2-way classifications, while (iv) corresponds to the 3-way classification.

Table 3.2 shows that the representation is very important for classification. The interval representation outperforming the absolute pitch representation is also consistent with humans' perception of melody. Although the absolute pitch method can represent the original work more objectively, the interval method is more compatible with humans' perception, since when people memorize, distinguish, or sing a melody, they usually do it based only on the intervallic information. The contour representation performed significantly worse than the intervallic representation for folk-music classification. This indicates that although contour-based representation is fairly compact for identifying a melody, the quantization procedure may cause the features for style discrimination to be reduced.

Classes	Rep. A	Rep. B	Rep. C	Rep. D
I-G	68%	68%	75%	72%
I-A	75%	74%	77%	70%
G-A	63%	58%	66%	58%
I-G-A	56%	54%	63%	59%

Table 3.2. Classification performances of six-state left-right HMMs using different representations. The first three rows correspond to two two-way classifications. The last row corresponds to the three-way classification. I: Irish music; G: German music; A: Austrian music.

The fact that the representation with duration did not outperform the representation without duration is not what would be expected. It seems to be inconsistent with humans' perception. We argue that this does not mean rhythmic information is useless for classification; instead, we suggest that the rhythmic encoding used (through repeated notes) in fact destroyed some characteristics of the melody, thus reducing the discrimination. [For comparison, see Sapp et al. (2004).

The experiment shows that melody is a significant musical feature. Although melody is not sufficient for music classification on its own, repertories from different countries show significantly different statistical profiles with respect to their melodies.

3.2 Melodic Matching and Song Identification

What are the significant features people use to identify a melody or to distinguish between melodies? How can the melodies be represented sufficiently as well as concisely? Dowling (1986) proposed that a melody schema is not likely to be a literal mental copy of the melody. An exact copy would have to be translated—expanded, contracted, and shifted both in time and in pitch—to fit any actual instance of the melody that might be perceived. Therefore, it seems likely that a melody schema should represent more general higher-order information than specific pitches at specific temporal intervals.

Query-by-humming systems can find a piece of music in the digital music repository based on a few hummed notes. Previous query-by-humming systems mostly propose using pitch contours to represent melodies. They seldom use rhythm in their melodic representation. However, rhythm is obviously important, because when identifying a melody, the listener perceives not only the pitch/interval information in the melody, but also how the notes correspond to particular moments in time. Rhythm is one dimension in which melodies in general cannot be transformed intact. A representation combining both pitch and rhythm information, which we call TPB representation, was proposed by Kim (2000) and adopted in our QBH system.

Additionally, how do people measure the similarity of melody? And how can we retrieve melody from our mind so easily even after it is transformed in some way? This problem is closely related to the representation problem. Levitin (1999) described melody as an "auditory object that maintains its identity under certain transformations...along the six dimensions of pitch, tempo, timbre, loudness, spatial location, and reverberant environment; sometimes with changes in rhythm; but rarely with changes in contour." Although rather broad, this definition highlights several important properties of melody. People are able to recognize melodies even when they are played on different instruments, at different volumes, and at different tempi (within a reasonable range). Based on the TPB representation, we also proposed new approximate string-matching methods to do the melody-matching task. The algorithms did not only take robustness into account but also efficiency.

The following sections present the melodic representation and the melody-matching methods we used in our QBH system.

3.2.1 Pitch Contour

It is clear that some type of interval information is important for representing melody, since melodic matching is invariant to transposition. However, instead of representing each interval exactly (e.g., ascending minor sixth, descending perfect fourth, etc.), the literature suggests that a coarser melodic contour description is more important to listeners in determining melodic similarity (Handel 1989). Experiments have shown that interval direction alone (i.e., the 3-level +/−/0 contour representation) is an important element of melodic recognition (Dowling 1978).

One possible reason for the importance of melodic contour is that this information is more easily processed and is at a higher (more general) level than interval information. But as one becomes more familiar with a melody and gains more musical experience, the specific intervals have greater perceptual significance (Edworthy 1985) (Levitin 1999).

There is, of course, anecdotal and experimental evidence that humans use more than just interval direction (a 3-level contour) in assessing melodic similarity. When recalling a melody from memory, most of us (not all!) are able to present information more precise than just interval direction. In an experiment by Lindsay (1996), subjects were asked to repeat (sing) a melody that was played for them. He found that while there was some correlation between sung interval accuracy and musical experience, even musically inexperienced subjects were able to negotiate different interval sizes fairly successfully. From a practical standpoint, a three-level representation will generally require longer queries to arrive at a unique match.

Given the perceptual and practical considerations, we chose to explore finer (5- and 7-level) contour divisions for our representation.

3.2.2 Rhythmic Information

It is first useful to define some terms. Duration is the psychological correlate of time. Beat refers to a perceived pulse marking off equal durational units. Tempo refers to the rate at which beats occur, and meter imposes an accent structure on beats (as in "one, two, three, one, two, three ..."). Meter thus refers to the most basic level of rhythmic organization and does not generally involve durational contrasts. Rhythm refers to a temporally extended pattern of durational and accentual relationships.

In Kerman (2000), music is defined as "the art of sound in time." Sound exists in time, and any sound we hear has duration—the length of time we hear it in minutes, seconds, or microseconds. Though duration is not an actual property of sound, like frequency, amplitude, and other of sound's attributes that are taught in physics courses, it is obviously of central importance for music. The broad term for the time aspect of music is rhythm. Rhythm is the driving force in the vast majority of music both popular and classical, music of all ages and all cultures. Figures 3.4a and b illustrate the importance of consistent rhythmic information in melodic description.

Figure 3.4. (a) First four notes of the bridal chorus ("Here Comes the Bride") from Wagner's Lohengrin; (b) first four notes of the German carol "O Tannenbaum."

It is apparent that these are two very distinct melodies, yet the sounding intervals and note durations are identical. The difference lies not only in the respective meters (time signatures) of the songs, but also in the positions of the notes relative to the metric structure of each piece. The time signature of the first example is 2/4, and the strong beats occur on the first beat of the measure, which correspond to the first note of the piece. The second example has a time signature of 3/4, and the strong beat is on the first beat of the measure, corresponding to the second note. From this example, we clearly see the advantages of incorporating rhythmic information in a melodic representation.

3.2.3 Melodic Representation for Matching

We use a triple <T, P, B> to represent each melody, which we will refer to as TPB representation. T is the time signature of the song, which can change, but often does not. P is the pitch contour vector, and B is the absolute beat number vector. The range of values of P will vary depending on the number of contour levels used, but will follow the pattern of 0, +, –, ++, – –, +++, etc. The first value of B is the location of the first note within its measure in beats (according to the time signature). Successive values of

B are incremented according to the number of beats between successive notes. Values of B are quantized to the nearest whole beat. Clearly, the length of B will be one greater than the length of P because of the initial value.

In case a melody has multiple time signatures, we can break the melody into multiple melodic segments, within each of which the time signature doesn't change. We can then apply the TPB representation to each melodic segment.

Additionally, we use a vector Q to represent different contour resolutions and quantization boundaries. The length of Q indirectly reveals the number of levels of contour being used, and the components of Q indicate the absolute value of the quantization boundaries (in number of half-steps). For example, Q = [0 1] represents that we quantize interval changes into three levels: 0 for no change, + for an ascending interval (a boundary at one half-step or more), and – for a descending interval. This representation is equivalent to the popular +/–/0 or U/D/R (up/down/repeat) representation. Q = [0 1 3] represents a quantization of intervals into five levels: 0 for no change, + for an ascending half-step or whole-step (1 or 2 half-steps), ++ for ascending at least a minor third (3 or more half-steps), – for a descending half-step or whole-step, and – – for a descent of at least a minor third.

Thus, given a melodic segment M and a resolution vector Q, we can get a unique contour representation:

$$getTPB(M.Q) = <T,P.B> \qquad (1)$$

For example, the TPB representation for the example in Figure 3.4 (a) using Q = [0 1 3] is <[2 4], [* 2 0 0], [1 2 2 3]>. The TPB representation for the example in Figure 3.4 (b) using Q = [0 1 3] is <[3 4], [* 2 0 0], [3 4 4 5]>.

In our system, both the symbolic music corpora and hummed queries are converted into the TPB format, so that the similarity between the song and the query can be measured by matching the strings in TPB representations. Please note that the beat numbers in the query are not necessarily absolute beat numbers as in the melodic segments, but they must be relatively correct.

3.2.4 Melodic Matching Algorithms

All the following matching algorithms have been implemented in our QBH system.

DYNAMIC PROGRAMMING MATCHING ALGORITHM (DPM)

Dynamic programming has been used in most existing query-by-humming systems. The algorithm uses only the pitch information for matching the query with melodies.

Dynamic programming is able to determine the best match of the two strings on a local basis. For example, using the two melodic fragments (typically one is a query and the other is a melodic segment), we would fill a matrix according to the following formula, where *c* represents the matrix; *q* and *p* represent the query melodic string and the piece to match against respectively; index *i* ranges from 0 to query length and index *j* ranges from 0 to piece length:

$$c[i,j] = \min \begin{cases} c[i-1,j]+d & (i \geq 1) \\ c[i,j-1]+d & (j \geq 1) \\ c[i-1,j-1]+e & (q[i]=p[j] \text{ and } i,j \geq 1) \\ c[i-1,j-1]+m & (q[i] \neq p[j]) \\ 0 & o.w. \end{cases} \qquad (2)$$

where *d* is the cost of an insert or delete, *e* is the cost of an exact match, and *m* is the cost of a mismatch. We used $d = 1$, $e = 0$, and $m = 1$.

Figure 3.5 gives an example of using DPM to match the melodic segment [* 0 0 –2 1 0 2 –1] and the query [* 0 –2 1 2 0]. The optimal matching has a minimum cost of 1, which occurs in one location. Tracing the path that led to the local minima results in the matches shown in this figure.

Melody String

Query String		*	0	0	-2	1	0	2	-1
	*	0	0	0	0	0	0	0	0
	0	1	0	0	1	1	0	1	1
	-2	2	1	1	0	1	1	1	2
	1	3	2	2	1	0	1	2	2
	2	4	3	3	2	1	1	1	2
	0	5	4	3	3	2	1	2	2

Figure 3.5. Dy namic Programming Matching (DPM) of the melodic segment [0 0 –2 1 0 2 –1] and the query [* 0 –2 1 2 0]. The optimal matching is marked by the arrows, which represent how the value pointed to was calculated and can be followed to determine the parts that have been aligned.*

The DPM algorithm was determined to be the best similarity measure compared with all the other previous matching methods proposed for the query-by-humming systems including n-gram counting, the longest common subsequence and the Ukkonen measure (Uitdenbogerd 1999).

In our QBH system, to get the similarity score instead of the above cost measure, we simply invert the sign of cost and normalize it to be between 0 and 1.

$$score = (-cost + QueryLength)/QueryLength \qquad (3)$$

THE TPB MATCHING ALGORITHM I (TPBM-I)

This is an algorithm we proposed to compute the similarity score s of a melodic segment m = $<T_m,P_m,B_m>$ and a query q= $<T_q,P_q,B_q>$ to evaluate how well they match. The main difference between it and the DPM algorithm is that it considers both the rhythmic information and the pitch information. A higher score indicates a better match. Both the melody and the query must be converted into the TPB representation using the same quantization vector Q.

The TPBM-I algorithm includes these steps:

1. If the numerators of T_m and T_q are not equal, then return 0.
2. Initialize the measure number, n = 1.
3. Align P_q with P_m from the nth measure of m.
4. Calculate the beat similarity scores for each beat (see below).
5. Average the beat similarity scores over the total number of beats in the query, resulting in the overall similarity score starting at measure n: S_n.
6. If n is not at the end of m, then n = n + 1 and repeat step 3.
7. Return s = max$\{s_n\}$, the best overall similarity score starting at a particular measure.

This is the beat-similarity algorithm:

1. Get the subsets of P_q and P_m that fall within the current beat as S_q and S_m.

   $i = 1; j = 1; s = 0;$
2. While $i \leq |S_q|$ and $j \leq |S_m|$

   if $S_q[i] = S_m[j]$ then $s = s+1; i = i+1; j = j+1;$

   else $k = j;$

   if $S_q[i] \neq 0$ then $j = j+1;$

   if $S_m[k] \neq 0$ then $i = i+1;$

   return $s = s/|S_q|$.

Thus, the beat-similarity score is between 0 and 1.

THE TPB MATCHING ALGORITHM II (TPBM-II)

TPBM-II is a generalized version of TPBM-I. Basically it ignores the time signature and meter information. Only pitch contour and relative beat numbers are used in this algorithm.

This is the TPBM-II algorithm:

1. Initialize the beat number, n = 1.
2. Align P_q with P_m from the nth beat of m.
3. Calculate the beat-similarity score as above.
4. Average the beat-similarity scores over the total number of beats in the query, resulting in the overall similarity score starting at beat n: S_n.
5. If n is not at the end of m, then n = n+1 and repeat step 2.
6. Return s = max{s_n}, the best overall similarity score starting at a particular beat.

3.2.5 Effectiveness of the Representation and Matching Algorithms

We first need to propose some measures for evaluating the effectiveness of a melodic representation and a matching algorithm for melodic retrieval purpose.

Two measures have been generally used in evaluating retrieval effectiveness in document retrieval systems.

> PRECISION is defined as the proportion of retrieved documents which are relevant. Precision can be taken as the ratio of the number of documents that are judged relevant for a particular query over the total number of documents retrieved. For instance, if, for a particular search query, the system retrieves two documents and the user finds one of them relevant, then the precision ratio for this search would be 50%.
>
> RECALL is defined as the proportion of relevant documents retrieved. Recall is considerably more difficult to calculate than precision because it requires finding relevant documents that will not be retrieved during users' initial searches. Recall can be taken as the ratio of the number of relevant documents retrieved over the total number of relevant documents in the collection. Take the above example: the user judged one of the two retrieved documents to be relevant. Suppose that later three more relevant documents that the original search query failed to retrieve were found in the collection. The system retrieved only one out of the four relevant documents from the database. The recall ratio would then be 25% for this particular search.

Figure 3.6 shows the concepts of precision and recall schematically in a Venn diagram and indicates the overlap between them. B = {relevant documents}, C = {retrieved documents} and $A = B \cap C$. Thus, from the above definition, precision = A/C [Eq. 4] and recall = A/B [Eq. 5].

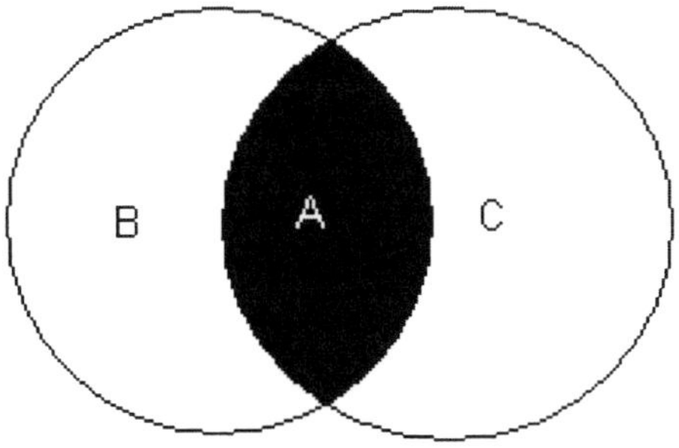

Figure 3.6. Concepts of precision and recall.

Theoretically, we would like to minimize C but maximize A to achieve maximum precision and recall. In practice, however, increasing one measure may cause the other one to decrease. So there is a trade-off between the two measures. The measures are affected by the matching algorithm (similarity between the query and the document) and how many documents are retrieved (similarity threshold).

In our particular case, we can still use the concepts while some special things need to be considered. Since for our melodic retrieval system, our main goal is to retrieve the song that is exactly the one the user wants to look for and not the songs that sound similar in some sense to the query, there should be only one song contained in B, except that there might be several copies in the database corresponding to the same song. If the right song is contained in the retrieved songs, then *recall = 1*. Ideally, the right song and only the song should have the highest score, so that if we retrieve only one song with the highest matching score, we will also get *precision = 1*.

However, such good performance is hard to achieve in practice. On one hand, we need the representation and matching method to be strict enough, so that when the query is perfect, it can guarantee that only the right song will get the matching score 1 and thus *precision = 1*. To this goal, exact matching is a good choice. On the other hand, we need the representation and matching method to be loose enough so that even if there are some errors in the query—which is typically true—it still can get a high matching score with the right song, so that it might be retrieved and thus *recall = 1*. To this goal, approximate matching is good.

Therefore, to solve the trade-off, we need a good representation and matching algorithm that can best characterize melodies and melodic similarity.

In Kim (2000), we did a complete evaluation of the TPB melodic representation and TPBM-I matching algorithm based on a small data set. Only perfect queries randomly generated from the data set were used in the experiment. The results we got include:

RESULTS I: IMPORTANCE OF RHYTHMIC INFORMATION

In spite of anecdotal evidence (such as the examples from Section 3.2.2), we wanted to explicitly verify the usefulness of rhythmic information in comparing melodic similarity. To test this, we used the simplest contour (3-level, $Q = [0\ 1]$) representations with and without the rhythmic information. Our results clearly indicate that rhythmic information allows for much shorter (and thus more effective) queries (Figure 3.7). A smaller number of matches indicates better performance.

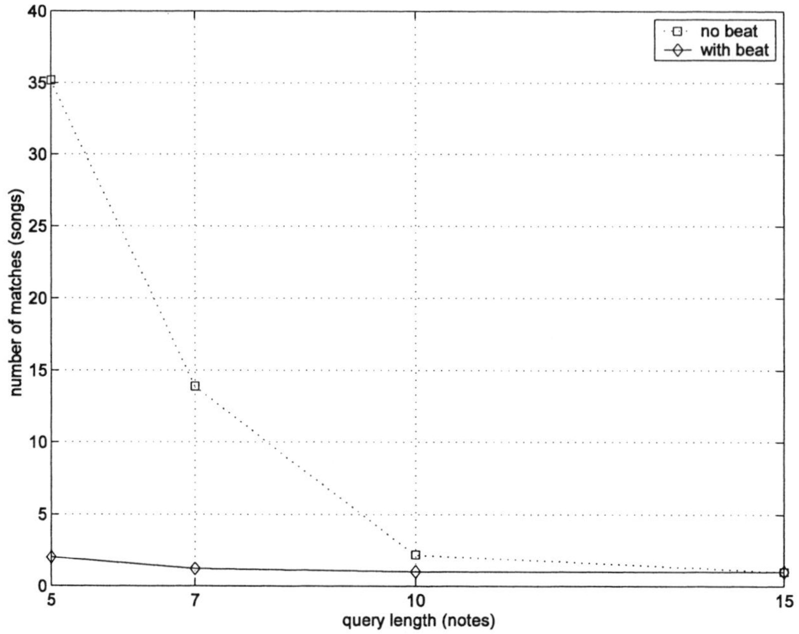

Figure 3.7. Importance of rhythmic information from Kim (2000).

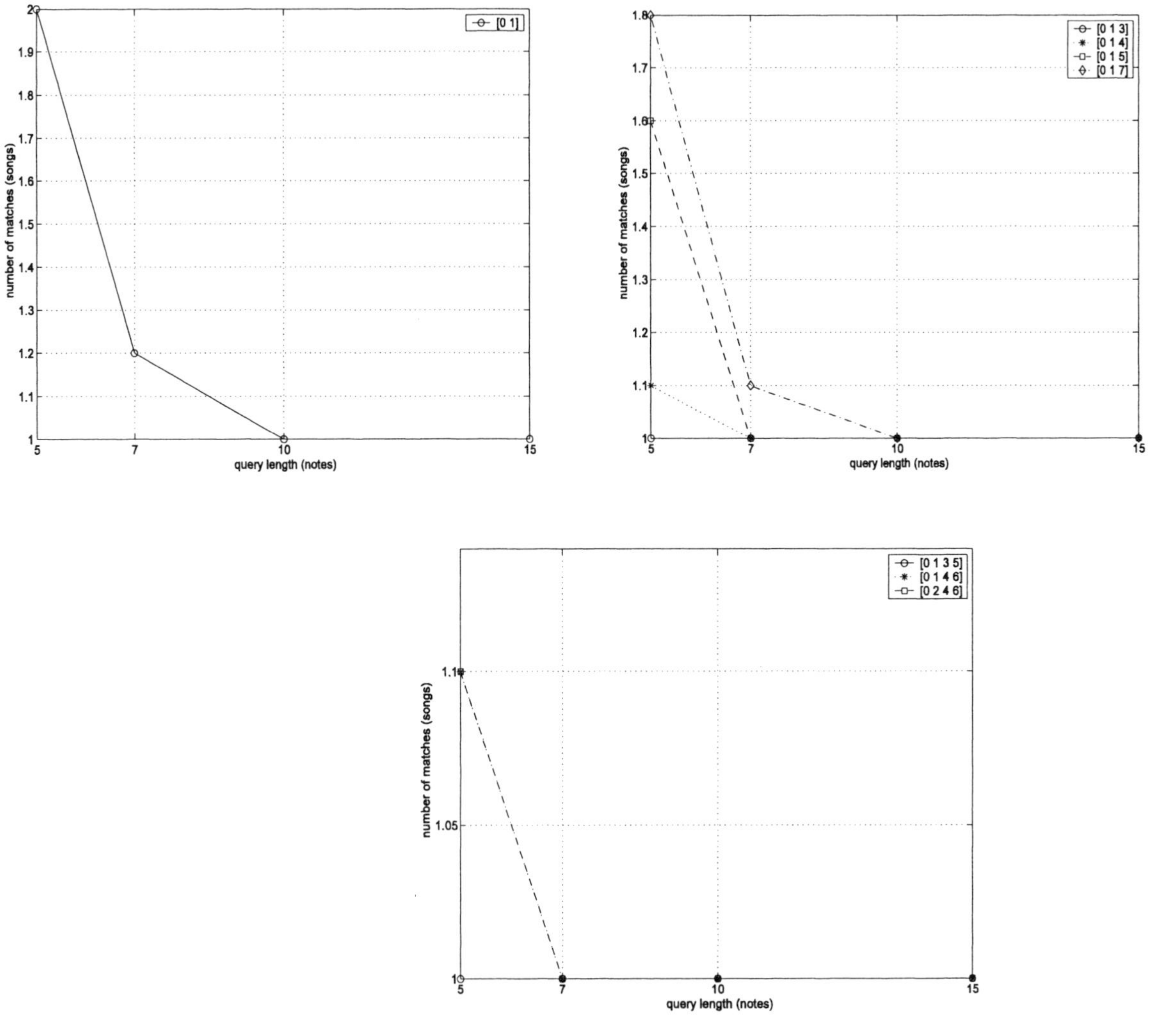

Figures 3.8 (a), (b), (c). Comparison of different quantization boundaries from Kim (2000).

RESULTS II: COMPARISON OF DIFFERENT QUANTIZATION BOUNDARIES

We examined 3-, 5-, and 7-level contour representations. For the 5- and 7-level contours, we also examined a variety of quantization boundaries (different quantization vectors Q). The results, in terms of average number of matches vs. query length (number of notes), are presented in Figures 3.8 a–c. It is clear that the 5-level contours perform generally better than the 3-level contours, with the 7-levels better still. For quantization vectors, we limited our search to Q_k = [0 1 x ...] cases only. Other values would have caused repeated notes (no interval change) to be grouped in the same quantization level as some amount of interval change, which does not make sense perceptually. It is an obvious result that greater numbers of levels in general result in more efficient searches. Clearly, more levels means more information, meaning fewer notes are needed to converge to a unique solution. What is more illuminating is that the best 5-level contour was able to equal the performance of the 7-level contour based on the rather small data set. This suggests that a 5-level contour may be an optimal trade-off between efficiency and robustness to query variation (more levels will cause more variations in queries).

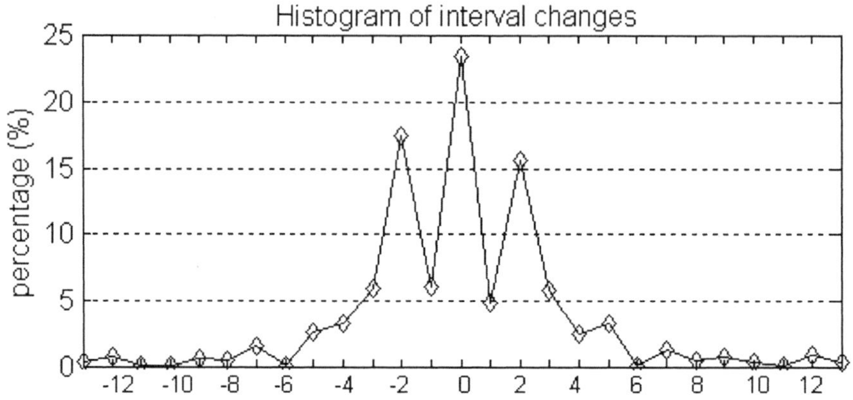

Figure 3.9. The interval histogram from Kim (2000).

Given our results, it is especially revealing to look at the histogram of interval occurrences in our data set (Figure 3.9). From this histogram, it is clear why certain quantization levels perform better than others. An optimal quantizer would divide the histogram into sections of equal area. Thus, for a 5-level contour we would like each level to contain 20% of the data. This is approximately true for the Q = [0 1 3] case, which has the best performance. No interval change (0) occurs about 23% of the time. Ascending half-steps and whole-steps (+1 and +2) are about 21% of the intervals, whereas descending half- and whole-steps (–1 and –2) represent approximately 23%. Other choices for quantization boundaries clearly have less optimal probability distributions, which is why they do not perform as well.

Although the above experimental results were based on a very small data set, the interval distribution of our current melody database containing 8072 songs, more than 536,181 notes (Figure 3.10), is amazingly similar to the smaller data set we used in Kim (2000). And the statistics of folk music from different countries did not reveal a significant cultural bias in the distribution of intervals. Compared with the results in Section 3.2.5, we may conclude that first-order pitch information (interval distribution) usually cannot capture the statistical difference between music from different cultures, while higher-order pitch information (e.g., modeled by HMMs) can do significantly better.

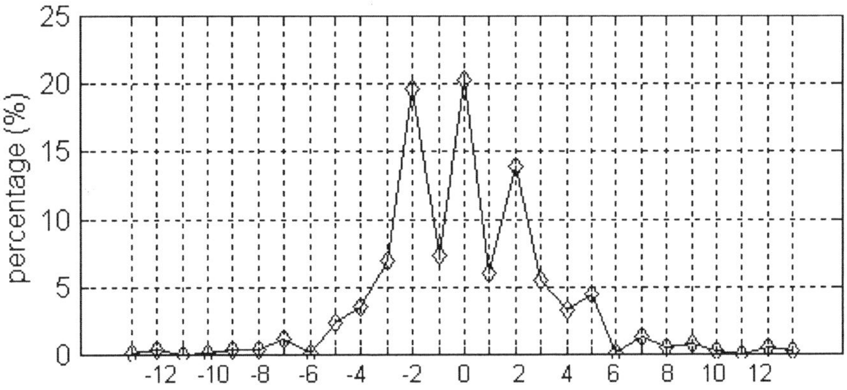

Figure 3.10. The interval histogram based on the QBH corpora.

The demonstration of effectiveness of the TPB representation and matching method is limited, though, because only perfect and randomly generated queries were used. Experimental results based on a much larger data set and real queries were presented in Chai (2001, Ch. 7).

3.7 Conclusions

This article presents theories and experimental results illustrating that melody carries statistical characteristics for musical style classification and song recognition. The experiments also show that designing melodic representations for different tasks is very important and can impact the system performance significantly.

References

Carpinteiro, O. and E. Itajubá (1998). "A Self-Organizing Map Model for Analysis of Musical Time Series," in *Proc. Fifth Brazilian Symposium on Neural Networks*, pp. 140ff.

Chai, Wei (2001). "Melody Retrieval on The Web." Unpublished M. Sc. thesis, MIT Media Lab. URL: *http://web.media.mit.edu/~chaiwei/papers/msthesis.pdf.*

Chai, Wei, and Barry Vercoe (2001). "Folk Music Classification Using Hidden Markov Models," in *Proc. International Conference on Artificial Intelligence.*

Cross, Ian (1999). "AI and Music Perception," *AISB Quarterly*, 102, 2–25.

Dowling, W. Jay (1978). "Scale and Contour: Two Components of a Theory of Memory for Melodies," *Psychological Review*, 85/4, 341–354.

Dowling, W. Jay and Dane L. Harwood (1986). *Music Cognition*. London: Academic Press.

Edworthy, Judith (1985). "Melodic Contour and Musical Structure," *Musical Structure and Cognition*, ed. Peter Howell, Ian Cross, and R. West, London: Academic Press, 169–189.

Handel, Stephen (1999). *Listening*. Cambridge, MA: The MIT Press.

Hewlett, Walter, and Eleanor Selfridge-Field, eds. (1998). *Melodic Similarity: Concepts, Procedures, and Applications (Computing in Musicology 11)*. Cambridge, MA: The MIT Press.

Huron, David (2000). "Perceptual and Cognitive Applications in Music Information Retrieval," in *International Symposium on Music Information Retrieval (ISMIR) 2000*.

Juang, B. and L. Rabiner (1985). "A Probabilistic Distance Measure for Hidden Markov Models," *The Bell System Technical Journal*, 64, 391–408.

Kerman, Joseph (2000). *Listen*, Brief Fourth Edition, p.2

Kim, Y., Wei Chai, Ricardo Garcia, Barry Vercoe. "Analysis of a Contour-Based Representation for Melody," in *International Symposium on Music Information Retrieval, Oct. 2000*.

Lerdahl, Fred, and Ray Jackendoff (1983). *A Generative Theory of Tonal Music*. Cambridge, MA: The MIT Press.

Levitin, Daniel J. (1999). "Memory for Musical Attributes" in *Music, Cognition, and Computerized Sound*, ed. Perry R. Cook (Cambridge, MA: MIT Press), 214–215.

Lindsay, A. T. (1996). "Using Contour as a Mid-Level Representation of Melody." M. S. thesis, MIT Media Lab.

Nettl, Bruno (1973). *Folk and Traditional Music of the Western Continents*, 2nd ed. (New York: Prentice-Hall).

Rabiner, L. (1999). "A Tutorial on Hidden Markov Models and Selected Applications in Speech Recognition," in *Proceedings of the IEEE, 77/2*, 257–286.

Roads, Curtis (1994). *The Computer Music Tutorial*. Cambridge, MA: The MIT Press.

Sapp, Craig Stuart, Yi-Wen Liu, and Eleanor Selfridge-Field (2004). "Search-Effectiveness Measures for Symbolic Music Queries in Very Large Databases," in *Proceedings of the Fifth International Conference on Music Information Retrieval (ISMIR)*.

Selfridge-Field, Eleanor (1998). "Conceptual and Representational Issues in Melodic Comparison," in *Melodic Similarity, Concepts, Procedures, and Applications (Computing in Musicology 11)*, ed. Walter B. Hewlett and E. Selfridge-Field (Cambridge: The MIT Press).

Singer, Jane (2002). "A Model of Melodic Representation: Towards an Implementation of Music Information Retrieval." Ph. D. dissertation, The Hebrew University, Jerusalem, 2002.

Sloboda, J. and D. Parker (1985). "Immediate Recall of Melodies," in *Musical Structure and Cognition*, ed. Peter Howell, Ian Cross, and R. West, London: Academic Press, 143–168.

Temperley, David (2001). *The Cognition of Basic Musical Structures*. Cambridge, MA: The MIT Press.

Uitdenbogerd, Alexandra L., and Justin Zobel (1998). "Manipulation of Music for Melody Matching," in *Proc. ACM, International Conference on Multimedia*.

Watkins, Anthony J., and Mary C. Dyson (1985). "On the Perceptual Organization of Tone Sequences and Melodies," in *Musical Structure and Cognition*, ed. Peter Howell, Ian Cross, and Robin Howell (London: Academic Press), 71–120.

4 Automating Motivic Analysis through the Application of Perceptual Rules

Olivier Lartillot[1] and Emmanuel Saint-James[2]

[1]University of Jyväskylä
Department of Music
PL 35(A)
40014 University of Jyväskylä, Finland
lartillo@cc.jyu.fi
[2]LIP6/SRC
Université Pierre et Marie Curie
4, Place Jussieu
75255 Paris, France
Emmanuel.Saint-James@lip6.fr

Abstract

Musical discourse may be described in terms of an intricate flow of local groupings. Such groupings, whose perception does not always reach a state of explicit awareness, mostly remain in an informal condition, except the most predominant of them, which contribute to more global constructions and will be remembered as the characteristic thematic materials of the musical piece. There have been some attempts, particularly in Reti's thematic analysis, to explicitly describe music at this level of detail. Such non-reductionist approaches to music analysis, facing huge complexity, desperately need automation and objectivity.

Current research in musical-pattern discovery, which may be considered to constitute the first steps towards this ideal, hardly discovers the basic musical structures expected by musicologists. This failure stems from the fact that current formalizations of musical patterns do not take plainly into account the essential characteristics of music as a perceptual phenomenon. Our approach to musical-pattern discovery is founded on perceptual heuristics, with the ideal aim of making explicit all the structural details that we more or less implicitly perceive. Basic principles and algorithms are described and illustrated, and early results are shown.

Music Query: Methods, Models, and User Studies (Computing in Musicology 13). Published by CCARH and the MIT Press, 2004.

4.1 Perceiving the Motivic Dimension in Music

4.1.1 Toward Motivic Analysis

One main reason for the growing interest of musicologists in computer tools is that large databases can be automatically searched for musical entities, either through a matching of a specific query or through an automated discovery of new configurations. Such user-defined queries and computer-defined discoveries are constrained to belong to certain musical categories, depending on the specific purposes for which these computer applications are designed.

For instance, such inquiry may focus on the *melody*, which is considered to be one of the most salient aspects of music, with the view to effectuate a discriminating characterization of works (see Selfridge-Field 1997-98). Multiple avatars of a particular melody may be retrieved among the corpora, be they exactly similar, slightly distorted, or significantly developed. It has been acknowledged, however, that the concept of melody cannot be applied universally, since some musical genres content themselves with constantly proliferating basic gestures instead (Figure 4.3).

Another musical concept around which these computer-aided analyses may be centered is the *theme*. Despite its confusing semantic similarities with the concept of melody, the thematic dimension of music may in fact be considered as an orthogonal vision. A theme is indeed any entity that characterizes a work because of its *reiterated* presence. A theme may be melodic, but its rhythmic and/or harmonic dimensions may be more stable than its melodic content. Conversely, a melody that does not share any specific redundancy with the rest of the work may be considered as non-thematic. What is interesting here is that the concept of theme is, contrary to that of melody, less dependent on cultural knowledge.

Since a theme is a specific configuration that is repeated several times throughout a piece, one may deepen the analysis by focusing on such basic configurations themselves, be they thematic or not. That approach, initiated by Rudolph Reti (1951), which considers music analysis to consist in the discovery of the specificity of each local aspect of the piece, contrasts with the reductionist approach that is frequently used by music analysts today. Reti's thematic analysis has been much criticized, perhaps in part because it desperately needs the help of automation. Indeed, the detailed analysis of local aspects easily "degenerates into a purely mechanical exercise in which the score is analyzed without ever really being read properly" (Cook 1987). Moreover, the foundation of Reti's methodology, which reveals his personal conception of music aesthetics, lacks objectivity. A computer implementation of his approach would require an explicit description of these mechanisms.

4.1.2 Perceptual Elements in the Theories of Reti, Nattiez, and Ruwet

Such analysis on the thematic level of music suggests another use for the computer in music analysis, which is as a tool for the explication of all pertinent structures in a score. Unfortunately, the implementation of procedures to carry out such a task confronts several obstacles. Today, only human intelligence is able to identify the subtle configurations of music. Does such idealistic artificial musical intelligence make sense, or should it be considered a utopian dream that cannot be practically achieved? To answer this question it is necessary to determine objectively the character of musical structures and to be able to answer questions on the possibility of exhaustive discovery of such entities.

This problem may be considered from a purely structural point of view. The analysis may focus on the "immanent configurational properties of a musical work," which is the "*analysis at the neutral level*" defined by Nattiez (1990); it differs from the "*poietic level*" of compositional procedures and intentions and from the "*aesthesic level*" of perceptual processes. According to this approach, musical entities may *exist* primarily in the score even before the listening or the analyzing process discovers them. However, such a distinction between subjective perception and objective analysis appears less evident when going into the details of what any neutral-level analysis really consists of.

The emblematic example of neutral-level analysis is the *paradigmatic analysis*, which was introduced by Ruwet (1987) and is based on a multileveled search for repeated patterns. Such an approach, if we suppose it to be temporally restricted to exact repetitions, may appear entirely objective at first sight. But where does the simple definition of a pattern as a contiguous sequence of notes, and not as a set of notes that are scattered throughout the score, come from, if not from perceptual properties?[1] For instance, an exact repetition of a pattern may equivalently be considered as the overlapping of groups of notes (Figure 4.1). This second representation is implicitly discarded simply because it does not correspond to what we actually perceive.

[1] According to Ruwet himself, paradigmatic analysis does take perceptual principles into account.

Figure 4.1. Mathematically speaking, a succession of two identical patterns of contiguous notes (solid lines) is equivalent to its dual representation as an overlapping of several identical patterns of two notes (dashed lines).

The phenomenon of approximate repetitions complicates this kind of analysis. As explained by Cambouropoulos (1998:12), "If similarity (i.e., not merely exact repetition) is taken into account, then analysis at the neutral level becomes unwieldy because any two musical sequences are similar in some respect. Analysis at the neutral level is useful only if guided by some sort of heuristics—for instance, based on general cognitive principles."

Such conclusions, calling into question the ideal of "neutrality," which, according to Nattiez (1990:13), "means both that the poietic and aesthesic dimensions of the object have been 'neutralised,' and that one proceeds to the end of a given procedure regardless of the results obtained," would rather lead us to defend the idea that musical structures cannot be separated from compositional or perceptual strategies.

4.1.3 Explicating the Implicit

There remain two levels on which the numerous musical structures may be envisaged—the *poietic* and the *aesthesic*. Reti, since he was himself a composer, envisioned thematic structure mainly on the first level: "the thematic phenomena are so manifold and complex that in a sense they evade academic tabulation. Though they can perhaps be described, they can hardly be comprised in an actual 'system.' They are too intimately connected with the creative process itself." (1951:233) But evidently, from the listener's point of view, composer intentions may show through the score.

Therefore, what is the use of musical analysis if a mere perception of music would suffice? The superiority of analysis over perception may be explained by a frankly elitist argument, stating that musical analysis shows the way we have to perceive music. Or it may be explained by the idea that analysis explicates what we perceive in a more or less implicit way. Once these inferences are made explicit, their perception will be made easier and more enjoyable. But at the same time, the potential of music perception is so rich that it seems really difficult, at first glance, to reduce it to a collection of explicit inferences.

4.2 Basic Principles of Pattern Perception

The quest for pertinent musical patterns (that is, for the building blocks of musical structures) remains an intricate challenge that has not yet been fully met. Here we approach the goal of automated musical analysis by investigating the possibilities for and obstacles to implementation of pattern-finding algorithms found in the theoretical literature.

4.2.1 Characterization of Patterns

A musical pattern may be defined in three ways. First, its existence may be explicitly and logically deduced from the constructive rules of a particular style. For instance, works in the classical style may be considered, roughly, as a hierarchical construction of patterns (e.g., formed by antecedent and consequent phrases) whose length is regular. When actual musical works deviate from this emblematic model, their melodic patterns are still understood by the listener. For this reason general characterizations of patterns may be considered as being independent of "style."

Patterns may also be discovered in a purely inductive way, following perceptual processes. Results offered by psychological studies such as Gestalt theory have been broadly applied in musical analysis by, among others, Meyer (1956) and Narmour (1990). In particular, groupings may result from segmentations that are ruled by local properties of the musical discourse. For instance, segmentation may be introduced between entities that contrast with each other along their pitch, time, onset, duration or intensity dimensions (see Lerdahl and Jackendoff 1983, Temperley 2001, and Cambouropoulos 1998).

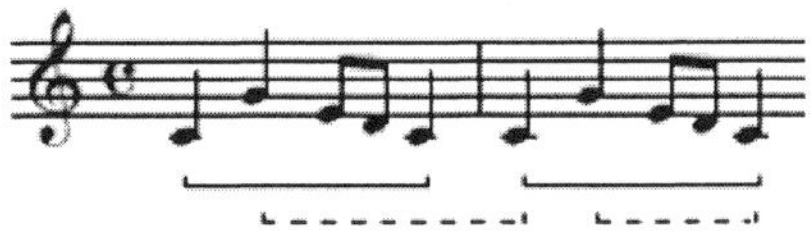

Figure 4.2. A pattern may feature contrasting steps.

Finally, a musical pattern may be defined as *a set of notes that is repeated several times* throughout the score. This last criterion, which has been studied primarily in linguistics (where paradigmatic analysis may be considered as a musical application; see Figure 4.2), conflicts with approaches involving local segmentation. Indeed, a musical pattern may be implicitly built through the aggregation of contrasting elements. In Figure 4.2 changes occur, for instance, in direction and intervallic size between the first and succeeding intervals but all belong to one pattern. A melodic pattern may be realized not by parametric repetition but by replication of some kind of dynamic evolution. In the remainder of this study, we will focus on this third (repetition-based) criterion,[2] but Gestalt principles will be considered too. All knowledge supplementary to melody (harmony, meter) will be discarded. Indeed, repeated patterns may appear in harmonically and/or metrically unstable places, as they do in the overlapping presentations of the fugal subject in a *stretto* passage.

[2] In GTTM Lerdahl and Jackendoff include the concept of repetition under "parallelism" and acknowledge that "a set of preference rules for parallelism has to be developed." They stipulate, however, that they are not "prepared to go further" in this direction. They admit that their "incapacity to flesh out this notion…is an important failure in [their] attempt to formulate a fully explicit theory of musical understanding" (1983:53). Temperley (2001:335) also notes that "because motivic analysis is influenced by a variety of factors, it seems likely that it…would be amenable to a preference-rule approach," but does not attempt it.

4.2.2 Cognitive Descriptions of Musical Patterns

The research projects dedicated to musical-pattern discovery are largely uniform in employing a pattern-extraction methodology which consists of similarity detection in a succession of musical elements (typically pitches or intervals formed by successive pitches). See, for example, Crawford et al. (1997-1998). Such a procedure, although a necessary condition for pattern determination, is not sufficient to insure a sound characterization. Simple examples may easily show that similarities of successions of notes do not necessarily characterize pertinent patterns. In Bach's *Prelude* in C, BWV 846 (Figure 4.3), some repetitions of successions of eight notes may correspond to actual motives (those marked with a solid line), but some may correspond to non-pertinent ones (those marked with dashed lines).

Figure 4.3. Two exact repetitions, one corresponding to pertinent patterns (solid lines), the other to non-pertinent ones (dashed lines).

If the previous example was not convincing enough, the simpler example shown in Figure 4.4, which contains only exact repetitions, may induce the inference of numerous non-pertinent patterns, due to the presence of a trill.

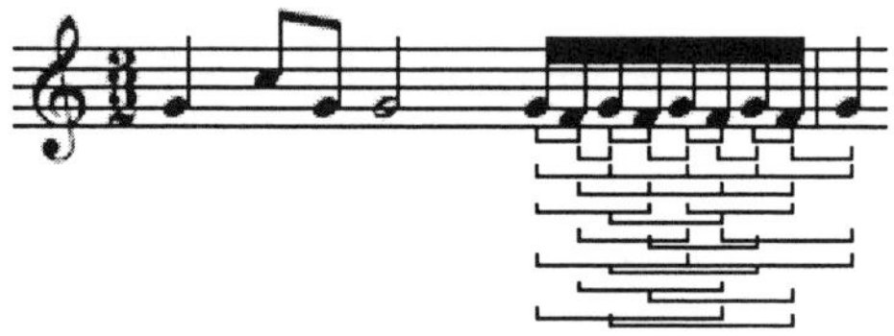

Figure 4.4. Non-pertinent patterns induced by the presence of a trill.

In order to avoid such bad inferences, Cambouropoulos (1998) proposed the addition of a specific constraint to guarantee the avoidance of overlapping patterns. However, such a constraint, if applied to general pattern-classes rather than to specific instantiations, cannot avoid the inference of patterns like FGF (Figure 4.4) or the dashed-line patterns (Figure 4.3).

Such conflicts may be resolved by considering the fact that patterns stem from conceptual inferences that are processed progressively during incremental listening. Each time a new note occurs, the set of inferences that are currently in process constitutes a context, which induces constraints upon the candidates for new inferences. In this cumulative process, non-pertinent inferences described in previous examples may be avoided.

4.2.3 Formalization of Pattern Classes and Occurrences

As we need to design a system that incrementally scans the score and progressively produces inferences that should depend on the score and on what has already been inferred, it may be convenient to construct these inferences directly on the score. First of all, we have to clearly distinguish the concepts of pattern class and pattern occurrence. A *pattern class* is an abstract concept that unifies all patterns of the score that are considered as similar. These patterns will be called *pattern occurrences* of the pattern class.

The characteristics of a pattern class are expressed through a list of properties shared by notes of the patterns and by the intervals between successive notes. Moreover, if we restrict our scope to monophonic music in a first approach, the notes of the pattern are totally ordered by chronology. Therefore, the entity of a pattern, be it a pattern class or a pattern occurrence, may naturally be formalized through a chain of states, where successive states correspond to successive notes of the pattern, and where each transition between two successive states corresponds to an interval between two successive notes (Figure 4.5).

Concerning the *pattern-class chain* (PCC), states and transitions feature the characteristic properties shared by the respective notes and intervals of its corresponding pattern occurrences. The *pattern-occurrence chain* (POC) interfaces the specific notes in the score with the associated PCC: each state of the POC is linked to one note of the score and one state of the PCC.

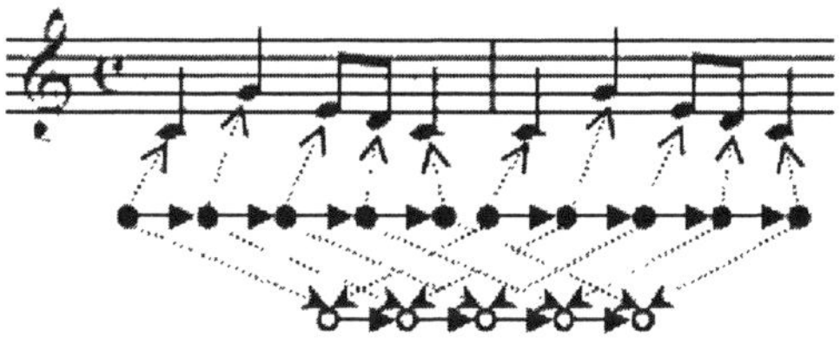

Figure 4.5. The two POCs (black circles) interface notes in the score with the corresponding states in the PCC (white circles).

Such formalization through graph theory enables one to easily implement the rules that should be added to the framework in order to insure pertinent inferences. For instance, there should be a rule generalizing our previous remarks concerning overlapping (see subsection 4.2.2) and stating that suffixes of patterns cannot be considered as new patterns, since they are already subsumed by current patterns (Figure 4.6).

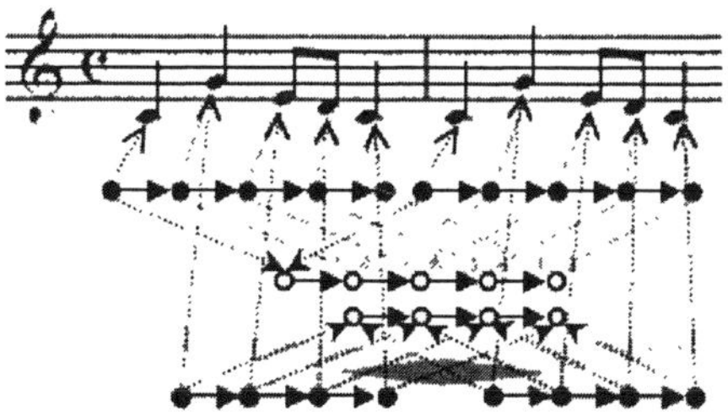

Figure 4.6. Suffixes (bottom POCs and PCC) cannot be considered as new pattern classes, since the associated notes of each of its POCs already belong to the POCs of the whole pattern (top POCs and PCC).

4.2.4 Pattern Associations

Music features multiple levels of pattern descriptions. Notes may indeed belong to several possible patterns in parallel. When discovering another occurrence of a pattern class that was associated to another pattern class, we may expect to retrieve the same association between these pattern classes. Therefore, pattern association may induce pattern *expectation*, as Leonard Meyer (1956) would say.

For this purpose, the association between patterns may be directly represented on the PCCs themselves. Every time a note of a pattern occurrence is associated to another pattern occurrence, on the corresponding state in each PCC is associated a new POC associated to the other PCC. Such pattern-association discovery induces a pattern-association expectation rule, stating that every time a new occurrence of such a pattern class is discovered, possible associated pattern classes are also expected. Such expectation may be formalized through the instantiation of new hypothetical POCs whose first state only is represented, waiting for further extension.

For instance, a pattern may include another sub-pattern. The eight-note pattern of Bach's *Prelude* in C features a repetition of two three-note patterns (Figure 4.7). Therefore, to the eight-note pattern class itself is added two three-note pattern occurrences.

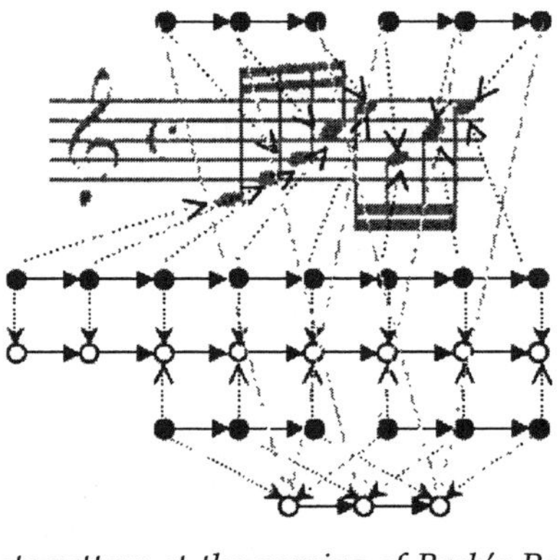

Figure 4.7. The eight-note pattern at the opening of Bach's Prelude in C Major (Well-Tempered Clavier, I) includes a repetition of two three-note patterns.

4.2.5 Pattern Reiteration

Music usually features successive repetitions of the same pattern class (Figure 4.3). If no new mechanisms were added, the system would consider each possible concatenation of these successive patterns as a new pattern. As noted above, these inferences, which do not correspond to human judgments and lead to combinatorial explosion, should be forbidden.

It may be remarked that such pattern repetition is a special case of pattern association. If each pattern is extended with the first note of the succeeding pattern, then this last note of such extended pattern may be associated to the first note of the same pattern class (Figure 4.8). This means that, in the extended pattern class, the last state is linked to the first state. The idea of pattern cycling is therefore explicitly represented.

The first note of each new occurrence, as soon as it appears, is immediately associated to a new pattern occurrence chain. An additional mechanism prevents the further extension of any pattern whose first note is also the last note of another occurrence of the same pattern.

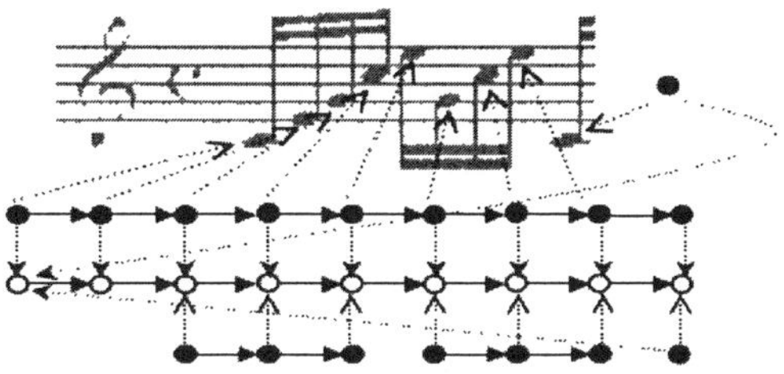

Figure 4.8. The last note of the nine-note pattern is linked to the first note.

4.2.6 Meta-Patterns of Patterns

The succession of pattern occurrences may be examined in exactly the same way as the previously considered succession of simple notes, provided that these pattern occurrences belong to the same pattern class[3]. For this purpose, a concept of "interval" between two successive pattern occurrences, that generalizes the traditional notion of an interval between two successive notes, is defined. A generalized interval simply consists of the list of all interval relationships between two respective notes *of the same rank* in each pattern occurrence.

[3] In future works, such a strong restriction may be replaced by a weaker one: for instance, pattern prefixes may be accepted too.

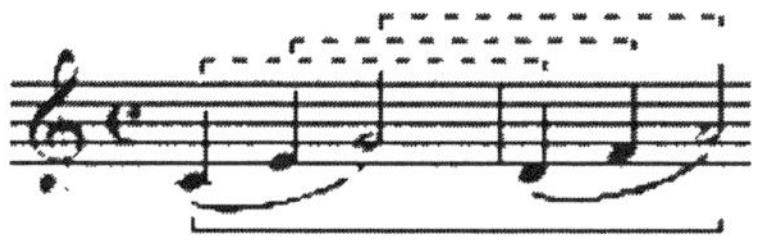

Figure 4.9. In a generalized interval between pattern occurrences, notes of the same rank are compared.

Meta-patterns of pattern occurrences will then be inferred when the successive generalized intervals of several successions of pattern occurrences are similar. It must be noted here that the similarity between two generalized intervals may consist of only a partial similarity along one or several ranks of the associated pattern occurrences. In this way, melody formed by the first note of each successive pattern occurrence, for instance, is considered (as in Bars 8-11 and 15-18 of the Bach *Prelude*). If the pattern occurrences are heard as chord arpeggiations, this generalized vision of pattern discovery may simply be understood as a horizontal (as opposed to vertical) approach to successive pattern occurrences.

Exact repetition of pattern occurrences may be considered to be a generalized "unison." The *Prelude* may then be modeled as a "perceptual" reiteration of a meta-pattern class that consists of two eight-note patterns in generalized unison (Figure 4.10). Moreover, this meta-generalization may be operated recursively and meta-patterns of meta-patterns may be considered too! Similar chord successions in the *Prelude* are special occurrences of such meta-patterns (Figure 4.11).

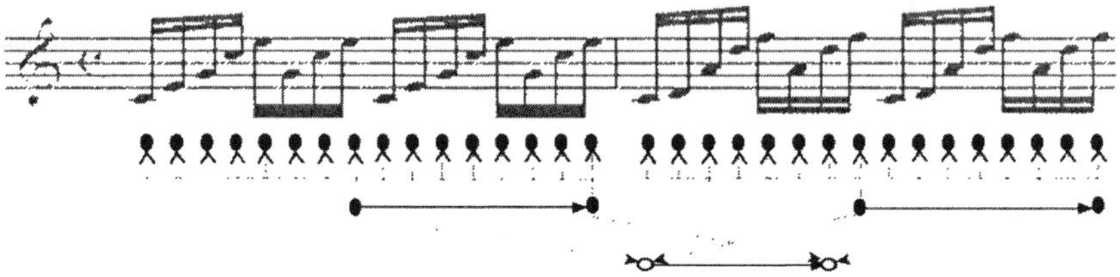

Figure 4.10. Each bar of the Bach Prelude contains the same generalized interval of "unison."

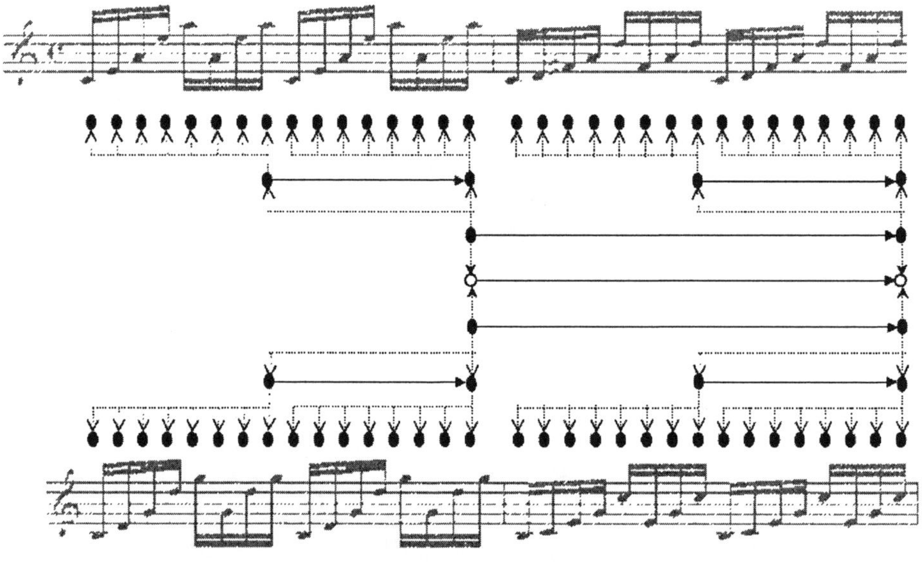

Figure 4.11. The Prelude also contains (hierarchically) meta-patterns of meta-patterns of eight-note patterns.

4.3 Modeling the Emergence of Similarity

4.3.1 Towards an Inductive Inference of Identities

So far, we have considered only exact repetition of patterns. The inference of identity relationships between patterns that are only similar is not obvious at all. One common idea consists of looking for identity along different "viewpoints" (see Conklin et al. 1995), or "levels of abstraction" (Dannenberg 2002) of the score.

Simply transposed patterns (Figure 4.12) may be detected by considering each pattern in its own pitch reference. For example, if patterns are described not with absolute pitch, but with relative pitch whose reference is the absolute pitch of the first note of the pattern, then such descriptions of transposed patterns are exactly identical.

Figure 4.12. A pattern and one transposition of it.

As for transpositions, slower and faster patterns (Figure 4.13) may be considered as identical to each other if a relative temporal representation is considered. For this purpose, the quotient between the duration of the current note and the duration of the first note is preferred to the absolute duration of the current note.

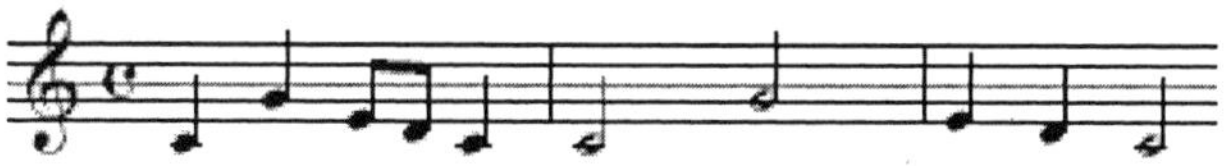

Figure 4.13. A pattern and one time-stretching of it.

But real music features much more complex transformations. In particular, pitch and temporal distortions may appear locally inside patterns. In order to handle such plasticity, more relative viewpoints of the pattern are considered. One commonly used description is the contour, which consists of the directions of the intervals between successive notes (downward, upward, or a repeat). Such a crude representation is so loose that non-pertinent repetitions may also be detected. Patterns with the same contour (for instance, up, down, down, down [Figure 4.14]) may be considered as nearly identical (first and second pattern), or as significantly different (first and third).

Figure 4.14. A pattern, a slightly distorted version of it, and a different pattern with the same contour description.

In fact, locally distorted patterns do not generally feature any explicit repetition. Repetitions are only hypothetical characteristics that have to be actively *induced* during perception (see Lartillot 2002). What also has to be taken into consideration are the local characteristics such as the quantitative distance between different intervals, or couples of successive notes. In the previous example (Figure 4.14), the first two patterns are similar because the distances between successive intervals are similar.

4.3.2 Local Contexts

If a pattern-induction algorithm has to mimic human capabilities, their basic principles first need to be described. In particular, we need to understand how a human listener, once s/he begins to hear the second occurrence of a pattern, is able to realize that what is being played has already appeared previously—exactly or similarly—even when such a pattern was not already explicitly defined.

Such cognitive capabilities seem to rely on the general characteristics of associative memory, where knowledge is indexed by content instead of being referenced according to an arbitrarily defined memory address. As patterns may be recalled even before being explicitly discovered, there exists a reproductive memory that associates local successions of notes that are similar to each other. Patterns may be defined as successions of local similarities.

These local similarities are built progressively from single intervals. Distances are computed first between single intervals, then between successions of intervals, or patterns.

Let n_1, n_2, n_3, n_4 be four notes whose respective pitches are p_1, p_2, p_3, p_4 and respective durations d_1, d_2, d_3, d_4. We propose, in a first approach, to formalize the perceptual distance between two intervals (n_1, n_2) and (n_3, n_4) as a weighted product of a pitch distance and a duration distance:

$$D\,[(n_1, n_2), (n_3, n_4)] = (\text{abs}\,[(p_2 - p_1) - (p_4 - p_3)] + 1) * (\max\,[d_1/d_3, d_3/d_1])^{0.7}$$

Here, only the duration of the first note of each interval is taken into consideration, since this duration is also the temporal distance between the successive notes. We may also remark that in music, pitches are subtracted, whereas durations are divided.

4.3.3 Step 1: Discovering Similar Contexts

Every successive local interval has to be memorized in an associative memory that is able to retrieve any interval similar to a query. For this purpose, a hash-table associates for each interval parameter the set of its occurrences in the part of the score that has already been analyzed. The similarity between current local interval i_1 and any old local interval i'_1 is computed with the hash-table.

If similarity between i_1 and i'_1 exceeds a certain threshold, previous local interval i_0 that precedes i_1 is considered, and compared to previous local interval i'_0 that precedes i'_1 (Figure 4.15). If the similarity between sequences (i_0, i_1) and (i'_0, i'_1) exceeds another threshold, then a pattern class that consists of this succession of two intervals is inferred.

Such an approach may now be immediately generalized to n intervals instead of 2, for any n greater than 2.

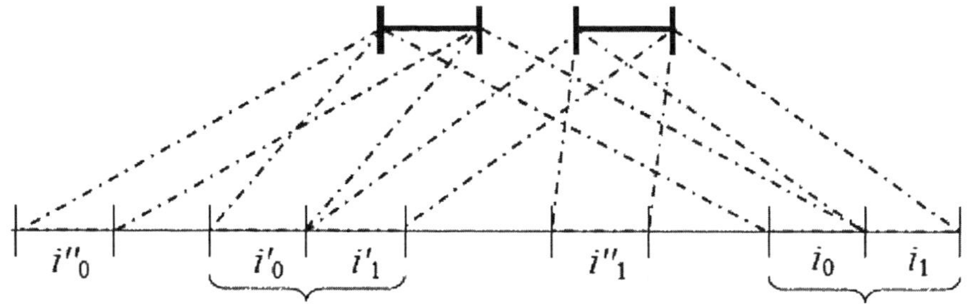

Figure 4.15. During Step 1, when two intervals i_1 and i'_1 are similar, preceding intervals i_0 and i'_0 are also compared.

4.3.4 Step 2: Prolonging Contexts

Once the similarity between the beginnings of two patterns has been detected, the inference of the similarity between the continuations of each pattern is far easier to process, since there is no need to discover new contexts any more. As present context induces expectation, the similarity threshold is higher here than for context discovery.

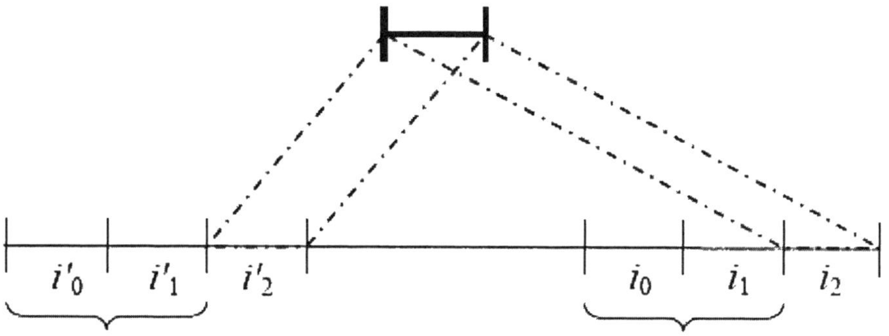

Figure 4.16. Step 2 simply consists of a comparison of each successive note of one pattern with the respective note of the other pattern.

Each successive note of the currently heard repetition is tentatively related with a possible successive note of the previously heard occurrence (Figure 4.16). In a pattern, each note may be disposed relative to the position of its preceding note, or also relative to the position of the first note of the pattern, and sometimes even relative to the position of another particular previous note of the pattern. In the 8-note pattern of Bach's *Prelude* in C (Figure 4.17), the similarity between the third note of each pattern is explained by its relative position with respect to the first note, and not the second note, since the two intervals between the second and the third note of each pattern are particularly different, whereas the two intervals between the first and the third note of each pattern are less dissimilar. On the contrary, the similarity between the fourth and fifth notes of each pattern may simply be explained by their position relative to their preceding notes.

Figure 4.17. Local referential relationships between pattern notes.

That is why the position of each note in a pattern may be considered relative to each possible previous note in the pattern, in order to find the minimum dissimilarity. More precisely, the distance between the two successions of notes $(n_1, n_2, \ldots, n_L)$ and $(n'_1, n'_2, \ldots, n'_L)$ is equal to:

$$D\,[(n_1, n_2, \ldots, n_L), (n'_1, n'_2, \ldots, n'_L)] = \min_{1 \le i < L} D\,[(n_i, n_L), (n'_i, n'_L)]$$

4.3.5 Discovering Further Occurrences

Once a pattern class has been discovered, its further occurrences should all be subsumed under the same pattern class. Therefore the discovery of these further occurrences cannot conform strictly to the pattern discovery algorithm described by previous steps 1 and 2. However, the distinction between context discovery and context prolonging still prevails.

In Step 1, when a similarity has been discovered between two different contexts, and before deciding to create any new pattern class, we have to make sure that such a context does not already exist in the beginning of one of the set of all discovered pattern classes (or more simply, in the set of pattern classes associated with the past context). If such a pattern class does exist, a new pattern occurrence simply associates the new discovered context with the retrieved pattern class.

Step 2 of pattern-occurrence discovery significantly differs from step 2 of pattern-class discovery. Since the beginning of a currently discovered pattern occurrence is already associated to a pattern class, each of its successive candidate continuations may simply be compared to the successive continuations along the pattern class. In this case, the current pattern occurrence does not need to be compared to old occurrences. The similarity threshold here is even greater than for pattern-class discovery, since the *expectation*, still in Meyer sense (1956), is explicitly represented within the pattern class.

4.4 *OMKanthus*: An *OpenMusic* Library

4.4.1 *Open Music*: A Graphical Music-Processing Language

Open Music was originally designed by Assayag et al. (1999) for computer-assisted composition. But since it was aimed at offering the most general tools possible for music processing, it may be used for any processing of abstract musical representations, and even for non-musical ones. This software offers a highly object-oriented visual environment for Common LISP programming, completed by numerous abstract music-processing tools. Objects are symbolized by icons that may be dragged and dropped all around. Most operations are then performed by dragging an icon from a particular place and dropping it in another. Several classes implementing musical data and behavior are provided. They are associated with graphical editors and may be visually subclassified by the user to meet specific needs. Different representations of a musical process are handled, which include common notation, MIDI piano-roll, sound waveforms, and break-point functions. A *patch* is a place where objects—functions, classes, instances, sub-patches, or *maquettes*—will be interconnected in order to specify musical algorithms. High level in-time organization of the music material is available through the *maquette* concept.

As *Open Music* was originally designed for algorithmic music generation, one first analytic application may consist of algorithmic reconstruction of specific musical works. In this way, compositional strategies may be exhibited.

Several musicological researches are associated with the *Open Music* project. In particular, Andreatta and Agon (2002) have formalized and implemented an algebraic approach to music theory, analysis and composition, presenting some well-known concepts, like Forte's PCS Theory, in a very elegant form by showing, at the same time, possible new strategies of generalization. Algebraic methods provide a fruitful way to formalize musical structures, in the pitch as well as the rhythmic domain.

4.4.2 *OMkanthus* Library

The concepts presented in section 4.3 have been implemented as an *Open Music* library called *OMkanthus*. It consists of a main function that analyzes MIDI files. In the current version, results are displayed as a list of texts that is not easy to understand. That is why the library is also provided with some basic tools for selecting and displaying the longest patterns, most frequent patterns, or most pertinent patterns, where pertinence is a product of length and frequency.

When asking for the pattern classes achieving the highest degree of pertinence in the beginning of Bach's *Prelude* in C, we obtain the 8-note pattern (Figure 4.18, first staff) and three-note patterns that are repeated inside the 8-note pattern itself (second staff). Such interesting results, discovered by a system that has no access to any prior cultural knowledge, have never been obtained by any previous algorithm.

Figure 4.18. Most pertinent patterns of the beginning of Prelude in C Major, BWV 846, by Bach.

When asking for the most pertinent pattern classes in the beginning of the *Fifth Symphony* by Beethoven, we obtain the 4-note pattern (Figure 4.19a-b, second staff) and the encapsulation of 3 times the 4-note patterns (Figure 4.19b, third staff). Note however that a non-pertinent occurrence has been found (dotted line). Non-pertinent encapsulation of 2 times the 4-note patterns (first staff) has also been considered.

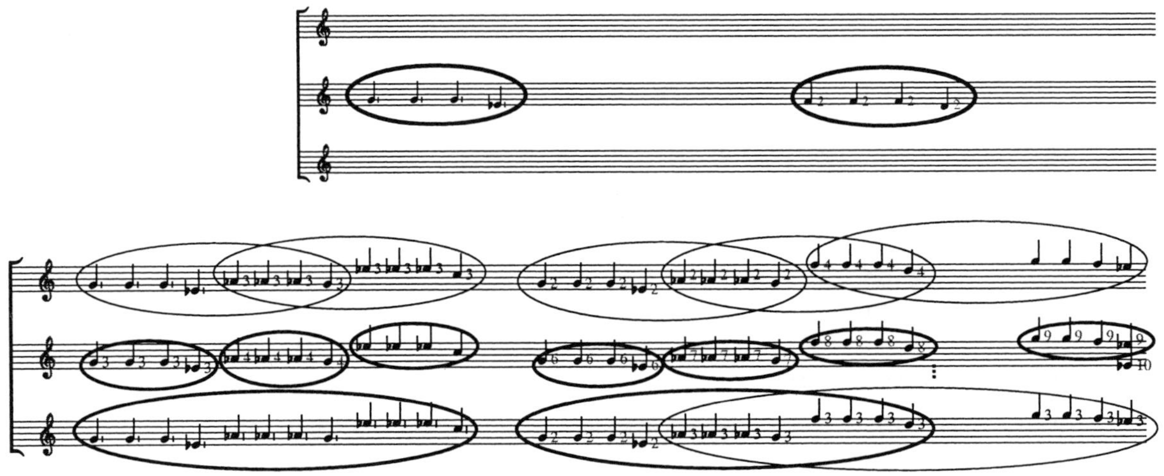

Figures 4.19a and b. Most pertinent patterns in the beginning of Beethoven's Fifth Symphony.

When asking for the most pertinent pattern classes in the beginning of the *Rondo alla turca* by Mozart, we obtain the five-note pattern (Figure 4.20a, second staff). Its prefix is also displayed (third line) because little patterns of four descending notes (Figure 4.20b) have been considered as occurrences of this pattern class. The algorithm is not well equipped to deal with polyphonic patterns. That is why we observe some failures in pattern detection (Figure 4.20a, first and fourth staves). Finally, the long pattern (fifth staff) pertinently encapsulates the repetitions of the five-note pattern, but cannot then integrate the following chords, due to the polyphony limitations.

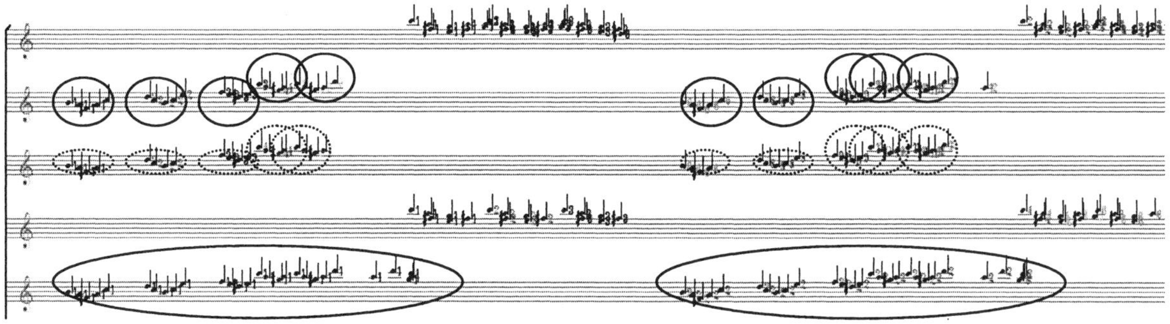

Figure 4.20a. Most pertinent patterns of the beginning of the Rondo alla turca by Mozart.

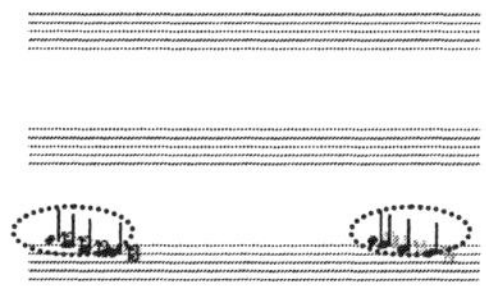

Figure 4.20b. continued (only the first three staves).

Such results may appear very simple and evident, compared to the complexity of the conceptual framework that has been developed for this purpose. But it has to be remarked that such results are very interesting for artificial intelligence research, and also for the understanding of the cognitive mechanisms of music perception. Moreover, now that the algorithm performance is starting to corroborate expected behavior, a little refinement of the model should offer more subtle results. An important study needs to focus on the optimization of the algorithms, as the current version, easily entering into combinatory explosion, cannot handle more than several hundred notes.

4.4.3 Future Work

Here are some issues we would like to tackle very soon, in order to improve the results. First, in each 8-note pattern of the Bach *Prelude*, the two occurrences of the 3-note pattern are in fact exactly repeated. Such a relationship should be explicated since it contributes to the essence of the 8-note pattern itself. It should also be noted that the 8-note patterns are also always repeated exactly twice.

Such conceptual repetitions cannot exist without a concept of similarity hierarchy. Indeed, in the Bach *Prelude*, if two occurrences of the 8-note pattern class are considered exactly identical, this means that they belong to a particular pattern class whose occurrences are all exactly identical. Also to be considered: the explicit representation of the class of all patterns consisting of the encapsulation of two successive exact repetitions of 8-note pattern classes. Such a particular class may be represented with the help of pattern associations and the still undefined notion of relative similarity.

There may be, inside patterns, "enclaves" of foreign notes not really belonging to these patterns. Patterns may also feature transitory states, such as passing notes or appoggiaturas. More generally, patterns may be included in a polyphonic flow. If this flow is represented as a single totally ordered sequence, pattern representations, here also, feature enclaves. Such a problem has already been tackled (see Meredith et al. 2002), but uniquely for exact repetition. Chords should also be taken into consideration and patterns of chords should be discovered.

An interface must also be designed, enabling browsing inside the score and the discovered structures. In the long term, such an approach may go beyond patterns and capture higher-level concepts. A project of automatic music-theory discovery may also be envisaged.

4.5 Conclusion

The new approach of musical-pattern discovery we proposed, based on modeling of cognitive mechanisms of music perception, leads to very promising results. The discovered structures correspond to basic patterns effectively perceived by human listeners. With some improvements, this algorithm should also be able to detect subtler patterns that are less easily discerned by listeners, but that participate in the complex flow of implicit reasoning, which constantly suffuses the mind of an experienced listener while enjoying music.

Up-to-date information about this project is available at:
www.ircam.fr/equipes/repmus/lartillot

References

Andreatta, Moreno, and C. Agon (2002), "Algebraic Methods in Music: Theory and Implementation," *17th International Congress of the International Musicological Society*.

Assayag, Gérard, C. Rueda, M. Laurson, C. Agon, and O. Delerue (1999), "Computer Assisted Composition at IRCAM: *PatchWork* and *OpenMusic*," *Computer Music Journal*, 23/3, 59–72.

Cambouropoulos, Emilios (1998). "Towards a General Computational Theory of Musical Structure." Ph.D. thesis, University of Edinburgh.

Conklin, Darrell, and I. Witten (1995), "Multiple Viewpoint Systems for Music Prediction," *International Journal of New Music Research*, 24/1, 51–73.

Cook, Nicholas (1987). *A Guide to Musical Analysis*. London: Dent.

Crawford, Tim, C. S. Iliopoulos, and R. Raman (1997-98), "String-Matching Techniques for Musical Similarity and Melodic Recognition," *Computing in Musicology 11*, 73–100.

Dannenberg, Roger (2002), "Listening to 'Naima': An Automated Structural Analysis of Music from Recorded Audio," *Proceedings of the International Computer Music Conference 2002*, 28–34.

Dowling, W. J. (1978), "Scale and Contour: Two Components of a Theory of Memory for Melodies," *Psychological Review*, 85/4, 341–354.

Lartillot, Olivier (2002), "Musical Analysis by Computer Following Cognitive Model of Induction of Analogies," *Proceedings of the International Computer Music Conference 2002*, 20–27.

Lartillot, Olivier (2003), "Discovering Pertinent Pattern Through Perceptual Heuristics: Why and How," *Proceedings of the International Conference on Music Information Retrieval*.

Lerdahl, Fred, and Ray Jackendoff (1983). *A Generative Theory of Tonal Music*. Cambridge, MA: MIT Press.

Meredith, David, K. Lemström, and G. A. Wiggins (2002), "Algorithms for Discovering Repeated Patterns in Multidimensional Representations of Polyphonic Music," *Journal of New Music Research*, 31/4, 321–345.

Meyer, Leonard B. (1956). *Emotion and Meaning in Music*. Chicago: The University of Chicago Press.

Nattiez, Jean-Jacques (1990). *Music and Discourse: Towards a Semiology of Music*. Princeton: Princeton University Press.

Narmour, Eugene (1990). *The Analysis and Cognition of Basic Melodic Structures: The Implication-Realization Model*. Chicago: The University of Chicago Press.

Reti, Rudolph R. (1951). *The Thematic Process in Music*. New York: Macmillan.

Ruwet, Nicolas (1987), "Methods of Analysis in Musicology," *Music Analysis*, 6/1-2, 4–39.

Selfridge-Field, Eleanor (1997-98), "Conceptual and Representational Issues in Melodic Comparison," *Computing in Musicology 11*, 3–64.

Temperley, David (2001). *The Cognition of Basic Musical Structures*. Cambridge, MA: MIT Press.

5 Towards a Measure of Cognitive Distance in Melodic Similarity

Eleanor Selfridge-Field

Center for Computer Assisted Research in the Humanities
Stanford University
Stanford, CA 94305-3076, USA
esfield@stanford.edu

Abstract

We propose a still preliminary cognitive-distance metric to rank possible melodic matches. Its primary purpose is to discriminate between literal matches and psychologically valid matches in searches of large symbolically encoded datasets. Cognitive weightings are based selectively on studies in several disciplines related to music. Examples are drawn from both "intentional" searches (those collected manually by musicologists and ethnomusicologists) and those culled in computer "automatic" searches (those collected by computer) of the same melodic prototypes. Two variants of a provisional scoring system are considered.

Music Query: Methods, Models, and User Studies (Computing in Musicology 13). Published by CCARH and the MIT Press, 2004.

5.1. Melodic Similarity and Feature Prioritization

The notion of similarity[1] (music excluded) is problematical in ways which arguably make it ill-suited to computer query. For tangible objects with such defining characteristics as shape, color, size, volume, texture, weight, and so forth, it is obvious that within a group of non-identical specimens, the number of combinatorial possibilities for matching one or more properties among all the pairs that can be formed is considerable, and that the feature categories themselves are of an arbitrary degree of complexity. Sound objects too contain an arbitrary number of properties (pitch, pitch fluctuation [ornamentation], duration, articulation, dynamic level, and so forth), many of which can be further refined. The ranking of these properties in relation to the establishment of discrete melodic identity has not been established. It seems fair to say that in similarity studies generally there is no obvious or inherently systematic way to rank objects by degrees, although that is what potential matches expressed as probabilities of an exact match purport to report.

[1]This paper is an adapted and expanded version of my talk "Accidental and Intentional Melodic Similarity: Towards a Measure of Cognitive Distance," *International Symposium of Music Information Retrieval (ISMIR), Paris, October, 2002.*

The phrase "melodic similarity" harbors a large array of goals which are divergent and depend on one's purpose. I shall cite four, although many others exist. (1) Musicians, like ordinary listeners, consider melodic similarity to be a concept which enables identification and location of a specific piece of music. Every potential match is correct or incorrect; judging degrees of similarity is usually irrelevant to the goal. (2) Publishers and copyright registrars want to know whether the same "essential" work has been printed or recorded before. The details need not be exactly the same in order for a violation of intellectual-property rights to occur. (3) Musicologists may be seeking to establish clusters of related melodies. These scholars may want to know how musical (or musico-social) identities were formed, preserved, and varied. (4) Music recommendation services, however, want to persuade customers who bought one product that a "similar" product has sufficient likeness to be worthy of their consideration. For them alone a list of probabilities in declining order lies on the direct path to the goal.

It falls to the community of music-query software developers to serve all of these needs. Even at this early date, there is much specialization within the field and little uniformity in the assumed definitions that inhere in these different realms of application. To date there has been little interaction between these developers and researchers in music cognition, where related research has frequently focused on Gestalt principles of melody (pattern completion, extension, expectation) and what is, in a sense, its obverse: segmentation and its tiers of generalization, with occasional consideration given to melodic associations with lyrics, with emotions, and sometimes with reference to specific qualities of memory and attention. Ultimately, music cognition is concerned with minds rather than music, but by offering important clues to the salient principles of melodic perception it identifies possibilities which deserve acknowledgment.

5.2. Towards a Cognitive-Distance Metric

5.2.1. Modeling Melodic Reduction: An Example

The human phenomena we associate with melody (hearing, recognizing, recalling, or performing a melody) exist within a paradoxical universe: the process of realization is necessarily sequential because it happens in time, while the process of "imaging" appears to be iconic and therefore static in time. What gives melodies their theoretical "shape"? We might presume that salient features of a melody, individually perceived and prioritized, play a role in the formation of these configurations.

The purpose of a cognitive-distance metric is to serve all sides of this relationship, to mediate between the experiential reality and the distilled idea. This implies mediation between time and non-time. On the real-time track, we begin by assigning an ordinal value from which the linear position of every sound event can be tracked. To get to the non-time (ideal) track, which retains a sense of time but does not operate in the same temporal space as sounding material, a qualitative weight which takes account of features of local and global importance within the melody is added.

This aim raises the question of note-functions within a melody. On the one hand, any single note in a melody contributes only its relationships, not its pitch content, to the melody as a whole. On the other hand, there are no firm rubrics for determining what the intermediate containers of musical meaning are, despite the fact that numerous models for melodic segmentation have been proposed (Lerdahl and Jackendoff 1983, Halperin 1990, Cambouropoulos 1999, Singer 2003). This chameleonic quality of melody is undoubtedly part of its charm.

Our sense of the simplicity of melody is imposed effortlessly by our minds, for the details of melodic fabric are frustratingly complex (see, *inter alia*, Selfridge-Field 1998). This discloses another paradox: when we try to model the cognitive process that makes melodies seems simple, we discover that the level of discarded detail varies from person to person and can move along the continuum of complexity—simplicity within a single melody. Apropos of this potential for shifting levels of reductions, Figure 5.1 shows a short example from a Bach minuet with three possible reductions.

Figure 5.1. Bach keyboard minuet in Bb Major (right hand on top staff) with three levels of melodic simplification: (a, b) mixed levels of reduction per bar, (c) scale reduction.

In Figure 5.1 Reduction (a) preserves the event-rhythm of Bars 1 and 3 but reduces that of Bar 2. Reduction (b) is an inversion of (a) in that it reduces the activity in Bars 1 and 3 by two levels but that of Bar 2 by only one level. Reduction (c) opts for the least amount of melodic activity required by implied harmonic change. [Obviously, many other reductions are possible.] There is no experimental evidence to suggest that any of these reductions or more or less valid than the others. There are faint indicators that as a collection they represent reductions that could each occur to some individuals. [Some might be more or less likely in different listening contexts, a subject which will not be discussed here.]

That harmonic implication plays some role in the cognitive dynamics of tonal melodies seems to be beyond dispute, even if the details require further investigation. Several studies call attention to the importance of harmonic implication in melodic recognition. Holleran and Jones (1995) suggest its primacy at a general level, while studies by Cuddy (1993) and Dowling (1994) underscore its relevance at a more specific level. Harmonic modeling by Sapp (2004) suggests that divergent harmonic inferences for identical musical passages operate systematically but (vis-à-vis Krumhansl 1990: 99–102) reflect distinctly different tiers of temporal resolution.

Harmonic implication can be seen to play an invisible role in the processes represented by Reductions (a) and (b). Reduction (c) is too shapeless to facilitate the modeling of melodic cognitive processes. A great many melodies of both classical and folk music can be reduced to scales by one means or another. Rhythmic patterning and pitch contour are essential to a fundamental sense of distinct identity.

Adjudicating between Reductions (a) and (b) is a more difficult task. A perfunctory search of the *Themefinder* database (for holdings see Sapp, Liu, and Selfridge-Field 2004), here using *c.* 40,000 incipits of European classical and folk music, culls only seven match-candidates (all of them imperfect) for works in a major key, in 3/4 meter, and initiated by the scale degrees 3–3–4–5. This suggests that Reduction (b) is adequately differentiated for searching purposes. It does not, however, indicate that (b) is more valid cognitively. Neither can one infer that melodies with similar rhythmic patterns could all be reduced as successfully with the (b) template. An implied harmonic change in Bar 2 could would call the reductions into question.

5.2.2 From Modeling to Metrics

Several efforts to create cognitively sensitive search tools for melodic representation and segmentation (Cambouropoulos 1999) have employed elements of the Lerdahl-Jackendoff (1983) hierarchical categorization model for listening. What the reductions shown in Figure 5.1 are intended to demonstrate is that perceptual feature-selection is likely to influence the results and therefore the efficiency of the resulting approaches. If one takes all three reductions and awards one point for the mere retention of each event on each tier, then the scoring shown in Table 5.1 results.

Event	**1**	2	3	4	5	6	**7**	8	9	10	11	12	**13**	14	15	16	17	18
Score	**4**	2	2	2	2	2	**3**	1	3	1	3	1	**4**	2	2	2	2	2

Table 5.1. Simple scoring method for each melodic event based on its presence in each of the reductions of Figure 5.1. Bold type indicates downbeats.

This approach avoids the difficult task of adjudicating between reductions. At the same time, each is retrievable: scores ≥ 4 produce Reduction (c), those ≥ 3 produce Reduction (b), those ≥ 2 Reduction (a).

A ubiquitous property of the Baroque repertory from which Figure 5.1 comes was its "sewing-machine" rhythms, from which buried melodies were to be excavated by the listener. Here the rhythmic figuration is monotonous. The ease with which listeners can construct something more tolerable in their minds is remarkable, but it is undetermined whether simple principles of reduction can be defined. It is premature to speak of a process whereby the "reduction" of a melody of this kind actually amounts to varying the weights of each item in its repetitive background to make the melody more definable.

While the scores of Table 5.1 contain no metrical information *per se*, they imply it. Here too there is something of a circular argument, for the coincidence of harmonic change precipitates the necessity to introduce notes which will be rendered essential to the melodic definition by most reductive approaches.

What can we learn from this example? One point is that metrical and harmonic information are indispensable elements of melodic identity. Whether they are captured implicitly or explicitly, some account must be made of them.

This simplistic approach to measurement attempts to get at the conundrum posed by Cuddy (1993), who asked [I paraphrase], "Why does a single note matter so much in one melody and so little in another?" One way of modeling a search designed to capture the notes that "matter so much" is to address the fact that some notes in a melody play multiple roles, which makes their presence essential, while others are simply present as "filler" and are hardly missed if absent. In the context of a given melody, some notes might be more salient than others because they complete a melodic leap which is out of character with the context of the surroundings, are associated with a rhythmic deviation (such as syncopation), or effect some other attention-getting feature (a change in articulation or dynamics, the presence of ornamentation, etc.). Narmour (1990) has investigated these kinds of deviations extensively in fleshing out his implication-realization model of melody. No attempt is made here to deal with this rich literature, nor with the variable weightings of particular features which are implied by different performances, nor to deal with the much-discussed question of phrase-boundary ambiguities. It is acknowledged, however, that some of the properties that may be captured in the proposed metric can be strengthened or weakened in particular performances and highlighted (or not) in refinements to this kind of approach. Further experimental investigation of all of these excluded areas is encouraged.

5.2.2. General Approach

Many authors have offered models of hierarchical weights in pursuit of a general model of melodic perception and cognition. Elements of this hypothetical approach can be found, *inter alia*, in Jones's concept of Joint Accent Structure (Ralson 1991, Jones 1993, Jones 1997), in the well-known Lerdahl/Jackendoff Generalized Theory of Tonal Music (GTTM 1983), and its extensions and refinements by Cambouropoulos for segmentation (1998) and by Temperley for music cognition (2001). Because actual implementation would require an immensely tedious set of procedures for multiple evaluations of every note in a set of melodies before search algorithms could be tested, some simpler means for representing some sense of this kind of searching are used for experimentation here.

The scheme proposed here is vastly oversimplified from a cognitive perspective, but it has the practical virtues that it can be implemented using existing data structures and algorithms and that it can therefore be tested on large databases of melodic material. The database we have used for testing is *Themefinder* (*www.themefinder.org*), on which see Sapp, Liu, and Selfridge-Field (2004).

The proposal as described here comes with several caveats:

1. **Metrical characteristics.** The criteria and methods for weighting are subject to "tuning" for specific repertories. Computer analysis of diverse repertories suggests wide variance in feature-frequency from one repertory to the next. For example, vocal music (particularly popular music) has a more restrained tessitura than instrumental music, so that octave differentiation may be more important for searching the latter than it is for the former. The attribute profiles of unmetered music (e.g., chant repertories, some Asian repertories of the present, French keyboard music of the seventeenth century) are obviously unsuited to this kind of evaluation. So too are improvised repertories which are characterized by syncopation (e.g., jazz) and those in which the use of melody is clandestine (e.g., chorale melodies in elaborate chorale preludes). As we know from the legacy of the mensural music of the fifteenth and sixteenth centuries, the arithmetic of triple and some compound meters is necessarily different from that of duple meter.
2. **Modal characteristics.** The behavior of melodies which come from works in minor keys is necessarily more complex than that for works in major keys, since ascending and descending versions of the scale are variable. This produces an expanded array of possible intervallic sizes and tonal qualities.

5.3. Feature Selection and Prioritization

Melodies have an uncalculated number of properties. We do not really know how many of them are essential to recognition. It seems likely that the number of relevant ones and, potentially, the relative weightings among them in the establishment of melodic identity may vary from one repertory to another. This possibility militates against one-size-fits-all solutions to melodic-search algorithms.

String-matching in melodic searches has thus far tended to mean iterative pitch-matching, irrespective of the labels used to describe them. While the recognizability of meter and accent (that is, beat organization) may play a strong role in song recognition and recall, temporal aspects of music are rarely considered in string-matching techniques. The most prevalent elaboration of one-dimensional string searching in musical applications has been edit distance,[2] but when applied to music it represents a categorically different set of problems from those considered here. Foreground/background distinctions, which bring the need of high relief to the representation of a linear process, are irrelevant to typing. Sophisticated varieties of edit distance have been introduced in several fields (primarily scientific) in recent years, but the results of edit-distance procedures in music retrieval are often unconvincing.

[2]The original goal of the Levenshtein edit-distance metric (1966) was automatic error-checking of a performance task (text input, in Russian) in the era of key-punches and paper tapes.

In art music, melodic "foreground" may be perceptible at different levels of temporal resolution, at variable lengths, and in multiple transformations. Melodic identity is considered to be singular even when successive presentations exhibit changes in order (inversion, transposition), key (modulation), and completeness (motivic development). Melodic manipulation has been one of the chief playgrounds of both the composers of European art music and the performers of the improvisational art music of the Middle East and the Indian subcontinent. By conferring a wide range of attributes—from internal coherence to human memorability to cultural significance—on music itself, melodic identity contributes significantly to the notorious elusiveness of "musical meaning."

Musical features which confound string searches come largely from the rhythmic domain. They include ties, rests, syncopation and, most particularly, accentuation, since it is not directly represented in musical notation or in representations of it. Experimental research in music cognition does not provide much guidance on the role that rhythmic and metrical features play in melodic recognition and recall. What are the expectancy thresholds for rhythmic deviation? Here no answers are forthcoming, despite a number of important results reported recently for the perception of rhythm generally and its role in individualizing musical performance.

5.4. Human Criteria for Melodic "Matches": A Case Study

The original purpose of the talk which underlies this study (ISMIR, Paris, 2002) was to adduce from human comparisons of melodies some general principles and then to contrast the results with those from computer searches for approximate matches. In the writing up, the characterization of human search criteria (to produce "intentional" matches) became unmanageable. It seems that some "monothematic" collections of melodies favor examples that satisfy individual criteria, while others are motivated by confirmation of social definitions of "belongingness." For this reason, the present examination considers a collection which I regard as "best of breed" in the first category, an expert system devised (without explicit criteria) by one individual.

Of several highly detailed longitudinal studies of tune preservation and dissemination in the early modern period, one by the noted Italian musicologist, organist, and harpsichordist Luigi Ferdinando Tagliavini (1994) affords a particularly fertile field for consideration. It provides 68 examples (of instantiations of one "tune"). Tagliavini has enjoyed a long career in professional performance, so his perceptual faculties might be considered to be somewhat superior to those of musically well-trained undergraduates. His sources come exclusively from printed sources of the sixteenth through eighteenth centuries. The prints are from various parts of Europe.

It is fundamental to the use of highly subjective expert systems to understand the expert's goal. Tagliavini's purpose is to show melodic persistence across centuries, language contexts, and titles. This has been a frequent goal in the study of mainly oral traditions (for example, of the preservation and dissemination of religious chant and folk songs). It has also received attention in the studies of the development of polyphonic music of the fifteenth and sixteenth centuries (often again with an emphasis on embedded chants). Tagliavini's focus heads off in a different direction, for it emphasizes printed music in collections assembled for diverse purposes and a range of instrumentations. His examples show many variations of meter, mode, ornamentation, and, less frequently, accentuation and harmonization. It is transcribed for many different instruments, and a few examples are transcribed from recordings. The theme he tracks is one which he identifies as the *ballo di Mantova* ("the dance from Mantua"), a generic title which in sixteenth- and seventeenth-century instances lacks lyrics but occurs under many titles. Like printed music itself, the audience for the *ballo* would have been Italian nobles. Over the next two centuries the *ballo* cropped up in France, Belgium, the Netherlands and elsewhere. Apart from record transcriptions, Tagliavini does not include nineteenth- or twentieth-century examples, but the theme of Smetana's "Ma Vlast" ("My Fatherland") and of Israel's current national anthem "Hatikvah" ("The Hope," adopted in 1948) would both qualify. In a way, this diffusion only tells us an obvious truth: music traveled in the heads of musicians as well as on paper.

Tagliavini's cache of examples raises two central questions about melodic identity. First, where are the outer limits of melodic recognition? In such a big sea of examples, which one should be considered the basic instantiation of the melody (i.e., the target) in a computer model of the selection process? A music historian would normally proceed as Tagliavini has and would select the earliest printed example as the target. Since the aim here is to compare the results with those produced in a computer search, a target most amenable to computer searching was selected instead. It is a texted instantiation called "Fuggi da questo cielo" and was printed in Florence in *c.* 1625. Its advantage in a computer model is simply that the melody is set syllabically, so that nothing considered at the time to be fundamental should be missing and, conversely (on account of the date and genre), nothing extraneous should be present. "Fuggi" and eleven of Tagliavini's variants are shown in Figures 5.2 (a–k).

Target: "Fuggi, fuggi, fuggi da questo cielo"—Florentine monody (*c.* 1625) attributed to Gherardo Pedrali as shown:

5.2a. Instrumental transcription—Gasparo Zanetti (1645).

5.2b and 5.2c. Rhythmic variants on transcription—(b) keyboard transcription attributed to Gio. Battista Ferrini (1661) and (c) keyboard transcription attributed to Gaetano Greco (*c.* 1715).

5.2d. Ornamental variant—transcribed from a twentieth-century violin performance (with guitar accompaniment) by Melchiade Benni.

5.2e. Harmonic variant—"Cecilia," from a Dutch anthology of 1700.

5.2f and 5.2g. Metric variants—"Cecilia" in (f) a Belgian variant transcribed *c.* 1850 by Jan Frans Willems and (g) as given in the Dutch collection *Evangelische leeuwerck* (1682).

5.2h. Rhythmic replacement of melodic tones—Nicolas Saboly (*c.* 1670).

5.2i. Rhythmic simplification (with retexting).

5.2j. Reharmonization—arrangement for Spanish guitar by G. B. Granata, 1646 (reharmonization).

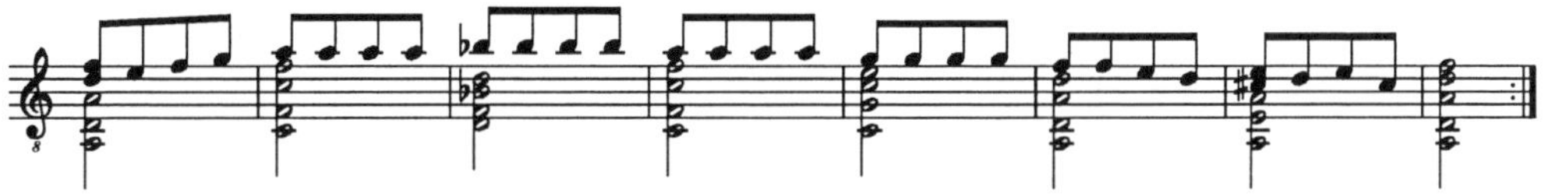

5.2k. Reharmonization with chordal arpeggiation (self-accompaniment, embedded notes, etc.)—anonymous transcription for lute or guitar, early 18th century.

Figures 5.2a–k. The target (the ballo di Mantova) and eleven match candidates provided in a musicological study by Luigi Ferdinando Tagliavini.

Tagliavini's selection is not so much representative of musicological studies of tune families (Selfridge-Field 2005) as it is of an ear steeped in classical music, particularly the keyboard repertory of the sixteenth through the eighteenth century. This is a repertory in which arrangements and transcriptions, some of significant complexity, are prevalent.

5.5. Computer-Produced Match Candidates

Before applying our provisional cognitive-distance metric to Examples 5.2a–k, we ran the first five notes of the *ballo* through *Themefinder* to see what match candidates would be produced by a linear search. Linear searches in *Themefinder* operate on pitch only at five levels on a continuum from generality (gross contour) to specificity (note and inflection names). The intermediate levels of search are refined contour (steps, skips, direction), scale-degree profile, and intervallic profile.

Wildcard searches are permitted. All levels can be filtered by meter and mode. Incipits in the *Themefinder* database come from three fundamentally different repertories: classical instrumental music, monophonic folk songs, and Renaissance polyphony. They are therefore somewhat different in character from many of the repertories represented in Tagliavini's collection (in it keyboard, lute, and string ensemble music make up a substantial portion). The component databases of *Themefinder* are searchable separately or together. The subset of data used included *c.* 12,000 classical incipits and *c.* 8,600 folk songs.

In a first-six-pitches search of *Themefinder*'s classical section at the (intermediate) scale-degree level, 22 matches were returned when no filters were applied, 6 when the search was limited to works in a minor mode, 4 when the search was limited to 4/4 meter, and none when both filters were in place. In other words, there was no candidate that might be termed "excellent" in its likelihood of matching the target. The pitches of repeated notes were ignored. (Because of the ambiguity that the treatment of repeated notes introduces into melodic profiles [e.g., should we substitute the sixth discrete pitch for the sixth event, which employs the same pitch as the fifth event?], we opted to exclude the sixth event in the melody.) A first-five-note search resulted in much higher rates of identification: 116 matches with no filters, 43 matches in the minor mode, 26 in 4/4, and 8 with both filters in effect. The most promising candidates from each search are shown in Figures 5.3a–b (5-note), and 5.3c–d (6-note).

In searches of the folk-music database, the statistics on machine matches for the 6-note search were 20 matches with no filters, 1 with a mode filter, 4 with a meter filter, and none with both filters. The results for a 5-note target were 45 without filters, 6 with mode filter, 12 with meter filter, and none with both.

Other statistical studies have demonstrated that the folk songs in *Themefinder* have a much greater concentration in regular $n/4$ and $n/8$ meters than do the classical incipits, where $n/2$ and $n/16$ meters are also encountered and where n's that are prime numbers proliferate in nineteenth- and early twentieth-century items. In both the classical and the folk-song portions of the database, examples in major mode are far more numerous than those in minor modes. This confers obvious biases when filters are used.

5.3a. Bach: Concerto for Two Violins and Orchestra, first movement.

5.3b. Grieg: Norwegian Dance, Op. 34, No. 4.

5.3c. Dutch folk song: "Die Schlangenkoechin Isabelle, mijn dochterken."

5.3d. von Suppé: from the overture to *Die schöne Galathea.*

Figures 5.3a–d. Accidental matches in Themefinder for the first six distinct pitches of the ballo di Mantova (repeated pitches ignored).

The positive effect of greater string length comes as no surprise, since studies by both computer methodologists (Selfridge-Field 1991, 1993; Uitdenbogerd 2003) and psychologists (Deliège, 2001) show that a more articulate target (suggested by greater length) produces more appropriate results than a less articulate one.

What is instructive in this group of match candidates is that the musical features which are most conspicuous in the examples which have been automatically culled are distinctly different from those collected by analogue means in Figure 5.2a–k. Excluding 5.3c, which resembles 5.2g in its metrical orientation (both come from Dutch folk songs), the other candidates all seem much more remote, in cognitive terms, from the target for a single reason: the relative accentual weights of the pitches that ostensibly suggest a match are privileged in the human collection and ignored in the machine collection. This difference is reinforced by the divergent harmonic implications of each set.

The cognitive-distance metric that we propose is tuned especially to this set of examples. That is, it attempts to model the privileges tacitly granted in Figures 5.2a–k over those of Figure 5.3a–d. This is hardly a scientific approach, but the opportunity to compare results for a fully automatic process and a fully human one where both provide ground for extensive investigation is actually quite rare.

5.6. Parameters and Scoring

The scoring system presented here is based on two goals—one perceptual, one practical. Whatever happens in a melody only attracts attention if it is conspicuous. Any downbeat is more likely to be noticed than any upbeat, although in future work it could be instructive to explore possible trade-offs between accent and other attention-attracters, such as intervallic leaps, changes of direction, or rhythmic deviations from an established pattern.

For easy computation of results, the provisional scoring system is a ten-point scheme. The first part assesses pitch in relation to metrical and accentual information. Because our patience with false matches has been sorely tried by the large caches of poor candidates that are retrieved from large datasets, we set fairly strenuous thresholds.

1. Basic Pitch-Accent Structure			Range = 0-4
A. If meter matches target			Max = 1.00
	and	If subunit (e.g., quarter note) is the same	Score = 1.00
	or	If subunit is different (e.g., 4/8 vs. 2/4)	Score = 0.50
Else			Score = 0.00
B. Percentage of matched pitches on primary beats*			Max = 2.00
If matching number of scale degrees = 100%			Score = 2.00
	or	If matching number of scale degrees => 90%	Score = 1.33
	or	If matched number of notes/unit => 80%	Score = 0.67
Else			Score = 0.00
C. Percentage of matched pitches on secondary beats			Max = 1.00
If matching number of scale degrees = 100%			Score = 1.00
	or	If matching number of scale degrees => 90%	Score = 0.67
	or	If matched number of notes/unit => 80%	Score = 0.33
Else			Score = 0.00

Table 5.2. Pitch-accent scoring.

The second part of the metric assesses harmonic conformance. This assessment will appear to be quite arbitrary, given that the database contains only monophonic material. The auditory context that a user brings to melodic incipits will, of course, make potential matches seem more or less appropriate. Yet it is clear from a close look at the *ballo di Mantova* candidates that some pairings with the target stand a low probability, at face value, of perceptual recognition because they are implicitly so distant harmonically.

Example 5.2k is a "bonus" example intended to show how a melody can be conceptually close to a model while appearing to be quite distant in a literal item-per-item search. It represents the ultimate challenge for a cognitive-distance metric, since the ideal metric would rank such a candidate highly. This is a self-accompanied melody, so the harmonic fabric is more nearly literal than implied. Because the harmonic "fill" falls off the beat, however, it creates a very different silhouette from source (2j).

Examples 5.2j and 5.2k raise a separate issue, too. It might be typified as a "real-life" problem which is not normally discussed in musical literature. The issue is that, as shown by Tagliavini, these examples (which are variants of one another) have an implied harmonization (the harmonization that the outline of the melody suggests) which is flawed (in comparison with familiar renditions). This kind of flaw is very commonly found in popular guitar books and lead sheets that rely on a very limited menu of chords in order to give beginners access to the repertory in some fashion. Practitioners will want to consider how best to accommodate these kinds of effects. For the sake of this theoretical discussion, we reharmonized. That is, we corrected the harmonization of four of the eight accented events present so that instead of the sequence i-III-VI-III-vii-i-V-I, which suggests a modulation to the major mode, the sequence was changed to i-i-iv-i-iv-i-V-i, which retains the minor mode except for the inevitably sharped third in the dominant at the cadence. (The harmonizations as given in 5.2j and 5.2k are not those in common use today, with the exception that Smetana's "Moldau" theme is harmonically similar, while being melodically slightly different.)

In the proposed metric, both examples would score well if the harmony is "corrected" (that is if the searcher were actually imaging in the i-i-iv-i-iv-i-V-i) but poorly if it were left unaltered. Example 5.2k has the potential for a much higher score than 5.2j because of its greater level of activity at the quarter-note level; its melodic deviations from the target fall on unaccented beats. The thresholds are slightly more liberal in harmonic-assessment sections because domino effects introduce a greater degree of interpretive uncertainty. One false step will push all subsequent events into a lower-scoring category, although in human cognition the damage to recognition may be much less dramatic. Obviously greater refinement is needed to deal with this possibility.

II. Basic Harmonic-Accent Structure		Range = 0-6
A. Mode of work (major, minor, other)		Max = 1.00
If modes match		Score = 1.00
Else		Score = 0.00
B. Percentage of matched chords on downbeat**		Max = 2.50
If unambiguous matches on primary beats => 90%		Score = 2.50
or	If unambiguous matches on primary beats => 80%	Score = 2.00
or	If unambiguous matches on primary beat => 70%	Score = 1.50
Else		Score = 0.00
C. Percentage of matched chords on secondary beats**		Max = 2.00
If unambiguous matches => 90%		Score = 2.00
or	If unambiguous matches => 80%	Score = 1.50
or	If unambiguous matches => 70%	Score = 1.00
Else		Score = 0.00
D. Percentage of matched chords on tertiary beats		Max = 0.50
If unambiguous matches => 90%		Score = 0.50
Else		Score = 0.0

Table 5.3. Harmonic accent scoring.

The method for computing the score of beat-sensitive items (5.1b, c; 5.2b, c, d) addresses each individual beat indicated in the numeral of the time signature as shown in Table 5.4.

Meter	**Primary**	**Secondary**	**Tertiary**
2 / 4	1	2	
3 / 4	1	2, 3	
4 / 4	1	3	2, 4
6 / 8	1	4	2, 3, 5, 6
12 / 8	1	7	4, 10

Table 5.4. Beat values for various meters.

As currently developed it is focused only on tonal works in regular meters. It is not suitable for music with persistent syncopation, such as much of the jazz repertory, without adaptation.

The rather stringent thresholds for any score to be achieved may be surprising to some, but in practical situations involving large quantities of musical data, it is essential to have fairly rigorous cutoffs. The difficult question is precisely how to retain what may be psychologically valid even when it may be quite remote on a note-per-note basis. For use with very large datasets such as the *Themefinder* database, we would set the thresholds considerably higher than they are here. At the same time it is acknowledged that ideas of what does or does not match an intended target may vary from user to user. We believe that the final selection of a match should therefore be determined by the user.

5.7. Tabulation and Comparison

In a first pass, the melodic/accentual and harmonic/accentual scores were to be added. Points were predicated on the notion of keeping the numbers simple. The scores obtained in this way are shown in Table 5.5.

Table 5.5. Scores for examples in Figure 5.2a–k (human matches), using addition as a basis for ranking.

Example	Pitch-Accent score		Harmony-Accent score		Total score (additive)	
	Raw	Ranked	Raw	Ranked	Raw	Ranked
2a	3.67	2	5.5	3	9.17	2
2b	3.67	2	5.0	4	8.67	3
2c	2.67	6	6.0	1	8.67	3
2d	1.17	9	4.5	5	6.67	8
2e	2.67	6	4.0	9	6.67	8
2f	2.33	8	4.5	5	6.83	7
2g	1.00	10	2.0	11	3.00	11
2h	3.50	4	4.5	5	8.00	6
2i	4.00	1	4.5	5	8.50	5
2j	1.00	10	4.0	9	5.00	10
2k	3.33	5	6.0	1	9.33	1

These results were then compared with scores for the machine matches from *Themefinder* (Table 5.6). (This comparison is flawed by the fact that there were so many fewer candidates.) The computed results are notably poorer, so much so that ranks were not assessed in relation to those of Table 5.5.

Example	Pitch-Accent score	Harmony-Accent score	Total score (additive)
3a	0.50	1.00	1.50
3b	1.33	1.00	2.33
3c	1.50	3.00	4.50
3d	0.83	1.00	1.83

Table 5.6. Scores for incipits shown in Figures 5.3a–d ("accidental" matches).

Since the "accidental" matches were not originally ranked, a comparison of scores by both approaches to it only serves to point out that their multiplicative scores are very low indeed. While that dramatizes their distance from the "intentional" matches, the additive scores make the categorical separation equally noticeable. Thus this approach could be of value in cases in which little is known about the underlying data or in which the quantity of potential matches is likely to be large.

5.8. Discussion

The most common way in which perceptually different melodies can appear (in sorted symbolic code) to be the same is when pitch alone is used as the yardstick, unless the level of pitch-definition is relatively precise (Sapp et al. 2004).

In relation to the literature on melodic cognition, the numerous studies of Mari Riess Jones (e.g., 1991, 1997) verify the important role of accentual information in human melodic assessment. Jones's concept of JAC is difficult to implement automatically because of its reliance on specific pitch-content in situations where, from our point of view, fuzzy searching may be required in the human-computer interface. Yet the idea of the coupling of accentual information with pitch and harmony separately (but without assessing "rhythm" or "accent" directly) is offered as a practical adaptation of this approach. Halperin's finding on the large degree of human tolerance for modal variability when coupled with the preservation of other musical features (1998) accounts for the low penalty in our metric for modal digression. The unpredictable relationship between detail and generalization in melodic comparison is highlighted in Cuddy (1993), wherein the variable effect of a single note on the recognizability of melody is confronted. We return to this study to underscore the author's attribution of this unpredictability to that fact that no parameters have been established for any aspects of melody other than accent.

The cognitive-distance measure proposed here does not go far beyond accent and it does not come with any claim for universal suitability. Its immediate purpose is to initiate more focused discussion of what those other attributes may be and how they should be tuned under different circumstances. Until these are better defined, search algorithms cannot dramatically improve what might be termed "cognitive satisfaction" levels. We do not know, for example, what the prevalent human ranking order might be for rhythmic substitutions. To what extent might the preferred rankings be accent-dependent? Are these rankings coincident with, stronger than, or weaker than other known attention-getters (melodic leaps, changes in melodic direction, accentual displacement, etc.)? Since the actual cognitive validity and relative cognitive weights of some of the factors included are still undetermined, we offer this material primarily as a basis for further discussion and experimental verification or refutation.

Acknowledgments

The *Themefinder* project was initiated by David Huron in 1996 for the purpose of capturing user-query information. The original user interface was developed by Andreas Kornstädt. Further development and management have been overseen by Craig Stuart Sapp for most of the intervening years. Most of the development work has been supported by the Center for Computer Assisted Research in the Humanities at Stanford University.

References

Cambouropoulos, Emilios (1998). "Towards a General Computational Theory of Musical Structure." Ph. D. thesis, University of Edinburgh.

Campouropoulos (2001). "Melodic Cue Abstraction, Similarity, and Category Formation: A Formal Model," *Music Perception* 18/3 (2001): 347–370.

Cuddy, Lola (1993). "Melody Comprehension and Tonal Structure" in *Psychology and Music: The Understanding of Melody and Rhythm*, ed. Thomas Tighe and W. Jay Dowling (Hillsdale, NJ: Lawrence Earlbaum Associates, Inc., 1993), pp. 19—38.

Dowling, W. Jay (1994).

Deliège, Irène (1997). "Cue Abstraction in the Representation of Musical Form" in *Perception and Cognition of Music*, ed. Irène Deliège and John Sloboda (Hove, UK: Psychology Press), 387–412.

Halperin, David (1990). "A Segmentation Algorithm and its Application to Medieval Monophonic Music," *Quantitative Linguistics*," 43, 107–119.

Holleran, Susan, Mari Riess Jones, and David Butler (1995). "Perceiving Implied Harmony: The Influence of Melodic and Harmonic Context," *Journal of Experimental Psychology: Learning, Memory, and Cognition* 21/3 (1995), 737–753.

Jones, Mari Riess (1993). "Dynamics of Musical Patterns: How Do Melody and Rhythm Fit Together?" in Thomas J. Tighe and W. Jay Dowling (eds.), *Psychology and Music: The Understanding of Melody and Rhythm* (Hillsdale, NJ: Earlham Affiliates, 1993), 67–92.

Jones, Mari Riess, and Peter Q. Pfordresher (1997). "Tracking Musical Patterns Using Joint Accent Structure," *Canadian Journal of Experimental Psychology* 51/4 (1997), 271–291.

Krumhansl, Carol L. (1990). *Cognitive Foundations of Musical Pitch.* New York: Oxford University Press.

Lerdahl, Fred, and Ray Jackendoff (1983). *A Generative Theory of Tonal Music.* Cambridge: The MIT Press.

Levenshtein, V. I. (1966). "Binary Codes Capable of Correcting Deletions, Insertions, and Reversals," *Soviet Physics Doklady*, 10/8, 707–710.

Muellensiefen, Daniel, and Klaus Frieler (2003-04). "Cognitive Adequacy in the Measurement of Melodic Similarity: Algorithmic vs. Human Judgments," *Music Query: Methods, Models, and User Studies (Computing in Musicology 13)*, 145–176.

Narmour, Eugene (1990). *The Analysis and Cognition of Basic Melodic Structures: The Implication-Realization Model.* Chicago: University of Chicago Press.

Ralson, Jacqueline T., and Mari Riess Jones (1991). "Some Influences of Accent Structure on Melody Recognition," *Memory and Cognition* 19/1, 8–20.

Sapp, Craig Stuart (2004). "Computational Harmonic Analysis of Western Tonal Music." Ph. D. thesis, Stanford University.

Sapp, Craig Stuart, Yi-Wen Liu, and Eleanor Selfridge-Field (2004). "Search-Effectiveness Measures for Symbolic Music Queries in Very Large Databases," *Proceedings of the Fifth International Symposium on Music Information Retrieval (ISMIR)*, Barcelona.

Singer, Jane (2003). "A Model of Melodic Representation: Towards an Implementation of Music Information Retrieval." Ph. D. thesis, The Hebrew University of Jerusalem.

Selfridge-Field, Eleanor (1991). "Issues of Representation in Melodic Comparison," *Computers in Music Research*, II (Queen's University, Belfast, 1991).

Selfridge-Field, Eleanor (1993). "Music Analysis by Computer: Approaches and Issues" in *Music Processing* (*Computer Music and Digital Audio Series*, 9; gen. ed. John Strawn), ed. Goffredo Haus. Madison, WI: A-R Editions, Inc., and Oxford: Clarendon Press, 1993, pp. 3–24.

Tagliavini, Luigi Ferdinando (1994). " 'Il ballo di Mantova', ovvero, 'Fuggi, fuggi da questo cielo', ovvero, 'Cecilia', ovvero..." in *Max Lutolf zum 60. Geburtstag: Festschrift* (Basel: Wiese), 135–175.

Temperley, David (2001). *The Cognition of Basic Musical Structures.* Cambridge, MA: The MIT Press.

Uitdenbogerd, Alexandra, and Justin Zobel (1999). "Matching Algorithms for Large Music Databases: A Technical Report," Melbourne: Dept. of Computer Science, RMIT University.

6 Transportation Distances and Their Application in Music-Notation Retrieval

Frans Wiering, Rainer Typke, Remco C. Veltkamp

Institute of Information and Computing Sciences
Utrecht University
P.O. Box 80.089
NL-3508 TB Utrecht
Netherlands
{*frans.wiering,rainer.typke,remco.veltkamp*}*@cs.uu.nl*

Abstract

This article introduces the representation of music notation as a weighted dot pattern and defines two distance measures—the Earth-Mover's Distance and the Proportional Transportation Distance. Their performance is compared in the ranking of melodic-match candidates.

Queries with both distance measures are evaluated and their applicability in music research is discussed. The research is related to the Orpheus project (*http://www.cs.uu.nl/centers/give/multimedia/music/*), which aims to develop efficient methods for content-based retrieval from large collections of encoded music notation producing meaningful results.

Music Query: Methods, Models, and User Studies (Computing in Musicology 13). Published by CCARH and the MIT Press, 2004.

6.1 Introduction

Suppose we are studying Handel's oratorio *Israel in Egypt* and would like to know more about sources the composer used to create this work. Take, for instance, the chorus "Egypt was glad when they departed". Just entering these words in Google gives the source of the text: Psalm 105, verse 38 (Hebrew/Protestant numbering; retrieved March 2, 2004, from *http://www.sacred-texts.com/bib/jps/psa105.htm*). However, were we to try to search the Internet for the beginning of the music (Example 6.1a), we probably would not be so lucky. If the data are there at all, then an obvious tool for searching them is lacking. To identify the musical source of Handel's chorus, a canzona by Kerll (Example 6.1b), we would depend on paper tools such as catalogs, thematic indices, and scores.

a

b

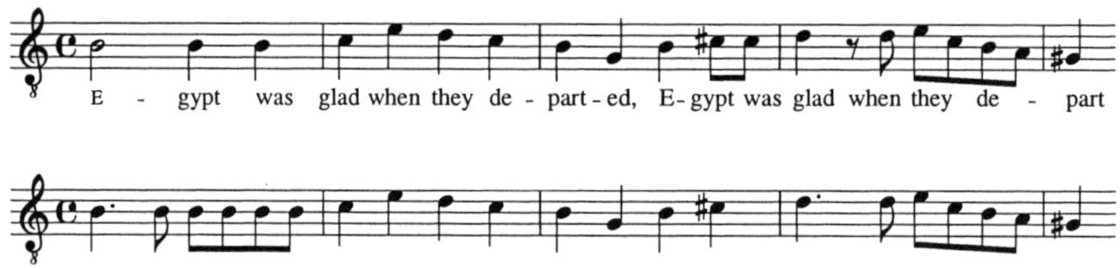

Example 6.1. (a) G. F. Handel, Israel in Egypt, HWV 54; (b) J. K. Kerll, Canzona 4 from Modulatio Organica super Magnificat (1686).

Human beings perceive the two melodies in Example 6.1 as very similar. There are some slight rhythmic differences in order to fit the text to the notes, but the melodic contour and the intervals are the same. We would expect a useful search engine to deal with musical similarity as humans do.

Despite several decades of research into computer analysis of music and music retrieval, the most frequently used way of searching notation is pattern matching in text representations. Generally, it is possible to search one dimension only: pitch (intervals being another way of looking at the same dimension). This makes it hard to take the relative importance of a note into account, which depends on such factors as duration and metrical position. As a consequence, a musical query may result in false negatives, when relevant items are missed, or false positives, when irrelevant items are retrieved. An example of the former would be not finding Example 6.1b when searching for Example 6.1a; this would happen when the query required the composition to begin with precisely three repeated notes. If, however, one would restrict the number of notes in the query to six (as in Example 6.2a) and allow an arbitrary number of repetitions of the first note, false positives such as Example 6.2b may result (retrieved September 26, 2003, from *http://www.themefinder.org*).

Example 6.2. (a) Query without pitch durations; (b) L. van Beethoven, Symphony No. 6, first movement.

The need for multi-dimensional music searching is widely acknowledged, yet only a few effective implementations exist. We have selected two that most resemble our approach for comparison, PROMS (Clausen et al. 2000) and C-Brahms (*http://www.cs.helsinki.fi/group/cbrahms;* Ukkonen et al. 2003).

In PROMS, the score is represented as a set of notes with two characteristics: MIDI pitch and onset time (but no duration). Queries, which may be polyphonic, are similarly encoded. PROMS tolerates missing notes by default, so long as the time structure is kept intact. Therefore, our two melodies in Example 6.1 would be matched, but it would be impossible to match Example 6.2a with these. One can construct a fuzzy query by specifying pitch alternatives for one or more notes. Such a fuzzy query is interpreted as a set of exact queries. There are indexes that allow fast queries over the test collection of *c.* 12,000 classical compositions. However, there is no way of finding rhythmical transformations of the query. Note also that this method is non-continuous: a small extra deviation from the pattern (e.g. a note that is just a semitone higher) may lead to an entirely different judgment (no similarity rather than similarity).

Ukkonen et al. (2003) represent notes as line segments in a pitch-time space. Example queries are all monophonic, but polyphonic queries appear to be possible too. Three algorithms are described that respectively find exact matches (P1), the largest common subset of onset times between the score and the query (P2), and the longest common shared time between the score and the query (P3). Algorithm P2 can be used to find partial matches with less than a given number of errors. The two melodies in 6.1 have 4 mismatches. One could also match Example 6.1 to Example 6.2b (assuming that 2b is rewritten with note values doubled), with 5 matching notes and 9 mismatches. Algorithm P3 allows another form of incomplete matching, where onset and offset times need not be precisely coordinated. The algorithms were tested in the C-Brahms project on a database of 10 times 279 musical documents. These methods too are non-continuous. In P2, one duration change, however small, will disrupt the match, as will the change of one melodic interval. P3 is somewhat more tolerant of duration change, but has the same problem with interval changes as P2.

Our method shares with the ones just described the "geometric" representation of music notation in a two-dimensional [pitch-time] space: we represent notes as dots with different weights that reflect their musical importance. Other than in PROMS, we do not compare dot patterns by deciding whether they match or not; we apply similarity measures to pairs of dot patterns that calculate their distance on a continuous scale. The hypothesis is that the smaller such a distance is, the more likely the two patterns resemble each other musically. Music retrieval would thus be improved by enabling ranking of the retrieval output. The C-Brahms algorithms already allow ranking, but this ranking is undercut by the algorithms' sensitivity to certain small deformations that are very common in musical practice. Our method is better able to handle these problems.

The similarity measures we discuss in this article are the Earth-Mover's Distance and the Proportional Transportation Distance. To evaluate these, we employed the RISM A/II collection (2002). This database contains bibliographic data about musical manuscripts dating (mainly) from the period 1600-1850. For most compositions, the beginning of one of the voices (an *incipit*) is given (or one for each movement), so that the work is characterized not only by its metadata but also by its initial musical content. Typically, incipits are *c.* 25 notes long, with considerable variation (a minimum of twelve pitches is required, though in practice some incipits are shorter). The data are used in several common musicological tasks, such as attributing a work to a composer, identifying its (physical) sources, or tracing musical relationships between different compositions. There were about 470,000 incipits in the version of the RISM A/II collection we employed.

Size was an important reason for selecting this collection. It is also maintained by a professional organization and designed to be used for a variety of representative scholarly purposes, so that both quality and usefulness are guaranteed. A search engine for musical incipits is missing in RISM A/II, although some user interfaces to the collection provide searches of the *Plaine & Easie Code* by which the incipits are represented [see Appendix I]. Finally, the similarity measures discussed here work best when comparing units of roughly the same size. Using the same measures for querying scores of complete works necessitates preprocessing, a step we wished to avoid in the early phases of our research.

6.2 Musical Notation as a Weighted-Dot Pattern

Rendition of a piece of music notation as a weighted-dot pattern works as follows. Each note onset is represented as a dot in a two-dimensional space. The axes are time and pitch; and the weight of the dot is an estimation of the note's importance to the melodic shape of the incipit. So far, we have assumed that a note's importance is proportional to its duration, but ultimately weights should be assigned on the basis of what is known from music perception. Rests are not encoded.

Pitch is encoded using Walter Hewlett's base-40 notation (1992). Like MIDI, this is a number-based notation, but with two additional advantages: enharmonic differences are respected, and enharmonically correct intervals can be calculated by subtracting pitch values. Durations and time coordinates are expressed by means of fractions of quarter notes (for the precise calculation see Typke et al. 2003).

Because of the base-40 pitch representation, the pitch range of an incipit is often much larger than its duration range. An extreme case is Example 6.2, with a pitch range of 46 and a duration range of only 5.5. To compensate for this, we multiplied the time coordinates by 3 for all examples in this article. For Handel's incipit, the values are given in Example 6.3.

Example 6.3. Handel's incipit as a weighted-point set. The parameters given inside parentheses are time, pitch, and weight.

6.3 Incipit Comparison using the Earth-Mover's Distance (EMD)

The Euclidian distance between the weighted dots acts as the "ground distance" for the calculation of transportation distances. The Earth-Mover's Distance (described in Cohen 1999) calculates the minimum effort needed to transform one dot-pattern into another. One can imagine this to happen as follows. One pattern (Kerll's incipit in Ex. 6.4) is represented as heaps of earth, the sizes of which correspond to the weights of the dots; the other pattern (Handel's incipit in Ex. 6.4) as holes with a certain capacity, likewise corresponding to the dots' weights. The task is to fill the holes with as little effort (that is, ground distance times weight) as possible. For our example, many heaps and holes have the same coordinates and size, so their contribution to the total effort is zero.

The heap of Handel's first note, however, is too big for Kerll's first note, and the remaining earth is moved to the second note. The effort is 4.5 x 0.5 = 2.25. Likewise, Handel's second and third notes are split up, each resulting in an effort of 1.5 x 0.5 = 0.75. On the other hand, the two C-sharps in Handel's measure 3 merge into one note in Kerll, also resulting in an effort of 0.75. Some capacity remains for the first note in Handel's measure 4, since all earth has been used: this has no effect on the EMD.

The total effort equals 4.5. The effort is normalized by dividing it by the total weight of the lighter pattern. The EMD is thus 4.5/16.5 = 0.2727. The mapping of weights is shown in Example 6.4. Note that for clarity the melodies are shifted apart; in reality, most of the notes are actually at the same coordinates.

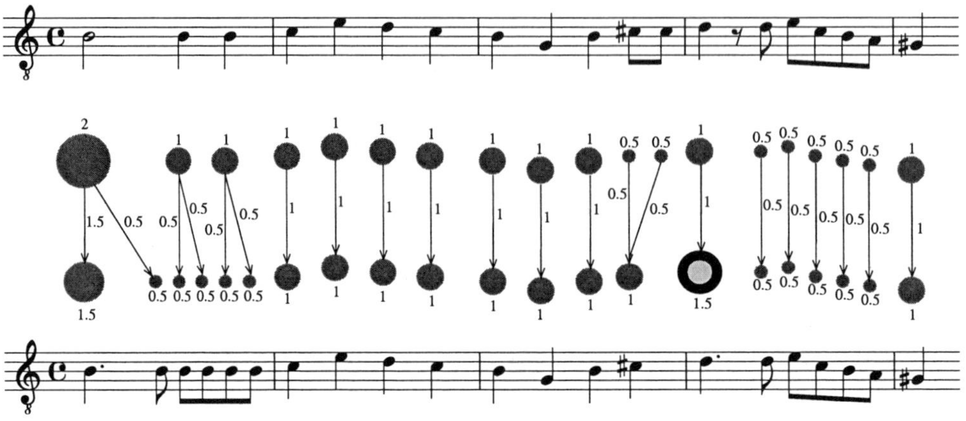

Example 6.4. EMD weight flow between Handel's and Kerll's incipits. The rim of Item 15 (lower row) corresponds to the matched part of the weight.

One interesting property of the EMD is that it allows partial matching. Compare for instance the first two measures of Handel's incipit and the complete incipit. The EMD is zero, as all "earth" in the former fits in the "holes" of the latter. That holes remain (or earth) is not an issue. The downside of this property is that the EMD is less suitable for constructing an index. (See Typke et al. 2003.)

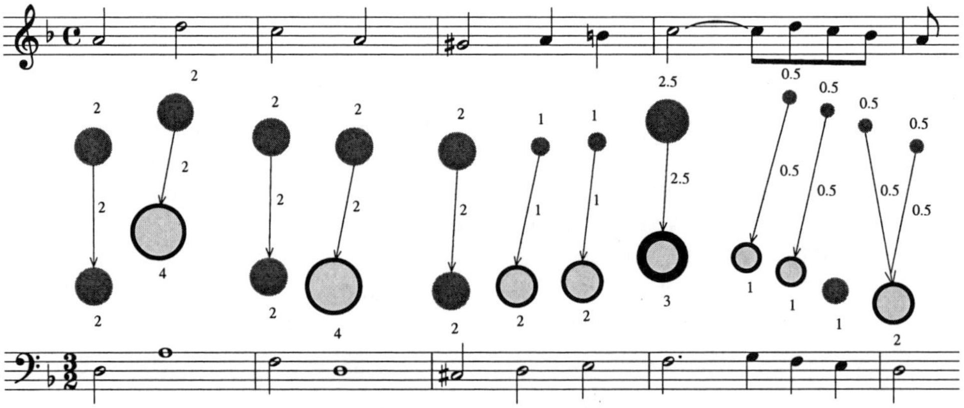

Example 6.5. J. S. Bach, Kunst der Fuge, BWV 1080: EMD weight flow between Contrapunctus 1, beginning of soprano (above) and Contrapunctus 12, beginning of bass (below). The EMD is 1.51256. In the lower row of circles, partial matching is indicated by a lighter shade of grey.

Example 6.4 is deliberately kept simple. Weight is only moved in the time dimension. It can also be moved in the pitch dimension, as in Example 6.5. But before computing the EMD, the two incipits need to be aligned. Durations are aligned by stretching the shorter incipit so that the beginnings of their last notes coincide (unless we are looking for a partial match). For pitch alignment we align the weighted average pitch. This is an approximation that may be improved in various ways. The diagram between the two incipits in Example 6.5 shows the optimum weight shifts needed to match them.

6.4 Incipit Comparison using the Proportional Transportation Distance (PTD)

To remedy the EMD's problem with indexing, Giannopoulos and Veltkamp (2002) developed another distance measure, the Proportional Transportation Distance. For the PTD, the total weight of both patterns is normalized to one; subsequently the EMD is applied. In terms of the earth metaphor, this means that all earth is always distributed over the holes proportionally to their capacity. Because of its different mathematical properties, the PTD can be used to construct an index, so that searching is much more efficient than when using the EMD (see Typke et al. 2003 for a discussion of the complexity of the algorithm). The price one pays is that partial matching is not possible with the PTD.

6.5 Applications in Music Research

Composer attribution is one of the three musicological tasks we mentioned in our introduction. The PTD was used in a "de-anonymifying" script that compared *c.* 80,000 anonymous incipits from the RISM (*Répértoire Internationale des Sources Musicales*) A/II database to all other incipits. In 13% of the cases, the system reported candidate attributions. A random sample of a hundred of these were checked manually. Fifty-five cases were matches with other anonymous works. Nineteen works could be attributed to a named composer because the compared incipits are identical. In eleven cases we could attribute the work although the incipits are not identical. Our method thus leads to the identification of about 3.9% (30% of 13%) of the anonymous pieces (see also Typke et al. 2003). Schlichte (1990) managed to identify only 2.08%.

Example 6.6 shows the process of assigning authorship in practice, with two candidate attributions for the anonymous incipit. Note that the incipits are similar, but not identical: there are differences in both rhythm and intervals. The individual character of the melody makes it very likely that we are dealing with closely related pieces, while the metadata enable us to establish that the anonymous work is probably a piano arrangement of Umlauff's aria.

Example 6.6. (a) Anonymous keyboard piece; (b) I. Umlauff/ A.F.J. Eberl/ W.A. Mozart, Ariette variée; (c) I. Umlauff, Das Irrlicht, aria "Zu Steffen sprach im Traume."

Whether the piece is identical to the *Ariette variée* ascribed to various composers cannot be established from the available data; for this the complete works need to be compared. The situation is thus no different from working with thematic indices, except that the speed and arguably the reliability are much greater. Also, the idea of being able to link directly to a score is tempting though as yet unrealized.

We tested the second task, the identification of physical sources, by means of the melody of "Roslin Castle," which was previously investigated by Howard (1998). Example 6.7 shows our results with both the EMD and the PTD. Howard, using an earlier version of the database, was able to retrieve 6 out of 13 known occurrences in his test set (46%). With the EMD, we were able to group together 11 out of 15 known correctly encoded occurrences (73%). The 16th occurrence is incorrectly encoded; as a consequence the EMD is greatly increased and the ranking is correspondingly low.

To retrieve the 15 correct occurrences with the PTD, we had to query three times, and the largest of these groups has only 6 incipits (for full results see Typke et al. 2003). The reason for this is that the PTD does not allow partial matching, whereas incipits of "Roslin Castle" in the database differ in length. Queries therefore need to have different lengths too, that is, 13, 16 and 21 notes. For the RISM database to be searched more efficiently by means of the present method, the musical data would need to be encoded according to more strict rules than is done at present. On the other hand, PTD-based searching could be improved by making it less dependent on length. One way to do so would be to add a weight component that is proportional to the inverse note number, thereby making notes progressively less important. Another would be to devise a way of dividing the incipits into chunks that can be better compared, and then to integrate the results.

The EMD Example 6.7 shows a number of false positives that are not at all musically similar to "Roslin Castle." This is caused by the partial-matching property: note that all false positives are relatively short. Here, too, a chunking strategy that produces chunks of similar size may be the solution. Rests within an incipit may cause trouble as well. A possible remedy is to replace note duration with distance-to-the-next-note in the weighting.

Example 6.7. "Roslin Castle," retrieved with one EMD-based query (left) and three PTD-based queries (right) in declining order of relatedness.

The third task, tracing musical relationships, is the hardest to perform. It seems that the EMD and PTD work well when variation is small, as in the case of Handel's borrowing from Kerll; when it is larger, the distances between related melodies are about the same as between unrelated ones. Example 6.8 shows two related themes from J. S. Bach's *Kunst der Fuge*; yet the EMD and PTD between these are greater than 5. In practice, the second theme will not be retrieved using the first as a query because there are too many intervening false positives. One way to get a better match between the principal theme and that of the Canon is to introduce other features into the weighting. Since in this case similarity is determined first of all by the notes that receive metrical stress, this feature is an obvious candidate.

Example 6.8. Two themes from J.S. Bach, Kunst der Fuge, with EMD and PTD distances.

There are many different levels of musical similarity. So far most of the examples have been about a specific kind of similarity, where different instances of one melody are compared. Example 6.8 is the exception: here some effort is required to see—or hear—the similarity between two melodies sharing the same underlying structure. From a historical or music-analytical perspective, searching for laxer forms of similarity is an important task. One may think of inter-textual relationships like allusion and emulation, and of searching for music that shares some generic quality, such as works of one artist, works belonging to the same genre, or works using a similar principle of construction. Listeners (as opposed to music professionals) may want to find music that "sounds like" or has the same emotional quality as a song they like. This type of search brings us to an area that is barely covered by present-day music retrieval techniques. Audio retrieval can be used to make a very general division of music into categories, one of which is often described as *classical music* (McKinney and Breebaart 2003). A finer granularity seems to be very hard to reach. Techniques for notation retrieval are so strongly tied to notes that concepts that abstract from these are hardly an object of retrieval—with the exception of some interesting experiments in harmonic retrieval (Pickens et al. 2002).

So far our approach has been strongly note-oriented, although obviously transportation distances could be used to measure the similarity of any other quantifiable musical property too (Berenzweig et al. 2003). Yet some queries we have performed using the *Orpheus* system suggest that it is possible to search for more generic resemblances too.

1. Hasse, Joh[ann] Adolf 1699-1783: Artemisia... - 0

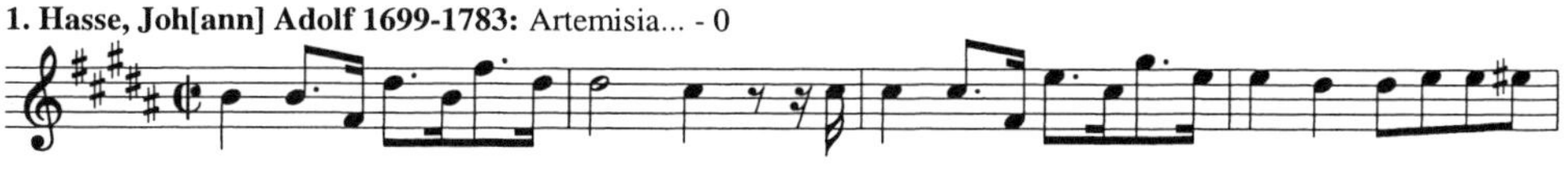

2. Anonymus: Allegretto...- 2.29331

3 Hasse, Joh[ann] Adolf 1699-1783: Romolo ed...- 2.8981

4. Anonymus: Totengrab...2.902

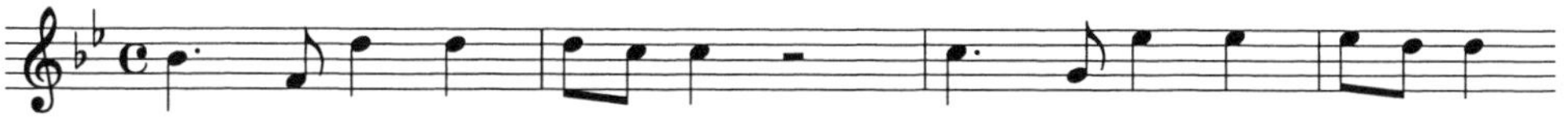

5. Carissimi, Giacomo 1605-1674: Democritus...- 2.94952

6 Henneberg,Johann [Baptist] 1768-1822: Te splendo...- 3.1108

7. Grétry, [André-Ernest-Modeste] 1741-1813: Fausse mag...- 3.17135

8. Aprile, Giuseppe 1731-1813: Bacio di N...- 3.3104

9. Tomasi, Gio[vanni] Battista 17.sc: Sesto Tarq...- 3.44386

10. Anonymus: LibertÁ...- 3.46176

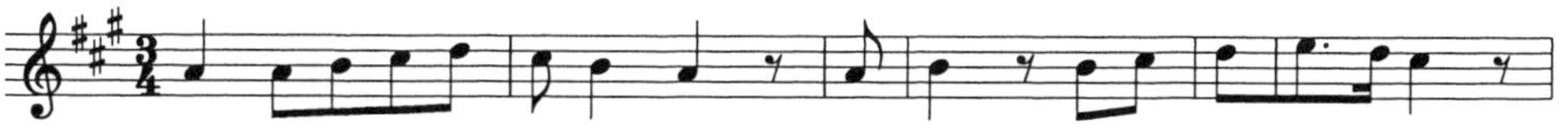

11. Vranicky, [Pavel]: Oberon Kö...- 3.50097

12. Hofmann, Leopold 1738-1793: Symphonies...- 3.53097

13. Anonymus: Dances fl...- 3.54719

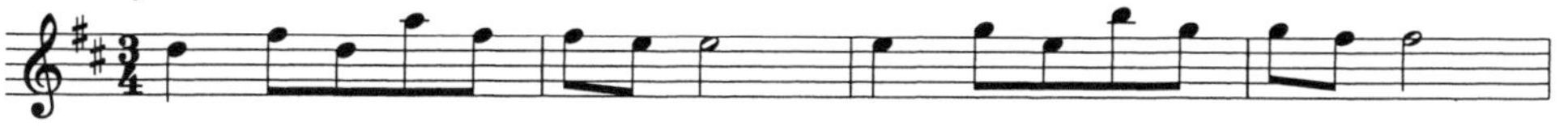

14. Anonymus: Altes Kirc...- 3.55255

15. Scopazzagatti, Michele: Sonatas or...- 3.56192

Example 6.9. Query for a melody by J.A. Hasse (no. 1) and first 15 hits sorted by transportation distance. Multiple hits for the same composition (nos. 1, 3, and 7) were removed.

In Example 6.9, a query was made for a melody from Johann Adolph Hasse's opera *Artemisia* by means of the EMD (duration weights only). Only hits for different melodies are shown, as variants of the same melodies (nos. 1, 3, and 7) show only minuscule differences. Surprisingly, several of the remaining hits show a conspicuous yet generic similarity to the query (nos. 2, 3, 4, 6, 7, 8, and 13; to a lesser extent, also 10 and 11). These melodies consist of two phrases, each beginning with a melodic ascent and closing with a descending second that acts as the resolution of a suspension. The second phrase is typically a second higher than the first. In addition, most of the incipits seem to be based on the very common harmonic framework I-II$_6$-V-I, as illustrated in Example 6.10.

Example 6.10. Inferred harmonic progression for J.A. Hasse's incipit.

Interesting as these results may be by themselves, they are no more than chance hits at this stage. If we inspect weight flows between pairs of incipits, as was done in Examples 6.4 and 6.5, some notes are matched very convincingly, while others may be split up and their parts matched to notes quite some distance apart. Weight flows for false positives such as no. 5 are not too dissimilar from those for the true positives, making it clear that the EMD by itself is not a sufficiently accurate model of human perception of similarity. Yet at the same time we can derive from this example the hypothesis that application of contour and harmony as additional criteria will increase the precision of our retrieval methods by eliminating false hits like nos. 5, 9, 12, 14 and 15.

6.6 Evaluation

Compared to Schlichte's and Howard's experiments with the RISM A/II collection using string-based techniques, we were able to attribute almost twice as many anonymous works to a composer, and to retrieve a distinctly higher percentage of instances of the "Roslin Castle" melody using the EMD. The reason for our better performance in computer attribution is, first of all, that we base our judgments on similarity rather than identity. It is unfortunate that Howard's data pertain to two melodies (from which we chose one) only, so that quantitative comparison of methods is impossible. As the RISM A/II database is large, high-quality, and generally available, it is useful to determine a ground truth for it, that is, a number of queries that have been evaluated by human experts against the whole database. This ground truth can then be used to benchmark the retrieval performance of search engines. We intend to compile and make publicly available a ground truth for RISM A/II in the near future.

Our hypothesis concerning the use of transportation distances for musical patterns is that *the smaller the distance, the more the two patterns resemble each other musically*. In the experiments described above, weights depend on duration only; corresponding query outputs show, in addition to many true hits, too many false positives to accept the hypothesis unconditionally. We still need to improve the way in which weights model the musical importance of notes—and test this by means of an established ground truth. Four factors that may improve weighting have been mentioned so far: note number, distance to next note, metrical stress, and contour. We expect the relative importance of such features to depend on genre. In plainchant, for example, metrical stress plays no role, and duration a minor one; contour is likely to be a major factor. Duration and metrical stress has an obvious place in dance music.

Finally, how does our work compare to other geometric approaches to music retrieval? The main advantage of our approach is that our distance measures have the property of *continuity*. Small changes of point sets (shifts of points and/or differences of weights) have a small effect on the transportation distance; if the changes in the point sets increase, then the transportation distance increases correspondingly, without sudden changes. It is because of this property that matches as in Example 6.9 are possible at all. Continuity is especially an improvement over PROMS (Clausen et al. 2000), where pitch may vary only within a range that has to be specified for each note, and duration may not vary at all. The C-Brahms P3 algorithm has some tolerance against duration change, but as soon as notes no longer overlap, matching is impossible. However, PROMS beats our present solution on two important issues. Searches are much faster due to efficient indexing techniques, and the underlying database consists of complete polyphonic scores rather than monophonic incipits.

6.7 Beyond Incipits

The ultimate challenge is to fully search large numbers of polyphonic scores in an efficient and reliable manner by means of polyphonic queries. Can our approach be used for this? We can only give a tentative answer. In any case, it makes no difference whether the dot patterns are polyphonic or not, as preliminary experiments using the EMD have confirmed. For matching queries against complete scores, the scores, and possibly also the queries, must be divided into chunks. One way to do so is by musical units such as measure, phrase or chord. Another is to set a fixed chunk size and divide scores and queries into overlapping chunks. This way presupposes no musical knowledge, which is an advantage. The application of the EMD for partial matching again raises the indexing problem. We are investigating how the EMD can be used to construct a usable index after all.

So far, all our searching has been melody-oriented. But polyphonic queries may partly or wholly consist of chords, and implicit harmony may have an important place in judging the similarity of melodies (see Example 6.10). Searching chords raises an interesting problem, as each chord can be expanded into a large number of pitch combinations. This relates to pitch representation. Currently we measure interval size, making an octave more related to a seventh than to a unison. If we order intervals by degree of consonance and use this order as the basis of distance calculation, this might offer a solution for dealing with different forms of the same chord, and at the same time better agree with perception.

To make our approach suitable for polyphonic "full-score" retrieval, computational, perceptual and musical issues need to be solved. If we solve these, we may be able to push music notation retrieval past its experimental stage and provide generic tools that help end-users and not just their developers.

References

Berenzweig, Adam, Beth Logan, Daniel P. W. Ellis, Brian Whitman (2003). "A Large-Scale Evaluation of Acoustic and Subjective Music Similarity Measures," in *ISMIR 2003: Proceedings of the Fourth International Conference on Music Information Retrieval*, ed. Holger H. Hoos and David Bainbridge (Baltimore, Johns Hopkins University), 99–105.

Clausen, M., R. Engelbrecht, D. Meyer, and J. Schmitz (2000). "PROMS: A Web-Based Tool for Searching in Polyphonic Music," in *ISMIR 2000: Proceedings of the 1st International Symposium on Music Information Retrieval* (Plymouth, MA); *http://www-mmdb.iai.uni-bonn.de/download/publications/promsIsmir 2000.pdf.*

Cohen, Scott (1999). "Finding Color and Shape Patterns in Images." Ph. D. thesis, Stanford University.

Giannopoulos, Panos, and Remco C. Veltkamp (2000). "A Pseudo-Metric for Weighted Point Sets," in *Proceedings of the 7th European Conference on Computer Vision (ECCV)*, ed. A. Heyden, G. Sparr, M. Nielsen, and P. Johansen (Copenhagen: Springer Verlag), 715–730.

Hewlett, Walter B. (1992). "A Base-40 Number-Line Representation of Musical Pitch Notation," *Musikometrika* 4, 1–14. *http://www.ccarh.org/publications/ reprints/base40/*

Howard, John (1998). "Strategies for Sorting Melodic Incipits," *Melodic Comparison: Concepts, Procedures, and Applications (Computing in Musicology 11)*, 119–128.

McKinney, Martin F., and Jeroen Breebaart (2003). "Features for Audio and Music Classification," in *ISMIR 2003: Proceedings of the Fourth International Conference on Music Information Retrieval*, ed. Holger H. Hoos and David Bainbridge (Baltimore: Johns Hopkins University), 151–158.

Pickens, Jeremy, Juan Pablo Bello, Giuliano Monti, Tim Crawford, Matthew Dovey, Mark Sandler, and Don Byrd (2002). "Polyphonic Score Retrieval Using Polyphonic Audio Queries: A Harmonic Modeling Approach," in *ISMIR 2002 Conference Proceedings: Third International Conference on Music Information Retrieval*, ed. Michael Fingerhut (Paris: IRCAM), 140–149.

Répertoire International des Sources Musicales (RISM) (2002). *Serie A/II, manuscript musicaux après 1600.* Munich: K. G. Saur Verlag.

Schlichte, Joachim (1990). "Der automatische Vergleich von 83,243 Musikincipits aus der RISM-Datenbank: Ergebnisse-Nutzen-Perspektiven," *Fontes artis musicae* 37, 35–46.

Typke, Rainer, Panos Giannopoulos, Remco C. Veltkamp, Frans Wiering, and René van Oostrum (2003). "Using Transportation Distances for Measuring Melodic Similarity" in *ISMIR 2003: Proceedings of the Fourth International Conference on Music Information Retrieval*, ed. Holger H. Hoos and David Bainbridge (Baltimore: Johns Hopkins University), 107–114.

Ukkonen, Esko, Kjell Lemström, and Veli Mäkinen (2003). "Geometric Algorithms for Transposition Invariant Content-Based Music Retrieval" in *ISMIR 2003: Proceedings of the Fourth International Conference on Music Information Retrieval*, ed. Holger H. Hoos and David Bainbridge (Baltimore: Johns Hopkins University), 193–199.

Appendix I. The RISM A/II Database

The RISM A/II Database, a work-in-progress for more than 50 years, attempts to provide bibliographical information on all music manuscripts, worldwide, for the seventeenth and eighteenth centuries. In some of the 60 countries which have collaborated to create this corpus of material, attention is now being devoted to manuscripts of the nineteenth century.

RISM (the *Répertoire International des Sources Musicales*) is headquartered in Frankfurt, Germany. The project referred to here (*http://rism.stub.uni-frankfurt.de/*) is currently directed by Klaus Keil. The designation A/II differentiates the music-manuscript project from a large number of text-based projects (printed music, music-theory treatises, et al.) also under RISM's jurisdiction.

Access to the RISM A/II Database *per se* is principally available via a CD-ROM (412,000 compositions with a total of 470,000 incipits) produced by K. G. Saur (Munich) and via library subscription (456,000 records) through NISC (Baltimore; statistics as reported in March 2004). Some national collections of RISM materials offer alternative means of access. For example, the musical incipits displayed for manuscripts in the Cambridge University Library are based on a separate implementation of *Plaine & Easie Code* (which is described in E. Selfridge-Field, *Beyond MIDI: The Handbook of Musical Codes*, The MIT Press, 1997).

7 Spontaneous User Behavior in "Vocal" Queries for Music-Information Retrieval

Micheline Lesaffre, Dirk Moelants, and Marc Leman

Institute for Psychoacoustics and Electronic Music
Department of Musicology
Ghent University
Blindijnberg 2, B-9000 Belgium
Micheline.LeSaffre, Dirk.Moelants, Marc.Leman@UGhent.be
Project website—*http://www.ipem.ugent.be/MAMI*

Abstract

We report the findings of a study of spontaneous behavior involved in vocal queries for music-information retrieval (MIR) systems. Two conditions were investigated: reproducing music purely from long-term memory, and imitation after listening to the piece. When participants are allowed maximal freedom in the formation of queries, a range of behaviors is found. We first give a global view on the characteristics of music queries, then consider the effects of long- and short-term memory. Our aim is to show that an informed knowledge of human approaches to music-information retrieval can provide valuable insights into appropriate development of user-friendly, content-based access to digital music collections.

Music Query: Methods, Models, and User Studies (Computing in Musicology 13).
Published by CCARH and The MIT Press, 2004.

7.1 Introduction

In a vocal-query system, the imperfections of human memory and inaccuracies of amateur performance both require accommodation. The user may not correctly recall a theme, or may not have the vocal skills to produce a good imitation of it. Most MIR research (see e.g. ISMIR conference proceedings) is focused on systems that can automatically extract information from an audio signal. User performance of vocal queries has been little studied although it is necessary to determine the most comfortable way for a user to reproduce a tune in a MIR system.

7.2 Query-by-Humming vs. Query-by-Voice

In the ideal vocal-querying environment, users can freely use different vocal methods for expressing the target content. Possible methods include singing lyrics, singing syllables, humming, whistling, or even speaking. Ghias et al. (1995) introduced the concept of "query-by-humming" (QBH) and considered it a natural approach to content-based music retrieval. Yet humming is in fact a highly problematic query method. Singing without opening the lips is somewhat artificial for the user, and produces legato and low-volume performance, which makes automatic recognition relatively difficult. Instead, it seems more natural to request that users sing well-defined syllables (e.g. McNab 1997).

In practice, QBH became a generic term. Researchers talk about 'query-by-humming applications' and 'hummed queries' without distinguishing between the methods used as input. Given the very limited meaning of the word humming, we prefer to speak of vocal queries and thus of "query-by-voice" (QBV) systems. By vocal query we simply mean a query produced by the voice and the vocal organs (i.e. vocal cords, tongue, lips, teeth).

We are not aware of experiments described in the literature that directly investigate the spontaneous user behavior in vocal queries. Many vocal-query experiments are carried out in view of processing queries to symbolic transcription without any concern for the user's preferences. Although the output should be representative of what can be expected as input to a QBV-system, clear constraints such as singing a specific syllable are imposed and queries are made by a small number of subjects. Experimenters assume that users are willing to accept certain constraints. It is argued that these constraints are compensated by a higher reliability of the system. However, these assumptions have not been justified. We simply don't know which vocal-querying method users prefer, and how frustrated users may become by imposing certain constraints.

Most systems rely on queries that are made by imitating music, thus using direct memory responses. However, one may assume that a great percentage of users of a QBV system might rely on long-term rather than on short-term memory for melodies. Within the MIR community very few studies investigate the impact of long-term memory. In studying long-term memory of absolute pitch, Levitin (1994) asked subjects to reproduce the pitch of the first few notes of their favorite rock 'n' roll song prompted by visual (and tactile) memory. His findings showed that subjects' long-term memory preserved a stable and accurate representation of musical pitch of highly familiar music, but also showed that subjects who heard the correct pitches internally could not always reproduce them with the same accuracy.

The question to be asked is why any constraints should be imposed. And if so, what is the most natural vocal method for users? Would they prefer to hum, sing in syllables, use lyrics, or whistle instead? So, instead of imposing constraints based on the limitations of a recognition system, our approach starts from the side of the user. We present the results of an experiment in which 72 subjects were asked to perform queries with as few constraints as possible. This allows us to describe some important features of spontaneous vocal querying behavior.

7.3 Description of the Query-by-Voice Experiment

7.3.1 Setup

The QBV experiment was designed to give subjects a maximal freedom of expression. After checking participants' familiarity with the music, they were instructed to vocally imitate a part of a piece of music using any vocal-query method and any combination of methods. We maintained maximal freedom of spontaneous behavior by allowing queries to refer to any fragment of the original music and to any voice (i.e. any melody, bass line or any particular instrument).

7.3.2 Subject Profile

The seventy-two subjects were recruited from students and staff members at Ghent University. The subject pool can be described as follows:

- They ranged in age from 19 to 56, with an average of 27.7 years.
- Twenty-eight subjects (39%) were female and 44 (61%) male.
- Thirty-seven (51%) played a musical instrument, practicing between 0 and 30 hours a week with an average of 6.1 hours; 38 (53%) had no musical education, 30 (42%) basic musical education, and 4 (6%) higher musical education (conservatory).
- On the combination of the results for the playing of an instrument and musical education, the subjects were divided into a group of 30 (42%) musicians and 42 (58%) non-musicians.

The native language of all subjects was Dutch. The experiment was anonymous and the participants were rewarded with a cinema ticket.

7.3.3 Stimuli

The experiment was based on a selection of thirty pieces of music from the MAMI target test collection.[1] The selection of pieces has been based on the criteria that the pieces selected should be:

- maximally familiar to the subjects
- easy to remember
- easy to imitate (reflecting the heterogeneous musical landscape)

Thus it contained different genres: besides popular music songs, ranging from chanson to heavy metal, it includes well-known Flemish children's songs and classical music.[2]

7.3.4 Procedure

Four vocal query methods were suggested to (but not imposed on) these subjects:

- humming,
- singing the lyrics,
- singing nonsense syllables, or
- whistling.

Methods could also be combined. The query length was limited to 30 seconds.

In a preparatory stage, titles and performers (or composers) of the thirty pieces were presented textually. Subjects were asked to indicate whether they knew the piece, and if so, whether they could remember it and would be able to imitate it.

In the first part of the actual experiment, subjects were asked to perform a vocal query for ten titles previously indicated as known and imitable. After each performance, the subjects were offered a second chance to produce another query for the same piece. Before moving to the next title, they were offered the possibility to make an additional query using another method (by sound recording or by typing text), or to propose alternative query methods.

In the second part of the experiment, four entire pieces of music, previously indicated as unknown or not possible to recall, were aurally presented. If there were less than four songs in this list, pieces indicated as imitable in the preparatory stage but not included in the first part of the experiment were used. The subjects were first requested to listen to

[1] An audio database of 160 pieces collected for the MAMI (Musical Audio Mining) project at Ghent University (see: http://www.ipem.ugent.be/MAMI).

[2] Permission to use this collection for the purpose of the project has been given by SABAM, the Belgian author rights association. For a complete list of the musical stimuli, see the Appendix.

the entire piece. They were asked if it was familiar and then to perform a vocal query, still following the instructions of the first part. Also here, the possibility to perform a second query was given. Figure 7.1 gives a schematic overview of the procedure.

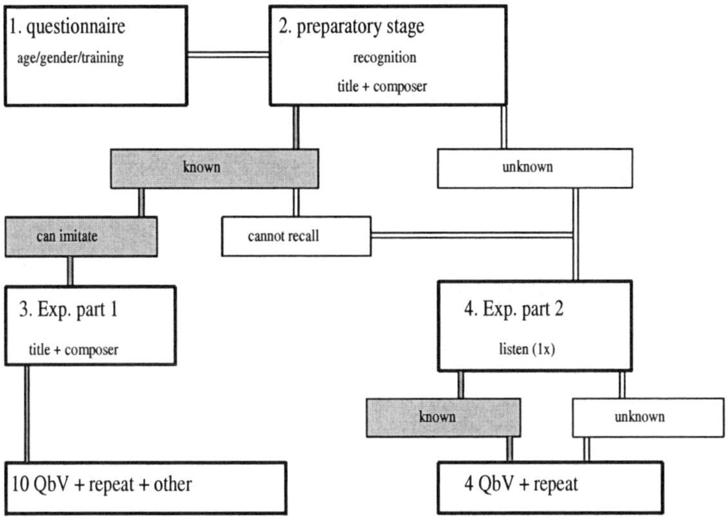

Figure 7.1. Schematic overview of the four steps in the procedure: (1) answering the questionnaire, (2) preparatory stage where the recognition of titles is checked, (3) first part of the experiment: queries relying on long-term memory, and (4) second part of the experiment: queries made immediately after listening to the piece.

7.4 Analysis Strategy

A team of musicologists manually annotated the 1,148 vocal queries resulting from the experiment. The annotation strategy was oriented towards general characteristics rather than a detailed analysis of, for example, issues of pitch and rhythm. The features investigated are: the length, beginning and end of the query, the vocal query method (singing lyrics, humming, whistling, etc.), performance style (melodic versus rhythmic), target similarity, and syllabic structure (what syllables are used). Some of these aspects are rather subjective, such as the assessment of the degree of similarity between query and original, and results are therefore rather tentative. Other aspects, such as temporal properties and method, allow a rather precise annotation.

Vocal queries could contain a mix of different query methods. In order to study the properties of the different methods, the queries were segmented according to the methods used. This resulted in a set of 2,114 segments, characterized by homogeneity of query method. In addition to the four suggested methods we found percussion (such as tapping along with the drum) and spoken comments.

7.5 Statistical Results

7.51 General aspects of the queries

General features are addressed using the original set of 1148 non-segmented queries.

7.5.1.1 BEGINNING AND LENGTH OF QUERIES

Seventy-eight queries (6.79% of the total) exceeded the 30-second limit of the recording time. In these cases the recording was stopped and the computer warned the performer. Twenty-six recorded fragments (2.26%) contained no query at all, as the subjects accidentally or deliberately stopped the recording before producing any kind of query. These files were not taken into account in our statistical analysis.

The average starting time of the query occurred 634 ms after the subjects started the recording, with 99.3% starting within 2 seconds. The mean length is 14.04 seconds, but the distribution is asymmetric, peaking towards 6 seconds and then slowly diminishing towards the maximum-allowed length of 30 seconds, with a peak between 5 and 15 seconds. However, large differences occur between subjects, with personal averages ranging from less than 5 seconds to close to the maximum-allowed recording time of 30 seconds. Also the average starting time shows huge differences between subjects, with personal averages varying roughly between 150 and 1500 ms.

7.5.1.2 NUMBER OF SEGMENTS, BASED ON QUERY METHOD

About 60% of the queries consisted of one homogenous query method and were treated as one single segment. Other queries contained different methods, as well as changes from one method to another and back (for example, lyrics, whistling, and back to lyrics, etc). The maximum number of segments observed in one single query was 12, but 97.8% of the queries contained a maximum of six segments. The distribution of the queries according to the number of segments is shown in Figure 7.2.

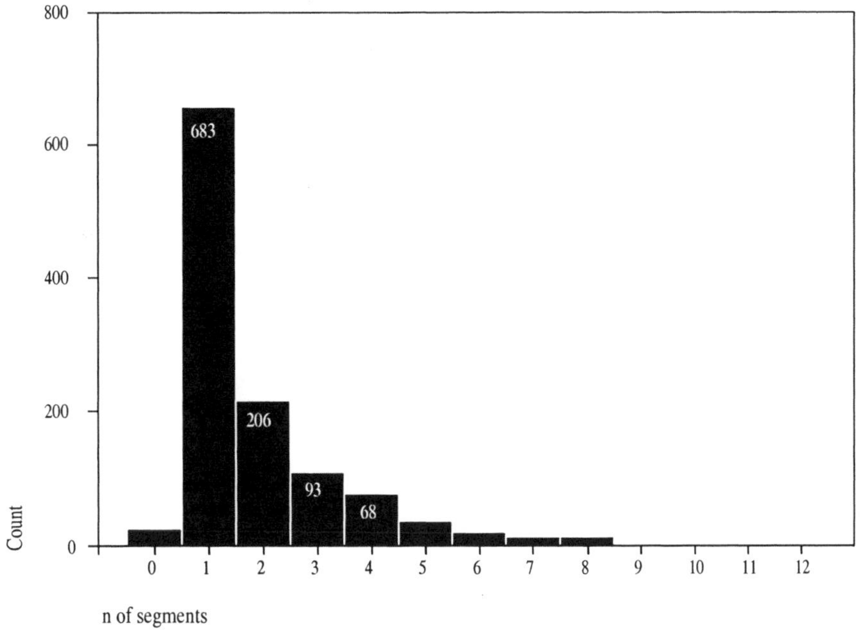

Figure 7.2. Distribution of the queries according to the number of segments. About 60% of the queries produced consist of only one query method.

7.5.2 Segment-Specific Aspects

For segment-specific aspects the set of 2114 segments was used.

7.5.2.1 Length of the Segments

Analogous to the analysis of the queries as a whole, the timing of the segments was investigated. As for the duration of the full queries, a similar asymmetric distribution is shown, but the average length is shorter, with a mean of 7.42 seconds and a sharp peak around two seconds.

7.5.2.2 Query Method

Figure 7.3 and Table 7.1 give an overview of the different query methods in terms of number of segments and total time within the output. The two most prominent methods are singing on text and singing on syllables. Together they account for 83.4% of the queries, and 78.2% of the total time. The frequency of text segments is higher, but the syllabic method is more prominent within the total time, which shows that syllabic segments are in general longer. Among the other methods, whistling is prominent, particularly because the average duration of whistled segments is rather long (with a mean length of 14.63 seconds, almost double the average). Thus, although only 8.6% of the segments are whistled, they take 17.1% of the total time. By contrast, 8.1% of the segments contain humming, percussion, or comments, but these methods combined take only 4.5% of the total time.

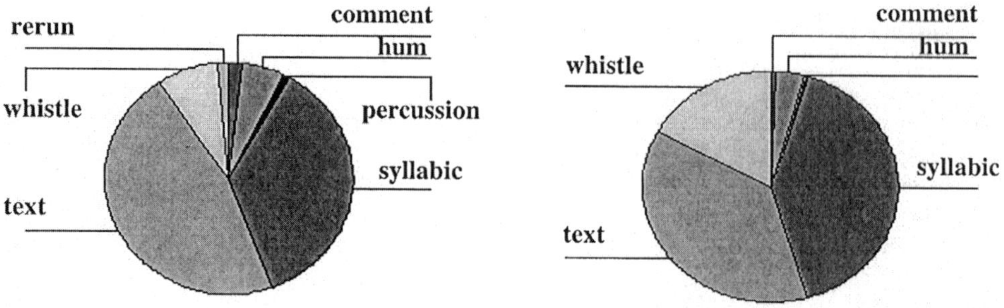

Figure 7.3. Pie charts showing the share of the different query types: textual, syllabic, whistled, hummed, percussive and comments. The left figure shows the types by count, the right figure by duration.

query method	n of segments	% of segments	total time	% of total time
text	926	45.60%	5558959	37.40%
syllabic	766	37.80%	6056644	40.80%
whistle	174	8.60%	2544864	17.10%
hum	101	5.00%	541815	3.60%
comment	42	2.10%	65108	0.40%
percussion	20	1.00%	77394	0.50%

Table 7.1. Occurrence of different query methods hierarchically ordered following the number of segments.

Within the syllabic segments, the syllables were analyzed according to their structural components: the onset (initial consonant or complex of consonants), the nucleus (vowel) and the coda (final consonant). Nucleus and coda together form the rhyme. In total 23 different onsets and 37 rhymes were found, but 99.3% of the total is organized in 11 onsets and 19 rhymes. The ten most common syllables are (in order of decreasing importance) [na], [n@], [la], [t@], [da], [di], [d@], [ta], [tu] and [ti], of which [t@], [na] and [d@] belong to the syllable repertoire of the largest number of subjects.[3]

[3] Syllables are transcribed using SAMPA (http://www.phon.ucl.ac.uk/home/sampa/home.htm), a machine-readable variant of the International Phonetic Alphabet.

7.5.2.3 PERFORMANCE STYLE

The annotation of performance style was aimed at distinguishing between melodic, rhythmic, and intermediate performances. A performance was considered to be melodic when a clear succession of different pitches, or melodic intervals, could be observed. A segment was labeled as rhythmic when no clear pitch intervals were noticed (such as in a spoken text or a percussive sequence). An intermediate category was necessary in order to classify segments where a sense of pitch was present, but without a clear melody (e.g. using a reciting tone). The distribution of these performance styles is given in Figure 7.4 and Table 7.2. Clearly, segments with melodic content are dominant, with 72.6% of the total number, and 76.7% of the total time. Intermediate and particularly rhythmic performance styles are much scarcer and in general also shorter than melodic segments.

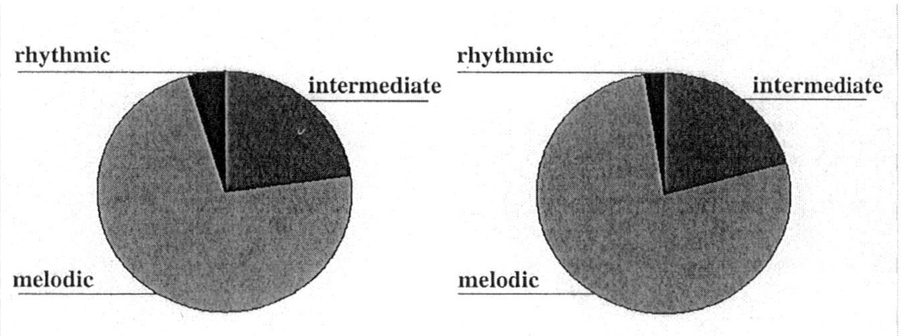

Figure 7.4. Pie charts showing the share of the performance styles: melodic, rhythmic and intermediate. The left figure shows the occurrence by counts and the right figure by length.

performance	n of segments	% of segments	total time	% of total time
melodic	1502	72.60%	11969478	76.70%
intermediate	469	22.70%	3264400	20.90%
rhythmic	98	4.70%	373249	2.40%

Table 7.2. Occurrence of performance types hierarchically ordered following the number of segments.

7.5.2.4 SIMILARITY BETWEEN SEGMENTS AND TARGETS

To each of the segments, a similarity rating was given on a six-point scale, from 0 (not recognizable) to 5 (sounds similar), focusing on melodic and rhythmic properties while, e.g., the timbre or the lyrics were neglected. The estimation of the degree of similarity between query segment and target, obviously, is subjective. Due to the subjectivity of the numbers, similarity measures are used only to compare large sets of data—to compare the efficiency of the different methods, the performance of different groups of users, and the effects of differences in memory recall.

7.5.3 Analysis of Query Methods by Subjects

The syllabic and textual query methods were the most widely spread among the subjects. Of the 71 subjects producing valid queries, 68 produced syllabic and 67 textual segments. Humming was used at least once by 39 of the subjects, whistling by 31 subjects. Twenty subjects gave comments, and 11 subjects produced percussive queries.

Looking at the distributions of the different methods for all subjects, different strategies can be distinguished. A small majority of the subjects (N = 38 or 54%) concentrated on one method (at least 60% of the query time). Eighteen subjects concentrated on text, 16 on syllabic queries, while a small group of 4 concentrated on whistling (2 produced only whistled queries). A quarter of the subjects (17), divided its query time between two methods (each taking between 30 and 60%, and together at least 80% of the time). In 15 of these 17 cases textual and syllabic queries are combined, while the combinations text/whistling and syllables/whistling each occur once. The remaining 16 participants used several methods (with three or four methods covering at least one eighth of the total query time); most common (N = 10) is a combination of textual, syllabic and whistled queries. In the other cases humming is added or replaces one of the three other methods.

Five different user profiles can thus be distinguished, four of which apply to about a quarter of the population each (text preference, syllable preference, two methods, mixed) and the fifth a small but rather distinctive group of 'whistlers.' The typical whistler is a young (mean = 24) male musician. This group produces the longest queries (mean = 19.3 s) with the highest overall similarity (mean = 4.12). They rarely switch methods within queries and if they use another method, they see the syllabic method as the only alternative. An ANOVA on the timing and segmentation aspects of the queries of the four remaining categories of subjects reveals significant effects on the mean number of segments [$F(3.63) = 1.418$, $p < 0.01$] and the mean segment length [$F(3,63) = 5.320$, $p < 0.01$]. As shown in Figure 7.5, subjects who divide their attention over two methods (average segment length = 6.60 s, average number of segments = 2.14) and subjects who use text as the dominant method (length = 5.92 s, number = 2.19) stand against subjects mixing more than two methods (length = 7.55 s, number = 1.59) and those who use syllabic queries as the dominant method (length = 9.29 s, number = 1.74).

7.5.4 Effects of Memory on the Timing and Accuracy of the Queries

A distinction was made between the queries from the first part of the experiment, based on songs indicated as "known, remembered and possible to imitate," entirely relying on long-term memory, and the queries from the second part of the experiment, made after hearing the complete song. Within the last category a distinction was made between songs indicated as "known" after listening and those indicated as "unknown."

For unknown songs, the subjects relied entirely on their short-term memory. For "known" songs they could combine with information recalled from long-term memory. Thus the experiment provided three classes of queries, each distinguished by a different use of memory:

- long-term memory (LTM) (833 queries from part 1),
- short-term memory (STM) (81 queries from part 2), and
- mixed (LTM+STM) (208 queries from part 2).

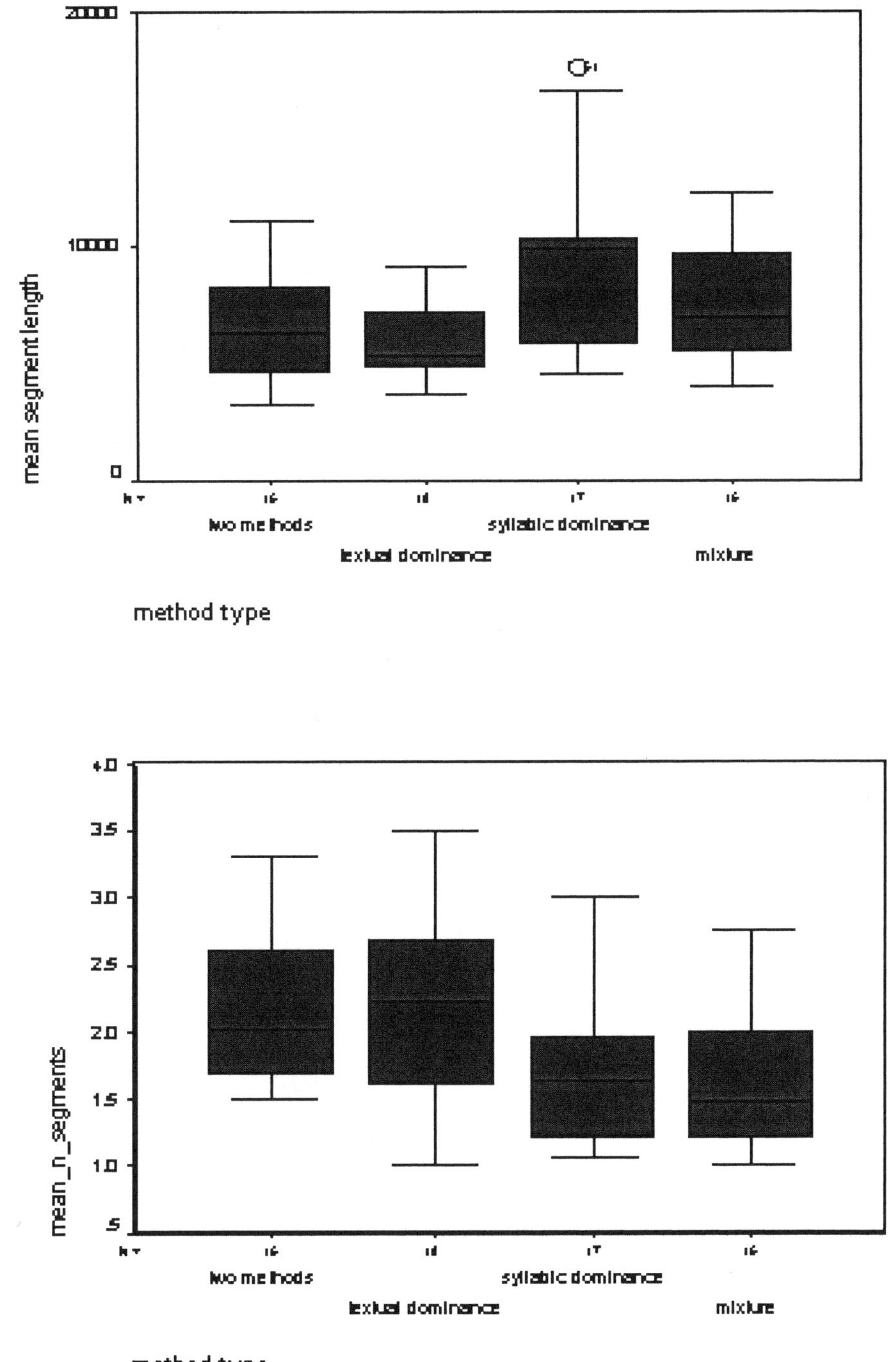

Figure 7.5. User categories according to the use of vocal query methods. Top: following the mean segment length. Bottom: following the mean number of segments.

The memory type had a significant effect on the start time and the length of queries, as well as on the similarity of the queries with the targets. There is a very clear effect on the query length [$F(2,1119) = 30.343$, $p < 0.001$], with these results:

- a mean of 13.21 s when using LTM,
- a mean of 12.78 s when using STM, but
- a mean of 17.87 s for LTM+STM (Figure 7.6).

This finding is reflected in a highly significant effect of memory category on the segment length [$F(2,2111) = 46.500$, $p < 0.001$]. The segments within the queries using LTM+STM are significantly longer (mean: 10.6 s) than those using only one type of memory (means: 6.8 s for LTM and 6.3 s for STM). Additionally, there is also a significant effect on the starting time of the queries [$F(2,1119) = 3.136$, $p < 0.05$]. When only relying on LTM (mean: 643 ms), subjects tend to start earlier than when using STM (mean: 685 ms), but when using LTM+STM they start still sooner (mean: 579 ms).

The type of memory used also has a highly significant effect on the similarity of the segments [$F(2,2111) = 10.571$, $p < 0.001$]. The distribution of the different similarity levels within the three categories (Figure 7.7) indicates only a small difference between LTM and LTM+STM but a drastic fall in similarity for the queries based on STM only.

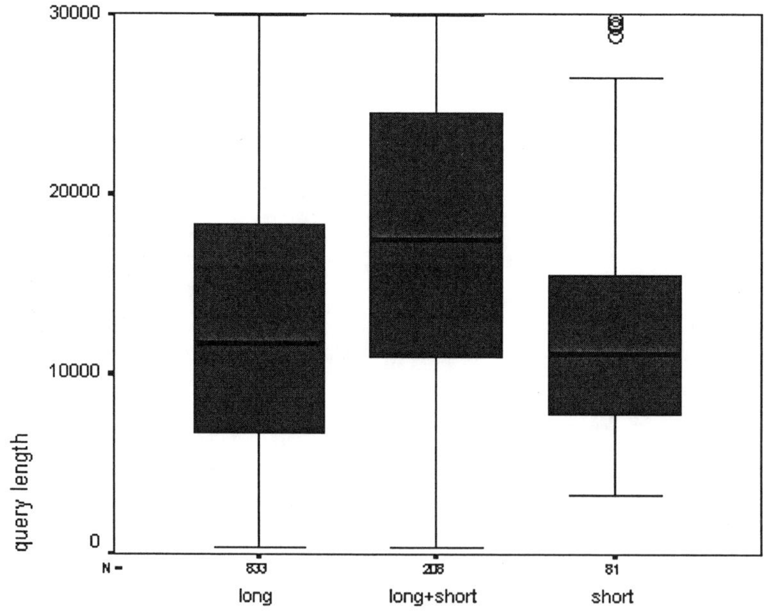

Figure 7.6. Effect of the three memory types on the query length.

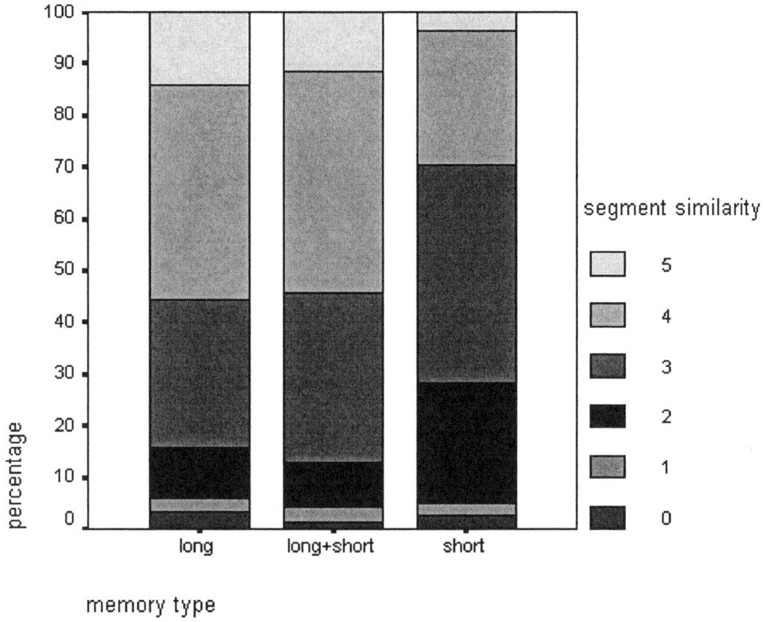

Figure 7.7. Distribution of the different similarity levels at the segment level within the three categories of memory.

Besides effects on timing and similarity, there is a clear influence of the memory type on query method and performance style. Figure 7.8 shows a change from a textual dominance to a syllabic dominance with a growing importance of short-term memory: for LTM, 48.7% of the queries are textual, taking 41.7% of the total time; for LTM+STM this becomes 39.7/33.3% and for STM 34.4/26.6%.

The importance of syllabic queries moves in the other direction: LTM 34.9/36.0%, LTM+STM 43.1/47.2%, and STM 49.1/58.3%. Parallel to this the importance of whistling decreases: LTM 8.6/18.0%, LTM+STM 9.5/15.3%, STM 4.3/8.0%. Also remarkable, finally, is the sudden increase in percussive queries when long-term memory is no longer present.

The influence of memory type on the performance style (melodic, rhythmic or intermediate) is shown in Figure 7.9. As with textual queries, the number of queries characterized by a melodic performance style decreases with a growing importance of short-term memory (LTM: 73.9/79.6%, LTM+STM: 69.0/73.7%, STM: 47.2/51.7%) in favor of intermediate (LTM: 19.1/18.2%, LTM+STM: 25.6/ 22.8%, STM: 45.5/41.9%) and, to a lesser extent, rhythmic style (LTM: 4.7/1.8%, LTM+STM: 3.7/3.2%, STM: 5.5/5.8%). The latter is only visible in the share of the total query time, which indicates that queries in a rhythmic style get relatively longer.

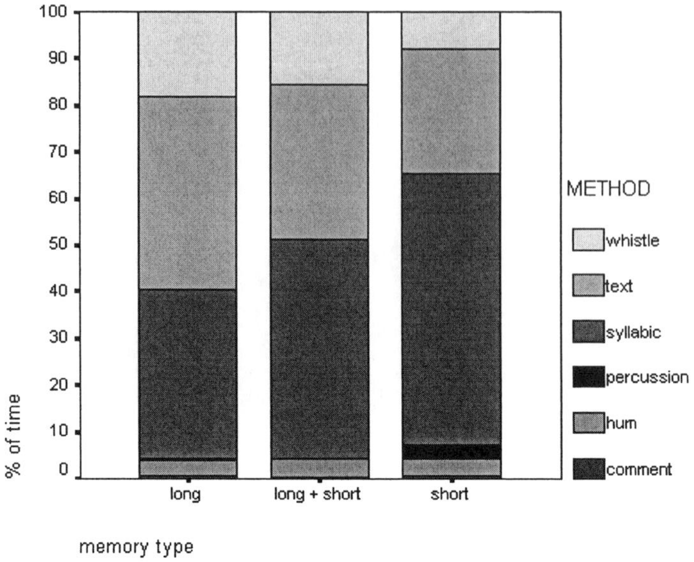

Figure 7.8. Change from textual dominance to syllabic dominance with a growing importance of short-term memory.

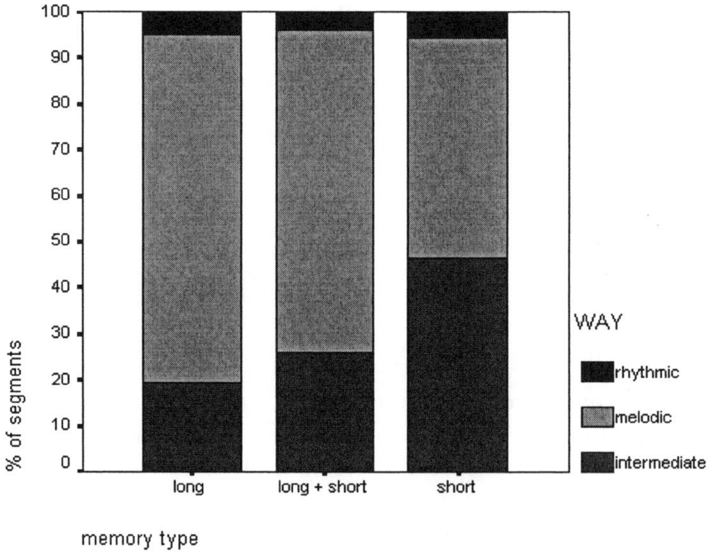

Figure 7.9. Influence of memory-type on performance style.

7.6 Discussion

Analysis of the timing characteristics of the queries shows a mean query length around 14 seconds; the start of the actual query occurs 634 ms average after the start of the recording. In both cases big inter-individual differences are found. Thus a user-friendly MIR system should be flexible in timing, expecting some people to start up to 2 seconds after the start of the recording, and expecting from a few seconds to over 30 seconds of information.

In classifying and segmenting the queries we distinguished between six methods: singing lyrics, singing syllables, whistling, humming, percussion and comments. In about 60% of the queries, subjects used only one method. In the other cases subjects used at least two methods, sometimes alternating two or more methods, but queries containing more than six segments are scarce.

The most common query methods are singing lyrics and singing syllables. Syllabic segments are in general longer than textual segments. Whistling is the third most popular method, while humming, percussion and comments occupy only a small share.

The use of certain methods is user-dependent. We could distinguish different types of users: (1) subjects that concentrate on one method (lyrics, syllables, whistling), (2) subjects that divide their query time between two methods (mostly a combination of textual and syllabic), and (3) subjects that mix several methods. These findings indicate that the ideal MIR system should be able to cope with changes in method. On the other hand, one could give users the choice of one specific method: text, syllables, or whistling.

Concentrating on one single method does not seem so attractive since some classes of users largely rely on one single method. This is most clearly illustrated by whistling. Less than half of the people used whistling as a query method, but a small group concentrated on whistling and moreover provided long, high-quality queries. Thus allowing only whistling (e.g. Prechelt and Typke 2001) does not seem to be a good choice, but excluding whistling would eliminate an interesting body of queries.

Around 75% of the query collection is performed in a melodic way, which supports the idea that melodic content is to be regarded as a salient feature of vocal queries (e.g. Chai 2001).

Since the use of syllables is one of the most important query methods, and most existing MIR systems require syllabic input, we further investigated the nature and structure of the syllables occurring in spontaneous queries. If a system requires specific syllables for ease of processing, it is desirable to choose some of the most common types. Some existing systems, however, ask the users to use syllables that hardly ever occur in spontaneous queries, e.g. [fa] (Pauws 2002). These syllables might be less comfortable for the users and thus might yield a larger number of errors, or diminish the attractiveness of the system for the public. Our finding that the most popular syllables end on a vowel and have no coda is in agreement with the syllabic constraints found in the experimental literature.

7.7 Conclusion

Although a large variety of vocal querying strategies was observed, we could establish some basic characteristics and distinguish some categories of users. These findings already generate some guidelines for the development of user-friendly MIR systems. The application of these guidelines would enhance the interactive process and open the way to make MIR systems more efficient and more attractive.

Acknowledgements

The research presented here has been carried out in the context of the MAMI (Musical Audio Mining) project (http://www.ipem.ugent.be/MAMI) at the Musicology Department at Ghent University. The aim of the project is to build a music-retrieval system using audio-mining techniques (Leman 2002, Leman et al 2002). The project is funded by the Flemish Institute for the Promotion of Scientific and Technical Research in Industry. It addresses research performed by an interdisciplinary consortium that is grounded in diverse fields such as signal processing, musicology and applied mathematics.

The authors gratefully acknowledge Koen Tanghe and Gaëtan Martens, members of the MAMI team, for the implementation of the application used for the experiment. We also wish to thank Jelle Dierickx and Liesbeth De Voogdt for their assistance in the annotation of the queries.

Appendix 1. Songs used in the experiments.

SONG TITLE	PART I			PART II		TOTAL
	recording			recording		
	1	2	3	1	2	
Blowin' in the wind	47	2	4	7	2	62
All I really want				23	1	24
Mooi, 't leven is mooi	68	12	7			87
De Marie-Louise	61	9	6	3		79
How do you do				19	1	20
Paloma Blanca				11	3	14
YMCA	67	10	4	2		83
When a man loves a woman	57	7	3	3		70
Don't worry, be happy	65	9	6	1		81
Walk on the wild side	44	7	1	6	1	59
Waterloo	60	3	3	5		71
Sunday, bloody Sunday	48	8	5	7	1	69
It's raining men	60	5	5	1		71
Without you				17	3	20
Ad mortem festinamus				22	2	24
My way	40	7	1	12	3	63
Rosa	17	2	2	16	4	41
Smells like teen spirit	10	1	1	20	3	35
Only happy when it rains	6	1		19	2	28
Temple of love	6		1	16	3	26
Highway to hell				13		13
Don't cry for me, Argentina	27	2	1	4	3	37
Klein klein kleuterke	17	1	2	6	2	28
'k zag twee beren	10	1		2		13

SONG TITLE	PART I			Part II		TOTAL
	recording			recording		
	1	2	3	1	2	
O Fortuna	4			11	1	16
Für Elise	2			12		14
TOTAL	716	87	52	258	35	1148

References

Chai, Wei (2001). "Melody Retrieval on the Web." M. S. Thesis, MIT Media Lab.

Ghias, Asif, Jonathan Logan, David Chamberlin, and Brian Smith (1995). "Query by Humming: Musical Information Retrieval in an Audio Database," *Proceedings of ACM Multimedia 1995*, pp. 213–236.

Leman, Marc (2002). "Musical Audio Mining," in *Dealing with the Data Flood: Mining Data, Text and Multimedia*, ed. J. Meij (Rotterdam: STT Netherlands Study Center for Technology Trends), chapter 5.5.2.

Leman Marc, Lieven P. Clarisse, Bernard De Baets, Hans De Meyer, Micheline Lesaffre, Gaëtan Martens, Jean-Pierre Martens, and Dirk Van Steelant (2002). "Tendencies, Perspectives, and Opportunities of Musical Audio-Mining," *Proceedings of Forum Acusticum Sevilla 2002*, special issue of Journal Revista de Acústica Vol. XXXIII, no. 3-4, abstract p. 79, full text: CD-ROM.

Levitin, Daniel J. (1994). "Absolute Memory for Musical Pitch: Evidence from the Production of Learned Melodies" in Perception & Psychophysics, 56, pp. 414–423.

McNab, Rodger J., Lloyd A. Smith, David Bainbridge and Ian H. Witten (1997). "The New Zealand Digital Library MELody inDEX," D-Lib Magazine, pp. 11–18.

Pauws, Steffen (2002). "CubyHum: A Fully Operational Query by Humming System" in *Proceedings of the Third International Conference on Music Information Retrieval*, ed. Michael Fingerhut (Paris: IRCAM–Centre Pompidou), pp. 187–196.

Prechelt, Lutz, and Rainer Typke (2001). "An Interface for Melody Input" in ACM Transactions on Computer-Human Interaction, pp. 133–149.

8 Cognitive Adequacy in the Measurement of Melodic Similarity: Algorithmic vs. Human Judgments

Daniel Muellensiefen[1] and Klaus Frieler[2]

[1]Christoph-Probst-Weg 8
20251 Hamburg
Germany
[2]Hopfenstraße 22
20359 Hamburg
Germany

Abstract

Melodic similarity is a central concept in many sub-disciplines of musicology, as well as for many computer-based applications that deal with the classifications and retrieval of melodic material. This paper describes a research paradigm for finding an 'optimal' similarity measure out of a multitude of different approaches and algorithmic variants. The repertory used in this study are short melodies from popular (pop) songs and the empirical data for validation stem from two extensive listener experiments with expert listeners (musicology students). The different approaches to melodic-similarity measurement are first discussed and mathematically systematized. Detailed description of the listener experiments is given and the results are discussed. Strengths and weaknesses of the several tested similarity measures are outlined and an 'optimal' similarity measure for this specific melodic repertory is proposed.

Music Query: Methods, Models, and User Studies (Computing in Musicology 13). Published by CCARH and the MIT Press, 2004.

8.1 Introduction

Melodic similarity is a key concept in several of musicology's subdisciplines. Among these are ethnomusicology (e.g. Bartók and Lord 1951, Seeger 1966, Kluge 1974, Bartók 1976, Steinbeck 1982, Jesser 1992, Juhász 2000), music analysis (e.g. Meyer 1973, Lerdahl and Jackendoff 1983, Baroni et al. 1992, Selfridge-Field 2003), copyright issues in music (e.g. Cronin 1998), music-information retrieval (e.g. Mongeau and Sankoff 1990, McNab et al. 1996, Downie 1999, Meek and Birmingham 2002, Uitdenbogerd 2002), and music psychology (Wiora 1941, Schmuckler 1999, Hofmann-Engl 2000, 2001; McAdams and Matzkin 2001, Deliège 2002). An overview of motivations, research paradigms, and related concepts is given in Volume 11 (1998) of *Computing in Musicology* (*Melodic Similarity: Concepts, Procedures, and Applications*) and the 2001 spring issue of *Music Perception* (Vol. 18, No. 3). For different research questions a variety of methodologies for measuring melodic similarity have been developed.

The motivation for the present investigation came from the area of music psychology. Following the research approaches to memory for melodies of Sloboda and Parker (1985), Kauffman and Carlsen (1989), and Dowling and colleagues (Dowling et al. 2002), a way to describe the memory representation of a melody is the goal of a current psychological research enterprise (Muellensiefen, in preparation). One necessary tool to find an adequate description of a melodic memory representation seems to be a similarity measure that relates an original melody to its (probably transformed) version in memory in a cognitively appropriate way. A proper measure for this purpose was already called for by Sloboda and Parker, complaining that "there is no psychological theory of melodic or thematic identity" (Sloboda and Parker 1985: 161).

The literature on similarity measurement for melodies of the last two decades does not suffer from lack of measurement procedures for melodic similarity but rather from their abundance. Different techniques for defining and computing melodic similarity have been proposed to emphasize distinct aspects or elements of melodies. Among features emphasized are intervals, contour, rhythm, and tonality, often with several options to transform the musical information into numerical datasets. Current basic techniques for measuring the similarity of these types of datasets are edit-distance, *n*-grams, correlation- and difference-coefficients, and Hidden Markov Models (HMMs). There are many examples of successful applications of these specific similarity measures: these include McNab et al. (1996) and Uitdenbogerd (2002) for edit-distance, Downie (1999) for *n*-grams, Steinbeck (1982) and Schmuckler (1999) for correlation- and difference-coefficients, Ó Maidín (1998) for a complex difference measure, and Meek and Birmingham (2002) for HMMs.

The basic question addressed in the present paper is, Which type of data and which similarity measures are cognitively most adequate? The aim of this investigation is to find the "optimal" similarity measure out of a set of basic techniques and their variants.

The "optimal" similarity measure would probably be the mean rating of a group of music experts. But since such a group of experts is not always at hand, the idea of this investigation was to model expert ratings with some of the basic measurement techniques just mentioned. So a rating experiment was conducted to compare expert ratings with the results of similarity algorithms. The "optimal" or most cognitively adequate measure would be the one that predicts the expert judgments best.

Not very many extensive studies comparing human ratings to algorithmic similarity measurement have been undertaken yet. Exceptions are Schmuckler (1999), Eerola et.al. (2001), McAdams and Matzkin (2001), Hofmann-Engl (2002), and very recently Pardo, Shifrin, and Birmingham (2004). The studies of Schmuckler (1999), McAdams and Matzkin (2001), and Pardo et al. (2004) come closest to the present approach, but the variety of similarity models and musical material employed here is far greater and closer to "ordinary" western music.

In the next section the different approaches to data transformations and similarity measures are defined and systematized. References to the original literature are made. Section 8.3 describes the rating experiment and the treatment of the collected data. Section 8.4 compares human ratings with the employed algorithmic models and proposes an optimization for a combination of different models. Section 8.5 discusses aspects of strength and weakness of the optimized model and points out musical dimensions of melodies that have not been covered by the basic models nor their combination presented here and that could be perspectives for future research.

8.2 Data Transformations and Similarity Models

For defining the general notion of a similarity measure, one has first to define what a melody is. An algorithmic or mathematically-based similarity measure has to find an abstract representation of a true musical melody sounding in time and space. For our purposes a melody will be simply viewed as a time series, i.e., as a series of pairs of onsets and pitches (t_n, p_n), where pitch is represented as a number, usually a MIDI number, and an onset is given by a real number representing a point in time.

The two components of this time series will be called "rhythm" and "pitch-melody" respectively. Most of the considered similarity measures work either on pitch or rhythm alone.

Furthermore, it is useful to view rhythm or pitch-melody as a vector in a suitable n-dimensional (real) vector space or as a string in a more computer-oriented sense. According to this, we discriminate different classes of similarity measures: vector, symbolic and musical measures. The musical measures use an abstract representation of melodies as well, but they rely on more or less detailed musical knowledge rather than on more abstract properties. We will concentrate here mainly on the vector and symbolic measures.

8.2.1 Definition

A similarity measure $\sigma(m_1, m_2)$ is a symmetrical map of the space of abstract melodies M mapping two melodies on a value between 0 and 1, where 1 means identity. It should be normalized, i.e., the similarity of a melody to itself should be 1. Furthermore, it should be invariant under transposition in pitch, translation in time and under tempo changes, i.e., dilation in time.

A general (and brute-force) way to achieve the desired invariances, which we adopted to some of the measures, is to take the maximum over all possible transpositions and/or translations/dilation. The algorithm by Ó Maidín (1998) employs a similar strategy.

The space of similarity measures is convex, i.e., if one has two or more similarity measures σi, a weighted sum, $\Sigma\ w_i\ \sigma_i$ with $\Sigma\ w_i = 1$, will yield another similarity measure. This will be exploited for finding an optimal measure by means of a linear regression over our data.

Looking at this abstract definition, it is intuitively clear that the space of similarity measures is enormous. The problem is not, as stated earlier, the lack of measures but to find the cognitively most adequate ones.

All of the herein presented measures typically follow some basic construction steps. First they transform the melodies with more fundamental transformations like the interval and/or duration representation, then they apply more elaborate ones, like Fourier transformation or fuzzification/classification. As a last step a standard method of correlation, like vector correlation or edit-distance, is adopted.

8.2.2 Representations of Abstract Melodies

Due to the invariance properties of a similarity measure, melodies are often written in duration and interval representations. The first goes from onset to onset, or by inter-onset intervals [IOIs] ($\Delta\ t_n = t_{n+1} - t_n$), and/or uses integral multiples of a common minimal duration for IOIs $\Delta\ t_n = k(n)\ \Delta T$. In the latter we will speak about quantized melodies and quantized representation, which are invariant under translation/dilation by construction. The second uses intervals, i.e. differences of pitches $\Delta\ p_n = p_{n+1} - p_n$, instead of absolute pitch. Any similarity measure using this representation already has the required invariance under transposition.

Another fundamental representation is achieved by rhythmical weighting. Similarity measures working on pitch alone use only the sequence order, but no absolute time information, giving shorter tones the same weight as longer ones. To account for this, and if one has quantized melodies (as we always had), one can substitute every pitch in the melody by n times the same pitch, where n is the duration in shortest time units of the tone. So, e.g., if one has the melody (in quantized representation):

$$(2, 64), (2, 66), (2, 68)$$

it becomes

$$(1,64), (1,64), (1,66), (1,66),(1,68)\ (1,68)$$

The concept of rhythmical weighting has been widely used in other studies (e.g. Steinbeck 1982, Juhász 2000, Hofmann-Engl 2002).

8.2.3 Transformations of Pitch

The most important transformations of pitch are contourization, fuzzification and Fourier transformation.

8.2.3.1 Contourization

The concept of contourization relies on the perceptual salience of melodic contour. The idea relies on the fact that the exact sequence of pitches is often not crucial, but the turning points of a melody are. Instead of considering all the pitches of a melody, contourization picks out only the local extremes of a pitch sequence and makes some kind of interpolation, mostly linear, between these anchor tones. Slightly different concepts of contourization were employed in the similarity measures by Steinbeck (1982) and Zhou and Kankanhalli (2003).

We used two different contourization procedures—the one used by Steinbeck (1982) and our personal one. The difference lies in the treatment of "changing tones" (a sequence of three notes in which the first and third are the same). The idea behind this is that changing tones, which always make for a local extreme, are irrelevant for contour perception. In our model a changing tone is substituted for the three events if the note before and the note after the candidate are the same. In Steinbeck's model, two tones before and after must be either strictly descending or ascending.

8.2.3.2 Fuzzification

The main idea of fuzzy logic is to allow a whole range of truth values between 0 and 1 for a logical statement, where 0 means "false" and 1 means "true". Accordingly, a fuzzy set (Zadeh 1965) is a set to which each element belongs only to some certain degree between 0 and 1. The advantage of this concept is that it offers an easy way to model fuzziness in perception and other areas.

The idea can be carried forward to intervals. Using fuzzy concepts with intervals reflects the fact that even an experienced listener is not always able to determine an interval exactly, but always has a certain perception of the magnitude of an interval. A listener will always be able to discriminate a step (one or two semitones) from a skip (three or more semitones).

We define certain classes of intervals and assign to each interval in the melody a vector of "belongingness" to these classes. But in fact our tested models use fuzzy sets, where each interval belongs to exactly one class, so it should be more precisely called a classification. The idea to reduce the intervals of the chromatic scale to a smaller set of interval classes is again very common in applications that use similarity measures (e.g. Pauws 2002). We took the nine interval classes shown in Table 8.1.

Class	Intervals	Name
-4	< -7	Big leap down
-3	-7, -6, -5	Leap down
-2	-4, -3	Big step down
-1	-2, -1	Step down
0	0	Same
1	1, 2	Step up
2	3, 4	Big step up
2	5, 6, 7	Leap up
4	> 7	Big leap up

Table 8.1. Interval classes used.

The intervals are counted in semitones. Taking the sequence (1,64) (1,65) (1,70) (1,68) (1,65) as an example, one gets the intervallic representation

1, 5, -2, -3

and the fuzzified melody

1, 3, -1, -2.

8.2.3.3 Fourier Transform

Another method adopted from Schmuckler (1999) is that of taking the (discrete) Fourier transform of the pitch-melody, more precisely the DFT of pitch ranks, i.e., the numbering of the pitches p_n as ranks r_n starting with 0 for the lowest pitch. The idea behind this, as stated by Schmuckler (1999), is that a Fourier transform detects inherent periodicities in a signal. The complex Fourier coefficients are given by the well-known formula

$$c_n = \sum_{k=-\frac{N}{2}}^{\frac{N}{2}} r_k e^{i\omega_n k}, \omega_n = \frac{2\pi n}{N}$$

and the amplitudes of the real positive power spectrum from this are then $p_n = c_n c_{-n}$.

8.2.4 Transformations of Rhythm

For similarity of rhythms, a field which seems to be neglected in the literature, we had to develop methods on our own. In principle every correlational technique, whether vector or symbolical, can likewise be used for rhythm vectors or rhythm strings. As preliminary transformations we used gaussification and fuzzification.

8.2.4.1 Gaussification

The idea of gaussification is to construct a continuous, integrable function out of a set of onsets by superposition of gauss functions with a mean at the point of an onset and fixed standard deviation. So, if t_n is a set of onsets, then

$$g(t) = \frac{1}{N}\sum_{i=0}^{N-1} e^{-\frac{(t-t_i)^2}{2\sigma^2}}$$

is called a rhythm gaussification. This transforms an n-dimensional vector t_n into an ∞-dimensional one, and as we will see later, one has to go from ordinary scalar products over to integrals.

8.2.4.2 Fuzzification

The technique of fuzzification, as explained above, can be applied to durations, too, but one has to relate the durations to a fixed duration, which we chose to be the most frequent duration (modus) d8 (of all durations) in a melody. We used the following five classes for the fractions $\Delta T_n / d_\infty$

Class	Fraction	Name
4	$f > 3.3$	Very long
3	$1.8 < f \leq 3.3$	Long
2	$0.9 < f \leq 1.8$	"Normal" beat
1	$0.45 < f \leq 0.9$	Short
0	$f < 0.45$	Very short

Table 8.2. Duration classes used.

This choice of classes is, of course, far from unique; it was inspired by the common categories of (binary) musical rhythm (Drake and Bertrand 2001: 24f).

8.2.5 Vector Measures

8.2.5.1 Correlational Measures

An important class of vector measures relies on the well-known correlation of n-dimensional vectors:

$$r(v,w) = \frac{\sum_i v_i w_i}{\sqrt{\sum_i v_i^2 w_i^2}} \in [1,-1]$$

For a similarity measure of pitch-melodies one has to ensure transposition invariance, and furthermore, one must transform the values to the interval [0,1]. The first can be done, for example, by transposing every pitch by the mean pitch of the melody. The latter can be achieved, for example, by setting any negative value to 0, as we did in most cases. This was done because we were not interested, unlike other investigations (e.g. Kluge 1974, Wiggins 2002, p. 308), in the degree of contrary or retrograde similarity.

Vector correlation was exploited by us by these means:

(1) Pearson-Bravais correlations of pitch-melodies (raw and rhythmically weighted, transposition by mean pitch): rawpcst, rawpcwst.

(2) Pearson-Bravais correlations of contourized melodies (unweighted, transposition by mean pitch): conspcst, conpcst.

(3) Pearson-Bravais correlations of Fourier-rank transformed melodies (weighted, unweighted): fourrst, fourrwst, fourri.

(4) Correlation of fuzzified intervals: difffuz.

(5) Correlation of fuzzified contourized pitch-melody: diffuzc.

(6) Correlation of rhythm gaussifications: rhytgaus.

(7) Harmonic correlation: harmcorr, harmcork, harmcorrc.

For the correlation of rhythm gaussifications, we have to adapt the scheme a little bit. First, one has to use integrals for the scalar products, which can be solved analytically. Second, one has to guarantee translation and dilation invariance. Translation invariance is achieved by translating each onset vector to start with $t_0 = 0$. Dilation invariance needs more sophistication in the general case. However, if one has quantized melodies, one can set the smallest time units of both rhythms to be equal and one arrives at the following formula for the scalar product of two gaussifications g and g′:

$$\langle g, g' \rangle = \frac{1}{N} \sum_{n,n'} e^{-\frac{(k(n)-k'(n'))^2}{2\sigma^2}}$$

Harmonic correlation belongs to the field of "musical measures" and will be discussed later.

The attentive reader will have noticed that the correlation is only defined for vectors of equal dimension (length). But in practice melodies seldom have exactly the same length. To accommodate possible differences, we shift the shorter melody along the longer one and compute a similarity for each section of equal length to the shorter one.

Additionally, to account for possible missing upbeats, we shift the shorter one up to 10% of its length or 8 minimal time units, whichever is greater, to the left of the longer melody. For each of these pairs of melodies of the same length we then calculate the correlations and take the maximum over all values as the true similarity.

8.2.5.2 Distance Measures

There is a natural link between distance measures on the space of melodies and similarity measures (e.g. Ó Maidín 1998). If one has a distance measure *d(m,n)* obeying translation, transposition and dilation invariance, a similarity measure can easily be obtained by $\sigma(m,n) = e^{-\frac{d(m,n)}{k(m,n)}}$, or, if *k(m,n)* > *d(m,n),* for all *m,n.*

We used just two out of this huge class of similarity measures: the mean absolute difference of intervals with different normalizations.

Set $z_i = \Delta m_i - \Delta n_i$, $\bar{z} = \frac{1}{N}\sum_i z_i, q_\infty = \max_i |\Delta m_i| + |\Delta n_i|$. Then $d(m,n) = N\bar{z}$ is a transposition invariant distance on pitch-melody space. The two similarity measures are given by:

$$\sigma_1(m,n) = e^{-\bar{z}}$$

$$\sigma_2(m,n) = 1 - \frac{\bar{z}}{q_\infty}$$

The first (diffexp) is merely a straightforward construct. The rationale behind the second one (diff) is to account for the size of steps or leaps of the individual melodies to be compared.

Melodies that consist of a series of large intervals and that result in a large mean absolute difference should have greater similarity values than melodies consisting of only small intervals with the same mean absolute difference.

8.2.6 Symbolic Measures

The symbolic measures view a "melody" (defined by either a series of pitches or durations) not as a vector but as a string, i.e., as a series of arbitrary symbols of finite length. Usually for strings in the computer science sense the symbols are taken to be ASCII characters. Accordingly, a string can be defined as a sequence of characters. But as we will see, the algorithm for the similarity measures used here rely only on the operation "test for equity," so arbitrary symbols like, say, real numbers are allowed. We used two common and well-known techniques: The edit-distance (or Levenshtein distance) and measures related to *n*-grams. This will be explained in the following.

8.2.6.1 Edit-Distance

The main idea behind the concept of edit-distance is to take the minimum number of operations ("edits") needed to transform one string into the other as a similarity measure for strings. The allowed operations are insertion, deletion and substitution. The calculation of edit-distance is done with a well-known dynamic programming algorithm. See Mongeau and Sankoff (1990) or Uitdenbogerd (2002) for details of the algorithm.

It is clear that the maximal possible edit-distance of two strings is equal to the length of the longer string, which enables us to define a similarity measure $\sigma(s_1,s_2)=1-\frac{d_e(s_1,s_2)}{\max(|s_1|,|s_2|)}$, where $|s|$ denotes the length of string s. We used this edit-distance in several ways:

(1) Edit-distance for raw melodies (rhythmically weighted and unweighted): rawed, rawedw. (Here we had to take the maximum over all transpositions.)

(2) Edit-distance for contourized melodies (Steinbeck-contourization and our own): consed, coned. (Again, we had to take the maximum over all transpositions.)

(3) Edit-distance for intervals: diffed.

(4) Edit-distance for fuzzified rhythms: rhytfuzz.

(5) Edit-distance of harmonic strings: harmcore.

8.2.6.2 *n*-grams

An *n*-gram is simply a string of length *n*. Strings of different lengths are denoted 3-grams, 4-grams and so forth. To make for a similarity measure of strings, one questions about the distribution of substrings of fixed length, the *n*-grams, in two strings to be compared. We used three different ways to account for a similarity measure: The Sum Common, the Count Distinct (or Coordinate) and the Ukkonen Measure. An in-depth discussion of *n*-grams as representations of melodies can be found in Downie (1999) and Uitdenbogerd (2002).

Sum Common Measure. Let s and t be two strings. We write s_n for the set of distinct *n*-grams in a string s. The Sum Common Measure sums the frequency of *n*-grams τ occurring in both strings.

$$c(s,t) = \sum_{\tau \in s_n \cap t_n} f_s(\tau) + f_t(\tau)$$

where $f_s(\tau)$ and $f_t(\tau)$ denote the frequencies of the *n*-gram τ in string s and t resp. The maximum frequency of an *n*-gram in a string s is $|s|-n+1$, so the maximum value of the Sum Common Measure is $|s|+|t|-2(n-1)$. A similarity measure is then given by

$$\sigma(s,t) = \frac{c(s,t)}{|s| + |t| - 2(n-1)}$$

Count Distinct (Coordinate Matching) Measure. The Count Distinct Measure resembles the Sum Common Measure, the only difference being that we do not sum the frequencies of the common n-grams, but just count them.

The Count Distinct Measure of the above example would then simply be 2, because there are two common n-grams.

For normalization we divide this by the maximum count of distinct n-grams of either string and arrive at the following similarity measure

$$\sigma(s,t) = \frac{\sum_{\tau \in s_n \cap t_n} 1}{\max(\# s_n, \# t_n)}$$

The Ukkonen Measure. The Ukkonen Measure is somewhat opposite to the Sum Common Measure for it sums differences of the frequencies of the n-grams not occurring in both strings. The formula is:

$$u(s,t) = \sum_{\tau \in s_n \cup t_n} |f_s(\tau) - f_t(\tau)|$$

For making a similarity measure we normalize by the maximum possible number of n-grams and subtract this from 1:

$$\sigma(s,t) = 1 - \frac{u(s,t)}{|s| + |t| - 2(n-1)}$$

Application: We combined these three measures with four different melodic representations:

(1) n-grams with pitch numbers as symbols (taking the maximum over all transpositions): ngrsumco, ngrcoord, ngrukkon.

(2) n-grams with fuzzified intervals: ngrsumcf, ngrcoorf, ngrukkof.

(3) n-grams with the alphabet S, D, U for intervals; assign "S" if the interval is the prime, "D" for a descending and "U" for an ascending interval: ngrsumcr, ngrcoorr, ngrukkor.

(4) n-grams for fuzzified rhythm: ngrsumfr, ngrcoofr, ngrukkfr.

For each variant we also took the maximum over n-gram lengths 3 to 8.

8.2.7 Musical Measures: Harmonic Correlations

From the class of musical measures we defined only measures for harmonic correlation here. There are actually some very interesting musical measures that look for similarities in several musical dimensions simultaneously, but they will be the subject of future investigations.

We used four different measures for harmonic correlation, all of them based on the tonality vector of Krumhansl. The main idea behind all four measures is to assign to each bar a tonality vector, which can be either major or minor. Hence, one gets a (vector of) harmonic vector(s) or a harmonic string, to which the usual techniques can be applied.

Krumhansl's Tonality Vector. Krumhansl and Schmuckler discovered (Krumhansl 1990, Krumhansl and Kessler 1982) that to each of the 12 semitones of the modern equally-tempered scale can be assigned a numerical value measuring its significance or relative strength for a given tonality. They proposed two 12-dimensional vectors, one for major and one for minor scales. The values are:

T_M = (6.33, 2.23, 3.48, 2.33, 4.38, 4.09, 2.52, 5.19, 2.39, 3.66, 2.29, 2.88) (Major)

T_m = (6.33, 2.68, 3.52, 5.38, 2.60, 3.53, 2.54, 4.75, 3.98, 2.69, 3.34, 3.17) (Minor)

The *n*th position in the vectors stands for the value of the *n*th semitone (modulo 12) above a given base tone. For example, a pitch of class "E" has a relative significance for C Major of 4.38 (4th semitone in major), whereas for D Minor it has only 3.52 (2nd semitone in minor).

For a bar, the relative strength of each tone in the bar (weighted by its duration) is computed for each of the 2 possible modes (major or minor) and 12 possible base tones giving two 12-dimensional vectors H_i and h_i.

For example, given a bar (3, C) (1, D) (2, E) (2, C) (in IOI pitch representation) the value for C Major (0th component of H_i) would be:

$$3 \cdot 6.33 + 1 \cdot 3.48 + 2 \cdot 4.38 + 2 \cdot 6.33 = 43.89$$

and for D Minor (2nd component of h_i)

$$3 \cdot 3.34 + 1 \cdot 3.52 + 2 \cdot 2.60 + 2 \cdot 3.34 = 25.42$$

Harmonic Vector Correlation I. For each corresponding bar of the melodies, two 12-dimensional harmonic vectors (major and minor) and their correlations are computed. (If one melody is shorter than the other, we simply ignored the supernumerary bars.) Next we computed the average correlations for all bars, again for major and minor separately. The maximum of the two values is the harmonic vector correlation I.

Harmonic Vector Correlation II. Instead of computing the vector correlation of corresponding bars for each mode separately and averaging the single correlations, one can use the 24-dimensional vectors directly. One gets a vector of these vectors for each bar of each melody, and for these vectors-of-vectors one can calculate the usual correlation.

Harmonic Edit-Distance. We also computed a single tonality value for each bar as the key, which had the maximum value of the 24 possible keys, taking values 0–11 as major keys and values 12–23 as minor keys. This gave a "harmonic string" for each melody for which we computed the edit-distance and got a harmonic similarity with the usual normalization. (See above.)

Harmonic Circle Correlation. A more elaborate version of correlating the 24-dimensional tonality vectors is based on the idea of the Circle of Fifths to reflect the fact that similarity of keys is in correspondence to their relative position on the circle. Therefore we retrieved first a harmonic vector for a melody by finding the maximum of the tonality vector as we did for the harmonic string. This gave a value ranging from 0 to 23 for each bar. Next this value was transformed into a relative position on the circle of fifths by using an angular variable in steps of $\omega = \frac{2\pi}{12}$. We arbitrarily set $\varphi_0 = Db = 0\omega$, $\varphi_1 = Ab = \omega$ and so on up to $\varphi_{11} = F\# = 11\omega$ for the major keys. The minor keys followed the same structure, with respect to their major parallels, but the angles were shifted by $\omega/2$, giving $\varphi_{12} = Bb^m = 0.5\omega$, $\varphi_{13} = F^m = 1.5\omega$ up to $\varphi_{23} = Eb^m = 11.5\omega$.

With the help of this transformation we now defined the correlation of two tonalities as the cosine of the difference of their angles:

$$r_i = \cos(\phi_i^1 - \phi_i^2)$$

This choice comes from the scalar product of two vectors on the unit circle in 2-dimensional space. The total correlation is then defined to be

$$r = \frac{1}{N}\sum_i^N r_i$$

where N is the number of bars and we set negative values to 0.

8.2.8 Implementation of the Models

We implemented a total of 48 models, counting all variants, of which 39 were used in this study. The implementation was done in C/C++ with GCC under Linux, and was also ported to Win32 platforms. It comprises over 5,000 lines of code. As input files we used .csv files, which were generated by extraction from ordinary MIDI files.

8.3 Experiments

8.3.1 Experiment 1

The idea of this study is to pick the similarity measures of the ones presented in the last section that best predict or approximate the similarity judgments of human music experts. For that reason two constraints were applied to the tested sample of subjects:

(1) Their judgments should be consistent over time.

(2) They should recognize identical melodies as highly similar.

In meeting these criteria a subject is expected to give reliable and stable similarity judgments that can be modeled algorithmically.

Subjects. A pretest with subjects with little or no music background showed that similarity judgments from many subjects were unstable and not consistent over time. Judgments of these subjects tended to be influenced by many non-musical factors such as position of the comparison item in the sequence of items and session length. As a consequence for the main study, only musicology students from introductory courses at the University of Hamburg were recruited as subjects. In all 82 subjects participated. Of these 82 subjects, the data of only 23 could be selected on the basis of the aforementioned criteria. The subjects' musical background was measured by an extensive questionnaire very similar to the one employed by Meinz and Salthouse (1998). Typically, musicology students have a long history of music-making (e.g., the mean number of years of playing an instrument was 12; the mean number of months of paid instrumental lessons was 71), but their most active musical phase is several years anterior, which is reflected in less time spent on current musical activities when compared to a more active musical phase in the past.

Materials. To obtain ecologically valid results, 14 existing melodies from western popular songs were chosen as stimulus material. Among these melodies were songs like "As Long as You Love Me" by the Back Street Boys, "Summer is Calling" by Aquagen, and "From Me to You" by the Beatles. All melodies were between seven and ten bars long (15–20 sec.). The melodies were selected according to several criteria: they should contain at least three different phrases and two thematically distinct motives, they should have a radio-like, popular character, and they should be unknown to the subjects to preclude effects from previous knowledge. In fact, some of the melodies were known to a few participants, as was evidenced by the questionnaire. But the ratings of the subjects who knew the songs did not differ from the other subjects' ratings in any respect. So data from these melodies and from these subjects were kept in the study.

For each melody six comparison variants with "errors" were constructed, resulting in 84 variants of the 14 original melodies. The error types and their distribution were done according to the literature on memory errors for melodies (Sloboda and Parker 1985, Oura and Hatano 1988, Zielinska and Miklaszewski 1992, McNab et al. 1996, Meek and Birmingham 2002, Pauws 2002).

Five error types with their respective probabilities were defined: rhythmic errors ($p = 0.6$), pitch errors not changing pitch contour ($p = 0.4$), pitch errors changing the contour ($p = 0.2$), errors in phrase order ($p = 0.2$), and modulation errors (pitch errors that result in a transition to a new tonality [p = 0.2]). Every error type had three possible degrees: 3, 6, and 9 errors per melody for rhythm, contour and pitch errors, and 1, 2, and 3 errors per melody for errors of phrase order and modulation. For the construction of the individual variants, error types and degrees were randomly combined, except for the two types of pitch errors, which were never combined in a single variant in order to evaluate their influence separately. As a result, 50% of the variants had between 4 and 12 errors in sum, with summed errors ranging from 0 to 16. As an example the test melody D, the chorus melody of the dance title "Wonderland" (as interpreted by Passion Fruit), is depicted in its original form (Figure 8.1) and its variant D1 (Figure 8.2), which contains 3 rhythmic errors (note repetition and deletions are counted as rhythmic errors) and 9 contour errors (accumulating mostly in Bars 7 and 8).

Figure 8.1. "Wonderland" by Passion Fruit, original version.

Figure 8.2. "Wonderland" by Passion Fruit, version D1.

Basically, the types and frequencies of errors in the test material are of fundamental importance to the comparison of different similarity models. Because of the unidimensional nature of most of the simple similarity measures discussed above, these measures perform quite differently according to the type and frequency of error (the error dimensions) that a particular set of melodies for comparison contains. So the errors were chosen according to the domain in which the optimal similarity measure should operate. In this case the domain is the reproduction of popular melodies from memory.

Procedure. Subjects were instructed to rate the similarity of pairs of melodic variants on a 7-point scale (with 7 representing maximal similarity). To make the task more realistic, they were asked to imagine that the first member of a comparison pair was a reference that could be played by a music teacher on a piano. The second member of each pair should represent a sung rendition of the same melody by a student. Sometimes the rendition could contain many errors, sometimes only few errors, and in some cases it could be without any error. With their ratings subjects should give "grades" to the imaginary student according to the "severity" of the errors in sum. They were encouraged to make use of the whole range of the rating scale. None of the subjects mentioned that they were unable to perform the task or that they did not understand it.

Each trial run consisted of a first exposure to the original reference melody to familiarize the subjects with it. After 4 seconds of silence, six pairs, each consisting of the reference melody and a different variant, were played to the subjects. The members of the pairs were separated with 2 seconds of silence, and the pairs were separated from each other with the announcement of the next pair and 4 seconds of silence. There was a break of 20 seconds after each trial, where the subjects had to indicate on the rating sheet if they knew the reference melody, and if so, to write down the title of the song. One test session consisted of 3 or 5 trial runs, each with a different reference melody, and took 17 to 23 minutes.

Subjects were tested in groups in their normal classroom environment. The melodies were played from a CD over suitable loudspeakers with a piano sound at a comfortable listening level (around 65 db). After the test session the subjects had to fill out the extensive questionnaire concerning their previous and current musical activities.

The design of the whole experiment was a test-retest design: subject groups were tested in one week and retested one week later. The design of the retest was identical to the test, but involved changing all but one reference melody. So, for example, one subject group was tested in week 1 with melodies A, B, and C and in week 2 with D, E, and A. In this way it was possible to compare the judgments of melody A from weeks 1 and 2 for each subject. Subjects were informed of the retest to take place one week later, but they were told that they would be retested exclusively with different melodies.

Results. The rating data of the subjects had to meet three criteria: subjects should have attended both test sessions, their ratings of variants containing 0 errors (identical to original) should be at least 6 in 85% of the cases, and the correlation of their ratings for the same variants from week 1 to week 2 should not be less than 0.5 as measured by Kendall's τ_b. Data of 23 subjects remained in the analysis. Of course different parameters or numerical values for the latter two selection criteria could have been chosen, but on this point there is no orientation in the literature. For example, the judgments of the subjects tested by Schmuckler (1999) and by McAdams and Matzkin (2001) do not seem to have been tested for reliability and/or consistency at all.

The 23 selected subjects may well be called "music experts" not only for their reliable and consistent similarity judgments, but also because of their musical activities. To give just a few statistics, none of them had been playing an instrument for less than 4 years (mean: 12.52 years), none was making music for less than 4 hours per week in his/her most active musical phase (mean: 21.35 hours/week), and only two had less than 6 months of paid instrumental lessons in their life (mean: 71.91 months).

Obviously, modeling the subjects' similarity judgments with algorithms only makes sense if the ratings of different subjects are quite similar, i.e. the inter-subject reliability is high. This would mean that there is something like a "true" similarity value for a given comparison pair, and that the subjects' ratings over- or underestimate this true value only slightly. To test this hypothesis Cronbach's α, among other measures, was calculated. This measure reflects how well all subjects' ratings measure a latent unidimensional factor ("true" similarity). For the two subject groups α-values of 0.962 and 0.978 were obtained. The Kaiser-Meyer-Olkin measure (KMO) reflects the global coherence in a correlation matrix and is frequently used to evaluate solutions in factor analysis. For the present correlation matrix of the subjects' ratings it yields values of 0.89 and 0.94 for the two tested groups. These values indicate a very high intersubject reliability. They are clearly higher than the α-values (around 0.84) obtained by Lamont and Dibben (2001: 253) in a comparable situation. From this result it can be inferred that there is something like a true or cognitively adequate similarity value for the comparison of melody pairs, at least for the population of "music experts."

Given the type of data collected in the experiment, many further results could be obtained, for example the dependency of the similarity ratings on the error types and degrees and the error position, the dependency of judgment reliability and stability on musical expertise, and the influence of the original melodic structure on the ratings. These results will be the subject of a detailed, more psychologically oriented analysis in the future.

8.3.2 Experiment 2

In tests prior to this experiment it was observed that some of the above described similarity measures tended to overestimate the similarity of melodies that do not come from a common original. Similarity values of up to 0.5 for completely different melodies were found. The idea of Experiment 2 was to collect expert similarity ratings for pairs of reference melodies and respective variants, and reference melodies and variants that have their origin in different reference melodies. In this sense Experiment 2 served as a control experiment for dissimilar material.

Subjects. The subjects were 16 musicology students from an undergraduate course; 11 of them were tested in one group, and 5 were tested individually. There were no observable effects of testing in groups vs. individual testing.

Material. Two of the melodies of Experiment 1 were chosen as reference melodies. The variants for comparison consisted of the same six variants as in Experiment 1 plus five or six new variants for Melody A and six new variants for Melody C that had their origin in different reference melodies and that seemed to be overestimated in their similarity to A or C by some of the algorithmic models. In contrast to Experiment 1, every variant was transposed to a key different from the reference melody, so that the subjects could not make use of absolute-pitch information for their ratings.

Procedure. Instructions and procedure were very similar to those of Experiment 1 with two exceptions: one trial with one reference melody consisted of 12 comparison pairs, and there was no retest session one week later. There were only two trials in one test session. To test reliability and stability, subjects should again rate identical variants highly similar and a comparison pair in one trial was repeated. The two identical comparison pairs should be rated with not more than 1 point difference.

Results. According to the two criteria, 12 of the 16 subjects were selected as music experts and their data remained in the analysis. The measures of inter-subject reliability, KMO and Cronbach's α, again yielded very high values of 0.811 and 0.9788 respectively. The music experts of the control experiment seemed also to estimate the "true" similarity values quite well. Like the music experts of Experiment 1, they had a highly active musical background. The results of the comparison between these human expert judgments and the tested algorithmic models are displayed in the following section.

8.4 Algorithmic vs. Human Judgments

According to an ANOVA with error type (interval vs. contour) as factor and rhythm, modulation, and phrase order errors as covariates, there was no significant difference ($p = 0.709$) between the similarity ratings for variants with interval and contour errors. Thus, further analysis treated variants containing these two types of errors equally.

8.4.1 Modeling Experts' Ratings with Linear Regression

To model the similarity ratings of the subjects and thus find the optimal similarity measure, the information of the several dimensions or parameters contained in the melodies must be combined to yield an effective measure (see Selfridge-Field 1998). The information contained in single-line melodies and relevant for human memory and similarity judgments can be classified in five dimensions: intervals, contour, rhythm, implied harmonic content, and characteristic motives. Each of the similarity measures explained above can be viewed as it measures the similarity of a melody and its variant along one of these five dimensions. A classification of the similarity measures is shown in Table 8.3.

Dimension	Definition	Measures
Interval	Difference, correlation, or symbolic measures operating on the sequence of pitches or intervals, or their fuzzified values	diff, diffexp, diffed, diffuz, rawed, rawedw, rawpcst, rawpcwst
Contour	Correlation and symbolic measures operating on the sequence of substituting contour values	consed, constpcst, coned, conpcst, fourrst, fourrwst
Rhythm	Correlation or symbolic measures operating on the sequence of fuzzified rhythm values or gaussified onset points	Rhythfuzz, rhythgaus, ngrcoorfr, ngrsumfr, ngrukkfr
Harmonic content	Correlation or symbolic measures operating on the sequence of harmonically weighted pitch values	harmcorr, harmcork, harmcore, harmcorc
Characteristic motives	Symbolic measures operating on subsequences of interval values or their directions or fuzzified substitutes	ngrsumco, ngrukkon, ngrcoord, ngrsumcr, ngrukkor, ngrcoorr, ngrsumcf, ngrukkof, ngrcoorf

Table 8.3. Melodic dimensions and tested measures.

As it is probable that human music experts make use of the information on several dimensions simultaneously, an optimal algorithmic model of the human ratings would encompass measures from several dimensions in a linear combination. So the optimization process takes two steps:

(1) For a given set of melodies and variants choose for every dimension the measure that has minimal Euclidean distance to the subjects' ratings. These are the "best" measures.

(2) With these five "best" measures perform a linear regression analysis to find the optimal combination and the optimal weights for the individual measures so that the subjects' ratings are best explained by the linear combination. The criteria for this step were: a positive sign for the weight of the factor (measure), a level of significance of $p < 0.05$ for each factor, the corrected R^2 should be maximal and the standard error should be minimal for the regression model.

This analysis was done for the three contexts of the 84 comparison pairs of Experiment 1, the 13 pairs with "real" variants that were manipulations of the reference melody in control experiment 2, and all 24 comparison pairs of control experiment 2.

Main experiment. For the main Experiment 1, the "best" measures with their respective Euclidean distance to the experts' ratings are: coned (5.29), rawedw (5.63), ngrcoord (5.94), harmoncore (6.18), rhythfuzz (10.43). Distances ranged from 5.29 to 12.8. Distances to all measures are found in the appendix.

Linear regression analysis with these measures yielded the best model according to the above-described criteria involving only two measures, rawedw and ngrcoord. Interestingly, in combination with other measures the overall best measure, coned, was not able to support explicative power to the model anymore, so that the p-value to its β-weight became insignificant in combination with rawedw or ngrcoord. Any model including coned yielded a lower overall fit than the one involving rawedw and ngrcoord.

The overall fit of the model is quite high: $R = 0.911$, $R^2 = 0.830$, corrected $R^2 = 0.826$, standard error of estimated values 0.66. This means that 83% of the variance in the rating data of the subjects is explained by this model, and the mean deviation for the estimated values is 0.66 points on the 7-point scale. The standardized β-beta-weights for the two factors are: rawedw ($\beta = 0.543$), ngrcoord ($\beta = 0.497$). The linear combination to best predict the subjects' ratings on the 7-point scale is:

$$\sigma_{best} = 3{,}355 \cdot rawedw + 2{,}852 \cdot ngrcoord$$

With this optimized similarity model we found a Euclidean distance to the subjects' ratings of 3.789. This means that the optimized model is by 28.5% better than the best single similarity measure tested (coned). This superiority of the optimized measure opti1 is shown in Figure 8.3.

Real variants in control experiment. For the 13 variants that had their origin in the reference melody in the control experiment the results were slightly different at first glance. The "best" measures from the five dimensions were: diffed (1.3), ngrsumco (1.88), harmcore (1.98), consed (2.11), ngrcoofr (3.09). Euclidean distances ranged from 1.3 to 5.96. A table with all the distances is found in the appendix.

The best model from regression analysis contained the two measures ngrsumco and harmcore. Very high values of fit were found for that model: $R = 0.960$, $R^2 = 0.922$, corrected $R^2 = 0.906$, standard error of estimated values 0.37. Thus, 92% of the variance in the rating data of the subjects was explained by this model, and the mean deviation for the estimated values is 0.37 points on the 7-point scale.

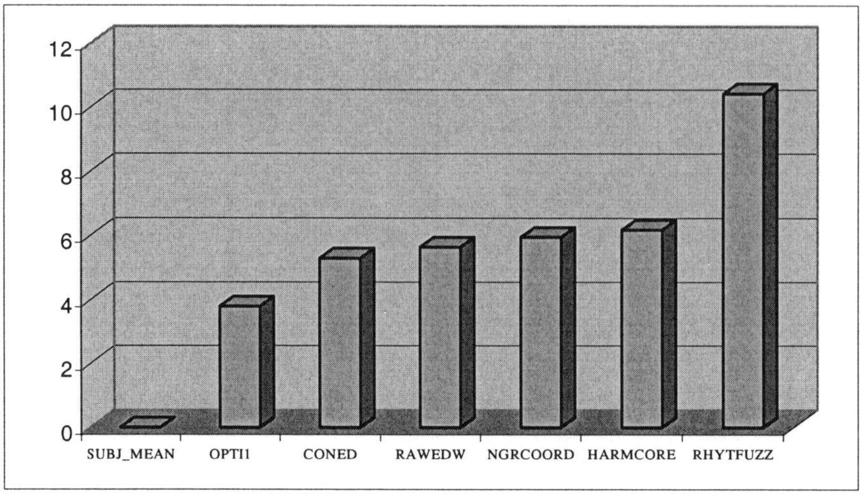

Figure 8.3. Performance of different similarity measures on data from Experiment 1.

To check the validity of the result of Experiment 1, a second row of regression analysis was performed using the best measures from the first experiment but with the data from the 13 "real" variants from the second. Again rawedw and ngrcoord in combination gave the best result. The model fit was also quite high: R = 0.946, R^2 = 0.895, corrected R^2 = 0.874, standard error of estimated values 0.43. At the same time, the regression model with measures from Experiment 2 on the data of Experiment 1 found high results as well: R = 0.884, R^2 = 0.781, corrected R^2 = 0.776 and standard error = 0.75.

The standardized β-weights for both models were approximately the same for each data set, weighting rawedw about 1.15 times more than ngrcoord, and weighting ngrsumco about the same as harmcore. So both models seem to give valid estimations of the subjects' ratings for the similarity of "real" variants and their respective reference melodies. But there are two reasons to assume the model including rawedw and ngrcoord resulting from Experiment 1 the superior one: firstly, the model including rawedw and ngrcoord was found to fit better for a larger data set (Experiment 1). Secondly, the difference of the corrected R^2 values to the second model for the data of Experiment 2 was smaller (0.906 - 0.874 = 0.032) than the other way around (0.826 - 0.776 = 0.05). So to model the similarity ratings of melodies and their variants by music experts, the above-stated linear combination including rawedw and ngrcoord is believed to be the optimal model, but with slightly different weights and a constant due to the overall shifting of the ratings towards the pole of maximum similarity:

$$\sigma_{best} = 2{,}254 + 2{,}61 \cdot rawedw + 1{,}72 \cdot ngrcoord$$

"Real" and "wrong" variants of the control experiment. For all 24 comparison pairs of the control experiment, including "real" and "wrong" variants, the five best measures were: diffed (2.04), ngrukkon (2.44), harmcore (2.98), consed (3.57) and rhythfuzz (3.65). Distances ranged from 2.04 to 7.73 as can been seen in the appendix. The best regression model was obtained with three measures: ngrukkon, rhythfuzz, and harmcore. Again, the model estimated the subjects' ratings very well: R = 0.96, R^2 = 0.921, corrected R^2 = 0.909, standard error of estimated values 0.49. A second try with the measures from the main experiment data set, rawedw and ngrcoord, yielded a clearly worse result with a corrected R^2 of 0.826. So the best linear combination for estimating the subjects' ratings on the 7-point scale is:

$$\sigma_{best} = 3{,}027 \cdot ngrukkon + 2{,}502 \cdot rhythfuzz + 1{,}439 \cdot harmcore$$

Again, with this optimized model we achieved a much better result than for any of the single measures. The Euclidean distance was 1.403, which is about 33.4% better than diffed. This is depicted in Figure 8.4.

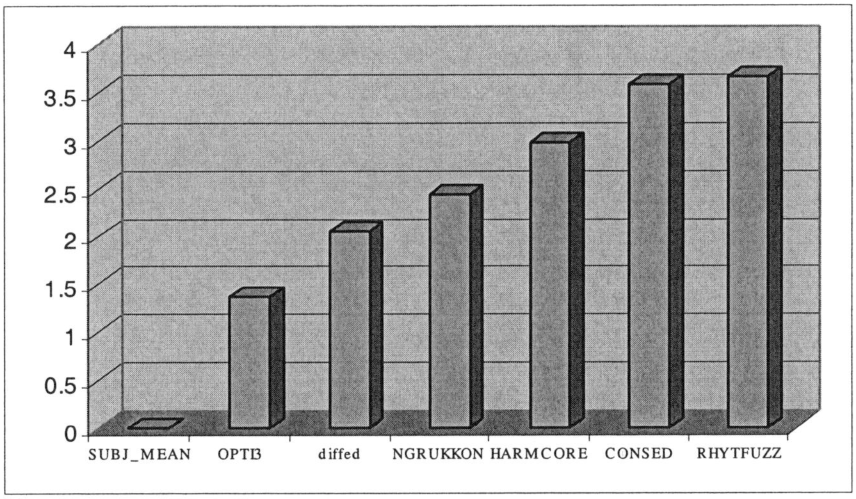

Figure 8.4. Performance of different similarity measures on data from Experiment 2.

Obviously, for the full data set of the control experiment, information from very different sources is needed to model the subjects' ratings. It seems very plausible that subjects make use of easy-to-detect dimensions like rhythm and harmonic content when the task is to distinguish different songs from variants derived from the same song. It is also interesting to note that, out of all *n*-gram measures, the Ukkonen distance performed best here, because it is the only *n*-gram measure that counts the differences between two symbol sequences rather than the common elements.

In any case, it seems that human music experts change their judgment strategy for melodic similarity ratings according to the task. With the more subtle differences in judging the similarity of "real" variants they make more use of individual pitch information, whereas with "wrong" variants to be judged they rely more on rhythm and differences in interval successions.

General observations about the performance of the employed measures. Apart from finding only the best combination of measures, the comparison with human judgments can teach us something about the general performance characteristics of the tested data transformations and similarity measures.

Looking at the data of the main experiment, we can ask: which measures perform best for the different types of transformed melodic data? A series of rank tests and inspections of the rank positions relative to the subjects' ratings was undertaken. Generally, contour measures came closer to the subjects' ratings than their raw-pitch counterparts. This holds true as much for the edit-distance as for the weighted correlational measures.

For pitch and interval measures, the non-parametrical Kruskal-Wallis Test was performed on the ranks of distance from the rating data. The test was significant with $p = 0.005$. Measures based on edit-distance performed best with a mean rank of 3, while *n*-gram measures had a mean rank of 6. Correlational measures and difference measures both lagged far behind with a mean rank of 13.5 in both cases.

A slightly different picture appeared when comparing measures for contour data. Edit-distance measures again produced the result that was by far the best, with a mean rank of 1.5, while correlational and Fourier-based measures shared the middle position, both with a mean rank of 8. Additionally, the *n*-gram measures that contained only directional information (Parsons 1975 alphabet) showed the poorest performance with a mean rank of 12.33. The test statistic approached the usual significance level with a p-value of 0.071.

Among the three different measures using the *n*-gram concept, coordinate matching (ngrcoord) was found to give the best result (distance to ratings in main experiment: 5.94), although the difference between the sum-common (6.16) and the Ukkonen measure (6.08) is not large. This is consistent with the observations by Uitdenbogerd and Zobel (1999, 2000), who found coordinate matching and sum-common to be the best overall *n*-gram measures.

In our data the *n*-grams based on intervals gave better results than *n*-grams using fuzzified interval classes and much better results than interval directions only, which proved to be the poorest measure of this family. The superiority of the *n*-grams consisting of intervals was true as well for the data of the control experiment. In any case, *n*-grams of length three gave the highest similarity values and were interpreted as the true similarity values. This superiority of short *n*-grams comes from the fact that shorter n-grams have a higher probability to match, because of the smaller number of possible n-grams.

Concerning the rhythm measures, the one using edit-distance on the sequence of fuzzified rhythm classes was best, with both data sets (distance to ratings in control experiment: 3.65) outperforming the Gaussian measures (3.81) and the n-gram fuzzy rhythm measures (3.92 to 4.64). As for the interval-based n-gram measures in the control experiment, the best rhythmic n-gram measure was the Ukkonen measure, which counts the differences in rhythmic n-grams in both melodies.

Compared to overall similarity measures that were employed with durationally weighted and unweighted options, these two types of options reached the same mean rank in a U-Test. So it is not possible to decide whether weighted or unweighted measures perform better in general. But looking at the distance table for the main experiment in the appendix produces a clearer picture for the individual measures: the edit-distance on the raw-pitch information performed better with the weighting for durations, while correlational measures for raw-pitch data tend to perform better without weighting. Lastly, the Fourier measures seem slightly better with weighting.

8.5 Discussion

The aims of this study were to systematize measures for melodic similarity and to find the "optimal" similarity measures. The optimal measure should mirror the similarity ratings of human music experts most closely. To this end two rating experiments were conducted. In the first experiment, music experts were asked to judge the similarity between a constant reference melody and several variants differing in the type and number of errors. The second experiment collected human rating data for a constant reference melody and "real" variants derived from that reference melody as well as "wrong" variants having their origin in a different melody.

As results, several observations that are central to the investigation and the modeling of human similarity judgments were made. The music experts showed a very high correlation among their similarity ratings. An inter-subject correlation as high as 0.978 (as measured by Cronbach's α) was found. This high reliability was corroborated by ratings of the same variants that were done by a different subject group in a different experimental context in Experiment 2. The significant correlation between these two groups' ratings of the same variants was 0.862. This leads to the conclusion that there is something like "true" similarity and that at least subjects with a strong musical background (music experts) can reliably estimate this true similarity. A reliable and stable similarity representation is a necessary condition for modeling human judgments.

The modeling started from the idea that comparing different aspects of the melodies would give better results than just employing one algorithmic measure. With the means of regression analysis an optimal compound measure was found for the main experiment. This measure includes the durationally weighted edit-distance and the coordinate matching of *n*-grams of length 3 based on intervals. This compound similarity measure came 28.5% closer to the human ratings than the best single measure. For the different task in Experiment 2 this combined measure still gave good results, but a combination of the Ukkonen measure for counting *n*-grams of intervals, the edit-distance of sequences of duration classes, and the edit-distance of the sequence of main tonalities of the individual bars was able to explain even more of the variance in the subjects' ratings (92%) and was 33.4% better than the best single measure.

From this outcome it seems obvious that for different experimental tasks, different types and lengths of melodies, and probably different subject populations, the individual similarity measures and their specific combinations vary in their predictive power. So, for applications employing melodic similarity measures this means that the optimal combination and optimal weights for that specific task (e.g. query-by-humming routines, symbolic searches in a melody database, the establishment of relations between melodic variants in ethno-musicological corpora) can be obtained. At the same time it would be interesting to find a compound similarity measure that is most robust and most sensible under a broad range of conditions, at least in one music culture. But to find this "best" similarity model for western popular music, for example, there is still much more experimental work to be carried out.

Apart from the experimental data that is needed to complete this investigation, it is also clear that the number of tested similarity measures, although already quite large, is still incomplete. So the next step should be to incorporate more measures of the same classes that have been systematized here. Among these measures are the TF-IDF from the *n*-gram family that was used by Downie (1998) and Uitdenbogerd (2002), and an *n*-gram measure that combines intervals and rhythm classes like the one proposed by Doraisamy and Rüger (2001). Also, more sophisticated measures for some aspects like harmonic content are possible, like the ones described by Temperley (1997) or Krumhansl and Toiviainen (2001). A melodic dimension that has not been used so far is meter or metric information that might serve to weight pitch information. Accent models like the ones by Boltz and Jones (1989) or Monahan et al. (1987) may give a more complete and more musical picture of the entire information that melodies contain. A very promising class of similarity measures is based upon the Hidden Markov Model approach (e.g. Pardo and Birmingham 2003). This class of measures is desperately waiting to be compared in its predictive power to the measures tested in this report.

Finally, the greatest simplification of this study is that the two melodies to be compared are of approximately the same length. But in most applications that use melodic similarity measures, a shorter query is compared to a number of much longer reference melodies, so most of the tested measures have to be adjusted to this type of task. With some measures like edit-distances the best adjustment is already known (local alignment in the case of edit-distance). With others like difference or correlational measures there are several possibilities to realize this adjustment. One promising solution is segmentation into individual phrases and their indexing of both the query and the reference melodies. But again for segmentation there are several possibilities such as accent or Gestalt laws, or models that look for repetition of melodic or rhythmic content. The choice of an adequate strategy would again depend on the type of task and data to be analyzed and compared for similarity.

Appendices

Table 1. Model names and abbreviations

Abbreviation	Model
RAWED	Raw pitch edit-distance
RAWEDW	Raw pitch edit-distance weighted
RAWPCST	Raw pitch P-B. corr, weighted, 0-1
RAWPCWST	Raw pitch P-B. Corr. weighted, 0-1
CONSED	Contour (Steinbeck) edit-distance
CONSPCST	Contour (Steinbeck), P-B. corr., 0-1
CONED	Fraunhofer qbh-measure (June 2003)
CONPCST	Raw pitch edit-distance weighted
FOURRST	Fourier (ranks), weighted, 0-1
FOURRWST	Fourier (ranks), weighted, 0-1
FOURRI	Fourier (ranks, intervals)
DIFFED	Intervals (edit-distance)
DIFF	Intervals (mean difference)
DIFFEXP	Intervals (mean difference, exp.)
DIFFFUZ	Intervals (fuzzy), edit-distance
DIFFFUZC	Intervals (fuzzy contour)
NGRSUMCO	*n*-grams Sum Common
NGRUKKON	*n*-grams Ukkonnen
NGRCOORD	Coordinate Matching (count distinct)
NGRSUMCR	Sum Common (interval direction)
NGRUKKOR	*n*-grams Ukkonnen (interval direction)
NGRCOORR	*n*-grams Coord. Match. (interval direction)
NGRSUMCF	*n*-grams Sum Common fuzzy)
NGRUKKOF	*n*-grams Ukkonnen (fuzzy)
NGRCOORF	*n*-grams Count distinct (fuzzy)
NGRSUMFR	*n*-grams sum common (fuzzy rhythm)
NGRUKKFR	*n*-grams Ukkonnen (fuzzy rhythm)
NGRCOOFR	*n*-grams Coord. Match. (fuzzy rhythm)
RHYTGAUS	Rhythm (gaussified onset points)

RHYTFUZZ	Rhythm (fuzzy), edit-distance
HARMCORR	Harmonic correlation (type I)
HARMCORK	Harmonic correlation (type II)
HARMCORE	Harmonic correlation (edit-distance)
HARMCORC	Harmonic correlation (circle)

Tables 2a-c. Euclidean distances between tested similarity measures and subjects' ratings

2a. Results for Experiment 1.

SUBJMEAN	0	DIFFFUZ	8.894
OPTI1	3.789	RAWPCST	9.182
CONED	5.292	RAWPCWST	9.481
RAWEDW	5.633	FOURRWST	9.720
RAWED	5.804	CONSPCST	9.844
NGRCOORD	5.940	NGRCOORR	9.923
NGRUKKON	6.084	FOURRST	10.105
NGRSUMCO	6.165	NGRUKKOR	10.132
HARMCORE	6.176	DIFF	10.173
DIFFED	6.301	NGRSUMCR	10.380
NGRUKKOF	6.684	RHYTFUZZ	10.431
NGRCOORF	6.718	RHYTGAUS	10.695
NGRSUMCF	7.211	HARMCORC	11.047
CONSED	7.295	NGRUKKFR	11.053
HARMCORK	7.586	NGRCOOFR	11.115
DIFFFUZC	7.744	NGRSUMFR	11.183
CONPCST	7.819	HARMCORR	12.796
DIFFEXP	7.943		

2b. Results for "real" variants only from Experiment 2.

SUBJMEAN	0	NGRUKKOF	2.024	RAWPCST	3.015
OPTI2	1.403	CONSED	2.105	FOURRWST	3.039
DIFFED	1.296	DIFFFUZ	2.217	NGRCOOFR	3.089
RAWED	1.593	CONSPCST	2.331	RAWPCWST	3.218
RAWEDW	1.771	HARMCORK	2.342	NGRUKKFR	3.418
NGRSUMCO	1.880	CONED	2.346	NGRSUMFR	3.506
NGRSUMCF	1.900	NGRUKKOR	2.500	CONPCST	3.819
NGRCOORF	1.964	NGRCOORR	2.561	RHYTFUZZ	3.881
HARMCORE	1.984	NGRSUMCR	2.574	HARMCORC	4.269
NGRUKKON	1.986	DIFFEXP	2.702	RHYTGAUS	4.319
DIFF	1.991	DIFFUZC	2.834	HARMCORR	5.960
NGRCOORD	2.019	FOURRST	2.895		

2c. Results for all variants from Experiment 2.

SUBJMEAN	0	HARMCORE	2.977	HARMCORC	4.94265794
OPTI3	1.403	NGRSUMCR	3.301	RAWPCWST	4.95775163
DIFFED	2.042	NGRCOORR	3.330	DIFFFUZC	5.25830586
RAWED	2.196	CONSED	3.572	FOURRWST	5.3029391
NGRUKKON	2.439	CONED	3.629	FOURRST	5.45782753
NGRCOORD	2.505	RHYTFUZZ	3.649	RAWPCST	5.49469773
NGRSUMCO	2.513	RHYTGAUS	3.805	CONPCST	5.55753837
NGRCOORF	2.5886	NGRUKKFR	3.91766035	DIFF	5.98850934
NGRUKKOF	2.599	HARMCORK	4.07437482	CONSPCST	6.06599364
RAWEDW	2.6612	NGRSUMFR	4.12671297	HARMCORR	7.72778626
NGRUKKOR	2.788	DIFFEXP	4.15603486	HARMCORC	4.94265794
NGRSUMCF	2.801	DIFFFUZ	4.2713198	RAWPCWST	4.95775163

References

Baroni, Mario, Rossana Dalmonte, and Carlo Jacoboni (1992). "Theory and Analysis of European Melody," *Computer Representations and Models in Music*, ed. Alan Marsden and Anthony Pople (San Diego: Academic Press), 187–206.

Bartók, Béla, and Albert B. Lord (1951). Serbo-Croatian Folk Songs: Texts and Transcriptions of Seventy-Five Folk Songs from the Milman Parry Collection and a Morphology of Serbo-Croatian Folk Melodies. New York: Columbia University Press.

Bartók, Béla (1976). "Why and How Do We Collect Folk Music?" *Béla Bartók Essays,* ed. Benjamin Suchoff (London: Faber & Faber), 9–24.

Cronin, Charles (1998). "Concepts of Melodic Similarity in Music-Copyright Infringement Suits," *Melodic Similarity: Concepts, Procedures, and Applications* (*Computing in Musicology 11*), ed. Walter B. Hewlett and Eleanor Selfridge-Field (Cambridge: MIT Press), 187–210.

Deliège, Irène (2001). "Introduction: Similarity Perception, Categorization, Cue Abstraction," *Music Perception*, 18/3, 233–243.

Dewitt, Lucinda A., and Robert G. Crowder (1986). "Recognition of Novel Melodies after Brief Delays," *Music Perception*, 3/3, 259–274.

Dowling, W. Jay and Fujitani, Diane S. (1971). "Contour, Interval, and Pitch Recognition in Memory for Melodies," *The Journal of the Acoustical Society of America*, 2/2, 524–531.

Dowling, W. Jay (1978). "Scale and Contour: Two Components of a Theory of Memory for Melodies," *Psychological Review*, 85/4, 341–354.

Dowling, W. Jay, Seyeul Kwak, and Melinda W. Andrews (1995). "The Time Course of Recognition of Novel Melodies," *Perception and Psychophysics*, 57 (2), 136–149.

Dowling, W. Jay, Barbara Tillmann, and Dan F. Ayers (2002). "Memory and the Experience of Hearing Music," *Music Perception*, 19/2, 249–276.

Downie, J. Stephen (1999). "Evaluating a Simple Approach to Musical Information Retrieval: Conceiving Melodic N-grams as Text." Ph. D. thesis, University of Western Ontario.

Drake, Carolyn, and Daisy Bertrand (2001). "The Quest for Universals in Temporal Music Processing," *The Biological Foundations of Music*, ed. Robert J. Zatorre and Isabelle Peretz (New York: New York Academy of Sciences), 17–27.

Edworthy, Judith (1983). "Towards a Contour-Pitch Continuum Theory of Memory for Melodies," *The Acquisition of Symbolic Skills*, ed. D. Rodgers and J. Sloboda (New York: Plenum), 263–271.

Eerola, T., T. Järvinen, J. Louhivuori, and P. Toiviainen (2001). "Statistical Features and Perceived Similarity of Folk Melodies," *Music Perception*, 18/3, 275–296.

Frieler, Klaus (2004). "Mathematische Musikanalyse: Theorie und Praxis." Ph. D. thesis, University of Hamburg (in preparation).

Hofmann-Engl, Ludger (2001). "Towards a Cognitive Model of Melodic Similarity," *ISMIR 2001 Conference Proceedings* (Bloomington, IN).

Hofmann-Engl, Ludger (2002). "Rhythmic Similarity: A Theoretical and Empirical Approach," *Proceedings of the 7th International Conference on Music Perception and Cognition*, Sydney 2002 [CD-ROM], ed. C. Stevens, D. Burnham, G. McPherson, E. Schubert, J. Renwick. Adelaide: Causal Productions.

Idson, Wendy L., and Dominic W. Massaro (1978). "A Bidimensional Model of Pitch in the Recognition of Melodies," *Perception and Psychophysics*, 24/6, 551–565.

Jesser, Barbara (1990). Interaktive Melodieanalyse: Methodik und Anwendung computergestützter Analyseverfahren in Musikethnologie und Volksliedforschung: typologische Untersuchung der Balladensamlung des DVA. Bern: Peter Lang.

Jones, Mari Riess, and Marilyn Boltz (1989). "Dynamic Attending and Responses to Time," *Psychological Review*, 96/3, 459–491.

Juhasz, Zoltán (2000). "A Model of Variation in the Music of a Hungarian Ethnic Group," *Journal of New Music Research*, 29/2, 159–172.

Kauffman, William H., and James C. Carlsen (1989). "Memory for Intact Music Works: The Importance of Music Expertise and Retention Interval," *Psychomusicology*, 8/1, 3–20.

Kluge, Reiner (1974). *Faktorenanalytischen Typenbestimmung an Volksliedmelodien*. Leipzig: VEB Deutscher Verlag für Musik.

Krumhansl, Carol L., and E. J. Kessler (1982). "Tracing the Dynamic Changes in Perceived Tonal Organization in a Spatial Representation of Musical Keys," *Psychological Review*, 89, 334–368.

Krumhansl, Carol L. (1990). *Cognitive Foundations of Musical Pitch*. New York: Oxford University Press.

Krumhansl, Carol L., and Petri Toiviainen (2001). "Tonal Cognition" in *The Biological Foundations of Music*, ed. Robert J. Zatorre and Isabelle Peretz (New York: New York Academy of Sciences), 77–91.

Lamont, Alexandra, and Nicola Dibben (2001). "Motivic Structure and the Perception of Similarity," *Music Perception*, 18/3, 245–274.

Lerdahl, Fred, and Ray Jackendoff (1983). *A Generative Theory of Tonal Music*. Cambridge: MIT Press.

Massaro, Dominic W., Howard J. Kallman, and Janet L. Kelly (1980). "The Role of Tone Height, Melodic Contour, and Tone Chroma in Melody Recognition," *Journal of Experimental Psychology: Human Learning and Memory*, 6/1, 91–105.

McAdams, Stephen, and Daniel Matzkin (2001). "Similarity, Invariance, and Musical Variation" in *The Biological Foundations of Music*, ed. Robert J. Zatorre and Isabelle Peretz (New York: New York Academy of Sciences), 62–74.

McNab, Rodger J., Lloyd A. Smith, Ian H. Witten, Clare L. Henderson, and Sally Jo Cunningham (1996). "Towards the Digital Music Library: Tune Retrieval from Acoustic Input," *Proceedings ACM Digital Libraries*.

Meek, Colin, and William Birmingham (2002). "Johnny Can't Sing: A Comprehensive Error Model for Sung Music Queries," *ISMIR 2002 Conference Proceedings*, IRCAM, 124–132.

Meyer, Leonard B. (1973). *Explaining Music: Essays and Explorations*. Chicago: University of Chicago Press.

Monahan, Caroline B., Roger A. Kendall, and Edward C. Carterette (1987). "The Effect of Melodic and Temporal Contour on Recognition Memory for Pitch Change," *Perception and Psychophysics*, 41/6, 576–600.

Mongeau, Marcel, and David Sankoff (1990). "Comparision of Musical Sequences," *Computers and the Humanities*, 24, 161–175.

Muellensiefen, Daniel (2004). *Varianz und Konstanz von Melodien in der Erinnerung*. Ph. D. thesis, University of Hamburg (in preparation).

Narmour, Eugene (1990). The Analysis and Cognition of Basic Melodic Structures: The Implication-Realization Model. Chicago: The University of Chicago Press.

Ó Maidín, Donncha (1998). "A Geometrical Algorithm for Melodic Difference in Melodic Similarity," *Melodic Similarity: Concepts, Procedures, and Applications (Computing in Musicology 11)*, ed. Walter B. Hewlett and Eleanor Selfridge-Field. Cambridge: The MIT Press.

Oura, Yoko, and Giyoo Hatano (1988). "Memory for Melodies among Subjects Differing in Age and Experience in Music," *Psychology of Music*, 16, 91–109.

Pardo, Brian, Jonah Shifrin, and William Birmingham (2004). "Name That Tune: A Pilot Study in Finding a Melody from a Sung Query," *Journal of the American Society for Information Science and Technology*, 55/4.

Parsons, Denis (1975). *The Dictionary of Tunes and Musical Themes*.

Pauws, Steffen (2002). "Cuby Hum: A Fully Operational Query-by-Humming System," *ISMIR 2002 Conference Proceedings*, IRCAM, 187–196.

Scherrer, Deborah K., and Philip H. Scherrer (1971). "An Experiment in the Computer Measurement of Melodic Variations in Folksong," *Journal of American Folklore*, 84.

Schmuckler, Mark A. (1999). Testing Models of Melodic Contour Similarity," *Music Perception*, 16/3, 109–150.

Seeger, Charles (1966). "Versions and Variants of the Tunes of 'Barbara Allen'," *Selected Reports in Ethnomusicology*, 1/1.

Sloboda, John A., and David H. H. Parker (1985). "Immediate Recall of Melodies," *Musical Structure and Cognition*, ed. Ian Cross, Peter Howell, and Robert West (London: Academic Press), 143–167.

Steinbeck, Wolfram (1982). *Struktur und Ähnlichkeit: Methoden automatisierter Melodieanalyse* (Kieler Schriften zur Musikwissen-schaft, XXV). Kassel, Basel, London: Bärenreiter.

Temperley, David (1997). "An Algorithm for Harmonic Analysis," *Music Perception*, 15/1, 31–68.

Uitdenbogerd, Alexandra, and Zobel, Justin (1999). "Matching Techniques for Large Music Databases," *Proceedings of the ACM Multimedia Conference*, Orlando, Florida, 57–66.

Uitdenbogerd, Alexandra, and Justin Zobel (2000). "Music Ranking Techniques Evaluated," *ISMIR 2000 Conference Proceedings*, Plymouth, MA.

Uitdenbogerd, Alexandra L. (2002). "Music Information Retrieval Technology." Ph. D. thesis, RMIT University, Melbourne, Australia.

Wiggins, Geraint A. (2002). "Hourses for Courses, or How to Change an Algorithm to Do What You Need," *ISMIR 2002 Conference Proceedings*, IRCAM, 308.

Wiora, Walter (1941). "Systematik der musikalischen Erscheinungen des Umsingens," *Jahrbuch für Volksliedforschung*, 7, 128–195.

Zadeh, Lotfi (1965). "Fuzzy Sets," *Information Control*, 338–353.

Zhou, Yongwei, and Mohan S. Kankanhalli (2003). "Melody Alignment and Similarity Metric for Content-Based Music Retrieval," *Proceedings of SPIE-IS&T Electronic Imaging*, SPIE, 5021, 112–121.

Zielinska, Halina, and Kacper Miklaszewski (1992). "Memorising Two Melodies of Different Style," *Psychology of Music*, 20, 95–111.

Table of Abbreviations

DFT	discrete Fourier transform
DPM	dynamic programming matching
EMD	Earth-Mover's Distance
FLNN	Fuzzy-Logical Neural Net
IOI	inter-onset interval
ISSM	Integrated Segmentation and Similarity Model
HMM	Hidden Markov Model
KMO	Kaiser-Meyer-Olkin measure
LCS	longest common subsequence
LTM	long-term memory
MIR	music-information retrieval
MKN	MIDI key number
MLP	Multi-Layer-Perceptron
MOT	musical onset time
MP	MIDI-to-PCM
PCC	pattern-class chain
PCM	Pulse Code Modulation
POC	pattern-occurrence chain
POT	physical onset time
PTD	Proportional Transportation Distance
QBH	query-by-humming
QBV	query-by-voice
SI	structural interpretation
SM	score-to-MIDI
SP	score-to-PCM
STM	short-term memory
TDB	template database
TPB	time signature/pitch contour/beat number representation

Index